Collection Management in Academic Libraries

Preface

Contents

1

Library: Backdrop and Growth

THE ROLE OF LIBRARIES IN MODERN SOCIETY

First, the general development of the information society is pushing to re-evaluation of all the institutions which work with information, data, and knowledge-indirectly also with culture. In this connection the roles of education and media have been discussed already quite largely also in the European Union.

But libraries-as well as other memory institutions like archives and museums-have not been considered. Still, there is a clear need in the information society to maintain an institution which is concentrating in collecting and organizing information and offering general access to it. Until now, this work has been underestimated, but I argue the situation will change! Libraries are especially important now when the whole idea of education is stressing more and more independent learning and acting.

All citizens must be able to find and use information. It is the key raw material-but it is a zero resource, if there are no access points to it and if documents are in chaotic order.

Here we can see libraries enter the stage:

- The unique function of libraries is to acquire, organize, offer for use and preserve publicly available material irrespective of the form in which it is packaged in such a way that, when it is needed, it can be found and put to use. No other institution carries out this long-term, systematic work. Culture must be nominated especially: it has an important and unique role in mobilizing resources of human beings. It has been described: To some extent, culture makes its influence felt more indirectly than knowledge, but it is impossible to imagine how people's creative powers could be fully activated without the impact of culture, which extends into the depths of the mind.

The challenge to modern societies is that the basic resource, knowledge, is developing from information in very individual, capricious and unpredictable process. It cannot be commanded. Still, societies can support this development, *e.g.*, by offering access to cultural and knowledge treasures.

This can even be translated into economic language: to get out the best from the human resources in Europe, this resource must be feeded up with rich and various cultural and information contents! I would like to stress especially the idea of organizing information by libraries. It is often shadowed by the second important side of library work: offering access. But in the life-long learning and new technology context just all forms of organizing documents are getting more to the focus. This is clear to anybody who has tried to find something from not-so-often-used Internet web sites.

NEW LINES IN THE EU-AND IN THE UNITED STATES

In accordance with these phenomenons, there are new political lines in the European Union: The Maastricht Treaty in 1992 launched the cultural aspects. This was only after a long discussion, which made it clear that we have to remember to separate the national view and the European view. The Amsterdam Treaty in 1997 declared citizenship as an important theme. A significant part of this are a ogranting information skills and access to information to every European.

In addition to this, the European future strategies need to meet the democratic aspects of the information society development. One of the crucial points is again general access to information. Libraries, especially public libraries, are a good tool in all of these new areas.

But the European union does not support whichever cultural or citizen concentrated projects in Europe. In the interests of the European Union there is always to find the European element. So, what can be done in library policy on the European level, taking in account that libraries are primarily a part of national education and cultural policies? *The own-initiative report "The role of libraries in modern societies," adopted by the European Parliament in October 1998, is the first effort to answer these questions.*

The same topics have been discussed in the United States. They have reached the point where especially the problems of those lacking access to digital resources have been studied. The report Falling Through the Net: Defining the Digital Divide by the U.S. Department of Commerce was released earlier in July 1999.

The report finds that minorities, low-income persons, the less educated, and children of single parent households, particularly when they reside in rural areas or central cities, are risk groups. The report calls for public policies and private initiatives to expand affordable access to critical information resources. But it also shows,, for the first time as far as I know, that libraries and community centres really can diminish the information gap between haves and not-haves.

The 1998 data from the U.S. demonstrates very clearly that community access centers, primarily public libraries, are particularly well used by those groups who lack access at home or at work: *e.g.,* unemployed groups used Internet in libraries three times as often as an average citizen.

EARLIER ACTIONS IN EU

In the European Union, there have been some efforts to mobilize "the treasures of the European libraries" since the mid-80'ies. These discussions and resolutions led to two special library programmes under the 3rd and 4th Framework programmes of research and development. The later programme has been known as "Telematics for Libraries".

They have been strongly concentrated in IT, because it has been seen as a good tool to produce better access to the existing, underused library resources. These programmes have had a clear impact in the European library co-operation and development. Benefits of this work come to public libraries indirectly: common standards and working methods help in the end all kind of libraries.

But a fact is, that nearly all the libraries active in these EU projects are national libraries or big research and university libraries. Two main exceptions are Publican, a network of European public libraries, and ECUP, which was a copyright awareness raising project, and reached public libraries as well. A new beginning was the so called Morgan report in 1997. In this report libraries were for the first time put clearly onto the place where they belong in the information society.

As one result of the Morgan report, the European Commission informed that it will produce a Green Paper about the role of libraries in the information society. For one or another reason, this was made quite ready but was never published. In this situation the Committee on Culture, Youth, Education and the Media in the European Parliament decided to produce an own-initiative report about libraries.

The main reason was that they wanted to influence the big issues under work in the EU, first of all the copyright directive and the 5th framework programme, which will have a direct impact to libraries. I was nominated the rapporteur of the own-initiative report. The report was adopted almost unanimously and with a very encouraging discussion in the Plenary session of the Parliament in October 1998.

DECISIONS OF THE EP CONCERNING LIBRARY POLICY

In short, when adopting the own-initiative report, the EP was calling the Commission and/or the member states to following actions:

- Libraries must be taken in account in national and EU information society strategies and in the respective budgets.
- Libraries need more resources for acquiring expensive books.
- The Green Paper on libraries by the Commission must be completed.
- The users position must be taken in account in the copyright directive process, the balance must be maintained-this was politically the most important decision in short run.
- Support to libraries was demanded from the 5th Framework programme of research and development, *e.g.,* for networking,

drafting standards, preserving, and transferring information; there is no more named library programme under the 5th framework programme

- A clearing-house to solve problems of long-term conservation should be founded.
- Studies concerning permanent paper should be done on European level.
- The member states should take care of digitizing their cultural heritage for future.
- There should be studies and concrete support to libraries in licensing matters, which are–will be the next big issue in library work.
- The EU cultural and information budget should be opened to libraries as well, libraries and their co-operation should be taken in account in planning new programmes.
- Problems of legal deposit in international and multinational materials, especially in electronic materials should be solved.
- The member states should provide all types of libraries with modern equipment, particularly with Internet connections.
- Free of charge use of public libraries, in the spirit of the UNESCO Public Library Manifest, was demanded.
- Free and easy access via libraries to material produced with the aid of tax revenues was demanded.
- The members states should organize for their library professionals up-dating education and training.
- A European Union focal point for libraries should be set up
- The member states should found European information points at libraries in countries where they do not yet exist.
- Library statistics should be better and more comparable both on national and European level.
- The national Parliament libraries should be opened to the MEP's in countries where this is not yet the practice.

In addition to these, the report strongly stresses that the library financing must be re-thought in the information society. Without new resources libraries are unable to do everything they are expected to do! After the EP adoption of this report, the European Commission informed that it will next prepare a communication about actions to do.

It was stated that the report had already served as a discussion paper, and so the need for the Green Paper had disappeared. The communication is in summer 1999 still under work in the Commission DGXIII/2.

TRADITIONS AND NEW FORMS OF WORK IN THE SAME HOUSE

The European Commission R&D framework programmes have concentrated in IT matters. The three cultural programmes, Caledoskope, Ariane and Raphael, have not been very useful for libraries, because their scope has been quite narrow. *E.g.*, the books and reading programme Ariane has concentrated in translations. In the coming framework programme Culture 2000 libraries will have more possibilities to get support also for their cultural actions.

What then will be the fate of the traditional tasks of libraries in general? Will the information society wipe out book loaning and poems?

THE PUBLIC LIBRARIES IN THE KNOWLEDGE SOCIETY

THE LIBRARIES IN A STATE OF FLUX

The municipal reform in 2007 had major consequences for the library service. The number of libraries decreased and the remaining libraries grew in size. The reform thus underlined and intensified various tendencies in library development over the past many years.

The public library is in a state of flux. *Library service to children* from 2008 that chose as its point of reference the changes in children's use of the library. Thus this report had a strong focus on one target group and on how the library can develop new services to that group. The present report also focuses on the target group, but slightly more on the institution–the public library.

Based on a number of societal needs and new opportunities the report also considers how the library can be developed as an institution.

The library offer is changing rapidly, but it continues to be much sought after. Two out of three Danes use the public library, and 29% of the adult population visit the library at least once a month. In 2008 the public libraries registered more than 34 mil. visits.

This makes the library one of our most popular, public cultural offers, and this has been the case for many years. But the way we use the library is undergoing a change. On the one hand the loan of physical materials–books, CDs etc.–is falling. In the period 2000-2008 the public libraries' loan of physical materials has thus fallen by 22%, from ca. 62 mil. to app. 48 mil. materials.

On the other hand the use of digital offers is growing, an offer that spans from downloads of music and e-books to renewals of loans via the library's homepage. Bibliotekernes Netmusik, where as a library user you can via your municipality download music for free, experienced over 2,5 mil. downloads in 2008–an increase of 48% compared with 2007.

One explanation of the change in borrowing patterns could be that the technology and media development has resulted in new media habits on behalf of the library users. At the same time the libraries' consistently high visiting show that they have succeeded in reorganizing and revitalizing themselves and continue to be attractive.

This happens by developing new library services, particularly digital services, but also by turning the library into something more than just a collection of materials, so that the physical library maintains its desirability. Today the library is also a place for being and meeting, where one for example gets instruction, uses the Internet or gets help in the local citizen service centre.

However, borrowing books remains the main reason why Danes visit the library. The latest cultural habits survey from 2004 shows that 85% of adult library users visit the library to borrow books and journals. The same tendency becomes apparent in more recent studies. In a Gallup poll conducted on behalf of the Danish Library Association, the Union of Danish Librarians and HK Kommunal (white collar workers' union (municipal) in 2009, "borrowing books" is the most frequent reason for visiting the library, followed by "borrowing electronic media", "taking the children to the library" and "watching events".

There is in fact also a growing interest in the library's non-users, as can be seen from the large number of new initiatives, which the libraries participate in at municipal level. In many cases these have a social aspect, and the library is here used as a partner in a targeted initiative towards certain target groups.

This effort is particularly relevant in the light of the challenges that globalization presents to less resourceful citizens. The focusing on non-users also has another angle, which is i.a. clearly expressed in former minister for culture, Carina Christensen's strategy Culture for everybody from 2009. Here the emphasis is on the value of participating in a cultural community and the individual citizen's benefit from cultural offers.

The strategy suggests that all citizens should be able to take advantage of the cultural offers and consequently–that the cultural institutions focus more purposefully on non-users.

THE POLITICAL BASIS FOR THE COMMITTEE'S WORK

The appointment of the Committee on the Public Libraries in the Knowledge Society was decided by the minister for culture in connection with several consultations in Folketingets Kulturudvalg (parliamentary cultural committee), which took place in the wake of a large number of public library branches being closed down during the first year of the municipal reform.

The discussion fuelled by this naturally included the media and technology development. A suggestion for a more extensive, interdepartmental committee work was rejected by the minister, who referred to the work that had already been done by the Globalisation Council. The committee's work builds on the report *Future library service to children* from 2008.

The report contains a number of recommendations as to how to make sure that a strong library offer continues to be available to all Danish children. In 2008 the Danish Agency for Libraries and Media also published the report *The public libraries after the municipal reform*, which analysed the development within the public library area with particular focus on any consequences due to the municipal reform.

The report concluded that the closure of the branches in 2006-2007 was a natural adaptation of the library service, and that at the same time it demonstrated a prioritisation in order to deliver a more up-to-date and value-enhancing library offer. With the report from the Committee on the Public Libraries in the Knowledge Society we now have a number of recommendations as to how this prioritisation can be made so that the public libraries also in future will be able to meet the public's need for enlightenment, education and cultural activity.

The committee presents its recommendations within an expenditure-neutral framework with the perspective that it may be both necessary and correct with local changes of priorities within the library field in order to support and strengthen the public library in the knowledge society.

THE COMMISSION'S ASSIGNMENT: MANDATE FOR THE COMMITTEE ON THE PUBLIC LIBRARIES IN THE KNOWLEDGE SOCIETY

The committee must focus on continuous development of the public libraries in Denmark. This includes the public libraries' interaction with other libraries and relevant institutions. Focus must be on the libraries as an easily accessible offer to everybody.

The committee must build on the report *Future library service to children* and pay particular attention to service to youngsters and adults. The committee must assess the public libraries' role in relation to the challenges facing the knowledge society, the globalisation strategy's focus on education, lifelong learning and societal cohesive force.

The committee must assess to which extent there is basis for establishing new concepts for a library service that meets the public's needs in terms of enlightenment, education and cultural activity, and close to the citizens. Likewise the committee must asses the possibilities for continuous development of traditional core services such as literature dissemination.

In particular, the committee must asses the need for further development of the libraries' digital infrastructure and the interaction between digital and traditional services. The committee must furthermore describe models for the mediation of digital cultural heritage and licensed digital media and models for various forms of learning and inspiration activities (*e.g.,* in relation to citizens with poor reading and IT skills).

The committee must likewise give examples of new partnerships, including inter-institutional cooperations and binding networking commitments. Finally the committee must assess the need for competence development of library staff.

On the basis of its analyses the committee must put forward recommendations and suggestions as to how the strategy's objectives can be realised within the present legislation and existing division of labour between state and municipalities. The committee's suggestions must be expenditure-neutral. The committee is composed upon appointment, so that the minister for culture appoints three members, while Local Government (KL), Danish

Library Association, Association of Library Directors, Danish Research Library Association, the Regional Libraries, Union of Danish Librarians and Børne-og Kulturchefforeningen each appoints a member.

The Danish Agency for Library and Media's director general is chairman of the committee, and the Agency is the committee's secretariat. The committee must have completed its work primo 2010.

DIGITAL LIBRARIES AND SOCIETY

Digital libraries are large, organized collections of information objects. Whereas standard library automation systems provide a computerized version of the catalog—a gateway into the treasure-house of information stored in the library—digital libraries incorporate the treasure itself, namely the information objects that constitute the library's collection.

Whereas standard libraries are, of necessity, ponderous and substantial institutions, with large buildings and significant funding requirements, even large digital libraries can be lightweight. Whereas standard libraries, whose mandate includes preservation as well as access, are "conservative" by definition, with institutional infrastructure to match, digital libraries are nimble: they emphasize access and evolve rapidly.

The five stages in this part provide an excellent illustration of the huge variety of interesting issues in digital library research that impacts the Asia Pacific region. Unlike the New World, where most of the research on technological aspects of digital libraries originates, Asia has an exceptionally rich cultural heritage.

This manifests itself in a huge legacy of documents, in various forms—from paper to palm leaves—and in various different conditions. The need to preserve this legacy is particularly pressing in today's world, where political instability is rife and climate change is beginning to have an effect. As recent events have shown, disasters, both manmade and natural, can have a devastating effect on fragile cultural artifacts. S.M. Shafi from the University of Kashmir, India, surveys the many issues involved with digital archiving of medieval manuscripts in Asia. Libraries are pillars of education, and it is natural to expect that digital libraries will provide new opportunities for innovative educational practices.

These will be particularly relevant to the Asia Pacific region because of the huge disparities in access to education between the different communities there. Peer-to-peer learning has always been a crucial factor in personal development, although it is frequently ignored in educational studies.

Natalie Lee-San from Nanyang Technological University, Singapore, describes her studies of how digital libraries can provide an innovative, perhaps revolutionary, environment for peer-to-peer learning amongst youths. She touches on many practical issues: gender differences, different learning styles, different levels of media and computer literacy, and age-related differences. Many economies in the Asia Pacific region are agriculturally-based.

Modern agriculture is a knowledge-based activity that can benefit greatly from digital libraries. Mila Ramos from the International Rice Research Institute in the Philippines describes a large-scale digital library system designed to support the growth, nurturing, harvesting, and distribution of that most Asian of staples, rice.

This digital library supports an institute whose goal is to improve the well-being of present and future generations of rice farmers and consumers, particularly those with low incomes. The institute's library houses the world's most comprehensive collection of technical literature on rice, and provides a widely-used international reference service.

As in many specialized libraries, digital library technology is seen to have special advantages in a world of shrinking library budgets. Intellectual property issues are a central driving force behind the market in information of which libraries are a part. And the questions become more complex as the nature of today's information shifts from a primarily book-based culture to one that embraces all types of multimedia objects, and large, carefully-curated, collections of such objects.

The stage on *"Multimedia digital library as intellectual property"* by Hideyasu Sasaki and Yasujshi Kiyoki at Keio University in Japan clarify the copyright situation as it affects multimedia collections and compilations. They go on to discuss the patentability of particular retrieval mechanisms, an essential component of digital libraries.

The fifth stage in this part on how digital library research impacts the Asia Pacific region is the present one, on digital libraries in society. Most existing digital library projects, being research-oriented, are predicated on state-of-the-art equipment and interfaces, academic and research institutions, special collections.

In contrast: digital library technology can and should be available to everyone, on all platforms, in all countries; and it can and should enable ordinary people to exercise their creative powers to conceive, assemble, build, and disseminate new information collections that are designed not just for western academics but for a wide diversity of different audiences throughout the world.

Though less glamorous, this may, in the end, be a more important goal for society. Digital libraries pose an inherent tension between the technologist's desire for advanced solutions that use the latest and greatest hardware and software, and the librarian's desire for wide, crossplatform availability and long-term preservation—as epitomized by the sustained success of paper as a delivery medium.

To achieve universal access for both information consumers and collection-builders is really a problem for HCI. We examine the social need for digital libraries, particularly in developing countries, by briefly sketching some trends in commercial publishing and contrasting them with a growing international perspective of information as a public good.

We draw out the implications for the user interface, which is the principal bottleneck in allowing non-specialist people to make public information available in focused collections that are universally usable. Then we introduce digital library technology and illustrate it with a particular example, the Greenstone digital library software, which is designed for a broad user base and is in widespread use in many corners of the world—from Uganda to the US, Kazakhstan to Canada, Nepal to New Zealand. Following that, we review a project that is applying digital library technology to the distribution of humanitarian information in the developing world, a context that is both innovative and socially motivated.

Next we discuss issues of universal access and illustrate them with reference to the Greenstone software. We include a brief demonstration of a prototype system that is intended to allow anyone to build and disseminate information collections, and illustrates some human interface challenges that arise when providing necessarily complex functionality to a non-computer-oriented user base.

We close with the hope that future digital libraries will find a new role to play in helping to reduce the social inequity that haunts today's world, both within our own countries and between nations.

BOOKS, LIBRARIES, AND THE SOCIALLY DISADVANTAGED

Today, the long-standing three-way tension between the commercial interests of publishers, the needs of society and information users, and the social mandate of public libraries, is being pulled and stretched as never before.

First, the very notion of a "book" is evolving in many different directions: books become more interactive; publishers rent content; books are distributed under restrictive conditions that mechanically prohibit sharing. While it would be premature to make specific predictions, it seems likely that these trends will further disadvantage the disadvantaged—particularly those in poorer countries who have yet to benefit from ready access to ordinary books.

Second, a huge body of information is becoming freely available on the Internet. Much is of questionable quality, but some is very good indeed. In many cases the information is provided for the "public good" rather than for commercial profit, and the redistribution of such information is likely to be encouraged, rather than prohibited, by those who make it available.

Initiatives like UNESCO's "Information for all" programme and the upcoming World Summit on the Information Society highlight the importance of public information; they are founded on the belief that information literacy will help alleviate many of the problems confronting human societies. Third, the implications for libraries are mixed.

Whereas new controls by publishers over how the content they own may be used presents libraries with significant problems, the ready availability of "public good" information meshes well with library philosophy. A new role is emerging for information professionals who can select material, index it, add appropriate metadata, and redistribute it in added-value form for the good of society.

Suitable technological infrastructure is being provided by the open source movement, which is making available high-quality software for repackaging and distribution of information (and not just on computer networks).

What future has the book in the digital world? The question is a complex one that is being widely aired. Authors and publishers ask how many copies of a work will be sold if networked digital libraries enable worldwide access to an electronic copy of it.

Their nightmare is that the answer is *one*: how many books will be published online if the entire market can be extinguished by the sale of one electronic copy to a public library? To counter this threat, the entertainment industry is promoting new *"digital rights management"* (DRM) schemes that permit a degree of control over what users can do that goes far beyond the traditional legal bounds of copyright need, the acronym is more aptly expanded as "digital restrictions management" because it is concerned solely with content owners rights and not at all with user's rights.

It is, in effect, a "private governance system in which computer systems regulate which acts users are and are not authorized to perform" nticircumvention rules are sanctioned by the *Digital Millennium Copyright Act* (DMCA) in the US.

The DMCA has been used, for example, to prosecute a Norwegian teenager for writing software to play a DVD that he had purchased on a computer for which no commercial playback systems exist, an DRM be applied to books? The motion picture industry can compel manufacturers to incorporate encryption into their products because it holds key patents on DVD players. Commercial book publishers are promoting e-book readers that, if adopted on a wide scale, would allow the same kind of control to be exerted over reading material basic rights that we take for granted—such as the ability to lend a book to a friend, resell it on the second-hand market, keep it indefinitely, continue to use it when your e-book reader breaks down, donate it to charity, preserve it for your grandchildren, copy excerpts without resorting to a handwritten transcription—are in jeopardy. DRM allows such rights to be controlled, monitored, and withdrawn instantly, and DMCA legislation makes it illegal for users to seek redress by taking matters into their own hands.

Fortunately, perhaps, lack of standardization and compatibility issues are delaying consumer adoption of e-books, and the realm of scholarly publishing, digital rights management is more advanced. Academic libraries license access to content in electronic form, often in tandem with purchase of print versions too.

They have been able to negotiate reasonable conditions with publishers—probably because they represent the lion's share of the scholarly market.

However, the extent of libraries' power in the consumer book market is moot. One can envisage a scenario where publishers establish a system of commercial, pay-per-view, libraries for e-books and refuse public libraries access to books in a form that can be circulated.

These new directions present our society with puzzling challenges, and it would be rash to predict what society's response will be. But one thing is certain: they will surely increase the degree of disenfranchisement of those who do not have access to the technology.

In parallel with publishers' moves to reposition books as technological artifacts with refined and flexible control over how they can be used, an opposing trend has emerged: the ready availability of free information on the Internet.

Of course, the world-wide web is an unreliable source of enlightenment, and undiscriminating use is dangerous—and widespread. As early as 1996 complaints arose that the Web's contents are largely unattributed, undated, unannotated, unreliable; information about author and publisher is unavailable or incomplete; far too many resource catalogues are chasing far too few original or non-trivial documents—complaints that are very familiar today.

But one thing has changed: search engines and other portals have enormously increased our ability to locate information that is at least ostensibly relevant to any given question. Teachers complain bitterly that students view the Web as a replacement for the library, harvesting information indiscriminately to provide answers to assignments that are at best shallow and at worst incoherent and incorrect.

One consolation is that the very same search facilities can be used to detect plagiarism.

Nevertheless, the Web abounds with accessible, high-quality information. Many social groups, non-profit societies and charities make it their business to create sites and collect and organize information there. To take a single example at random, a Google search for *diabetes* returns three national diabetes associations in the top ten hits, and of course many more exist. Such of these sites offers a cornucopia of valuable information on the disease, which is not commercial and provided for the public good.

Widespread use is strongly encouraged, and it seems likely that arrangements could be made for re-distribution of the material presented there, particularly it was intended as a not-for-profit service and appropriate acknowledgement was made. And of the key problems with information distribution via the Web is that it disenfranchises developing countries.

Although the Web does not extend into the homes of the socially disadvantaged in developed countries either, various national programmes are working to provide access. But network access varies enormously across the world. Whereas in 1998 more than a quarter of the US population were surfing the Internet, the figures for Latin America and the Caribbean was

0.8%, for Sub-Saharan Africa 0.1%, and for South Asia 0.04%. Schools and hospitals in developing countries are poorly connected. Even in South Africa, the bestconnected African country, many hospitals and 75% of schools have no telephone line.

Universities are better equipped, but even there up to 1,000 people can depend on just one terminal. The Internet "is failing the developing world". Prompted by this inequity, the importance of information, and particularly public information, is today being highlighted by prominent international bodies.

For example, UNESCO's "Information for all" programme was established in 2001 to foster debate on the political, ethical and societal challenges of the emerging global knowledge society and to carry out projects promoting equitable access to information.

It reflects a growing awareness that information is playing an increasing role in generating wealth and human capital, and that participation in the "global knowledge society" is essential for social and individual development. Information literacy is described as "a new frontier" by the Director of UNESCO's Information Society Division. The Inter-national Telecommunications Union has established a World Summit on the Information Society, held in Geneva in December 2003 and Tunis in 2005, to promote a global discussion of the fundamental changes that are being brought about in our lives by the transformation from an industrial to an information society, and to confront the extreme disparities of access to information between the industrialized countries and the developing world.

What is the librarian to make of all this? The mandate of today's public libraries, in sharp contrast to that of publishers, is to facilitate the open distribution of knowledge.

Librarians strive to enable the free flow of information. Their traditions are liberal, founded on the belief that libraries should serve democracy. To help fulfil their mission as resource centers for citizens, public libraries maintain collections of records, policy statements, government documents, and so on.

A recent promotional video from the American Librarian's Association exults that "the library is democracy's place of worship". The impending redefinition of the book as a digital artifact that is licensed rather than sold, tied to a particular replay device, with restrictions that are clearly laid out and mechanically enforced, is an innovation that goes right to the heart of libraries. The changing nature of the book may make it hard, or even impossible, for libraries to fulfil their mandate by providing quality information to readers.

And on the other hand, the emergence of a vast storehouse of information on the Internet poses a different kind of conundrum. Librarians, the traditional gatekeepers of knowledge, are in danger of being bypassed, their skills ignored, their advice unsought. Search engines send users straight to the information they require—or so users think—without any need for an inter-mediary to classify, catalogue, cross-reference, advise on sources. The ready availability of information on the Internet, and its widespread use, really presents librarians with an opportunity, not a threat. Havvy users realise they need help, which librarians can provide.

A good example is Infomine, a cooperative project of the University of California and California State University. Infomine contains descriptions and links to a wealth of scholarly and educational Internet resources, each of which has been selected and described by a professional academic librarian who is a specialist in the subject and in resource description generally.

Participating librarians see this as an important expenditure of effort for their users, a natural evolution of their traditional task of collecting and organizing information in print. What kind of technical infrastructure is needed to support and promote this kind of work? Open source software is a powerful ally for librarians who wish to extend liberal traditions of information access.

These systems make the source code freely available for others to view, modify, and adapt; and the very nature of the licensing agreement prevents the software from being appropriated by proprietary vendors. But the open-source movement is more than just a vehicle for librarians to use: its link with library traditions goes much deeper.

Public libraries and open source software both enshrine the same philosophy: to promote learning and understanding through the dissemination of knowledge. Both are pervaded by a sense of community, on the one hand the kind of inter-institutional cooperation exemplified by interlibrary loan and on the other teams of designers and programmers that frequently cross national boundaries. Few trends in information access present librarians in developed countries with difficult and conflicting challenges.

Meanwhile, however, the situation in the developing world is dire. Here, traditional publishing and distribution mechanisms have failed tragically. For example, whereas a US medical library subscribes to about 5,000 journals, the Nairobi University Medical School Library, long regarded as a flagship center in East Africa, last year received just 20 journals. In Brazzaville, Congo, the university has only 40 medical books and a dozen journals, all from before 1993, and the library in a large district hospital consisted of a single bookshelf filled mostly with novels.

Traditional libraries are substantial institutions that occupy physical space, present a physical appearance, and exhibit tangible physical organization. When standing on the threshold of a large bricks-and-mortar library you gain a sense of presence and permanence that reflects the care taken in building and maintaining the collection inside. Digital libraries, in contrast, are lightweight.

But they provide potentially far greater accessibility, which means that they will have even greater social effects. Once created, they can, without significant institutional support, continue to serve users.

They can be distributed throughout most of the developed world over the Internet. In developing countries and remote corners of the developed world they can be circulated on removable media—CD-ROM, DVD, or 100 Gb disk units the size of videocassettes—and updated over radio. Issues of copyright pose difficult problems, but they are manageable. For example, there is plenty of non-copyright material, or material whose owners are prepared to donate copyright for socially useful purposes, and trends towards more open access to academic and humanitarian information are visible.

Not everyone sees digital rights management and the DMCA as the way forward, and in the longer term publishers, to remain viable, will have to investigate alternative revenue models for the information they own. No wonder international organizations such as the United Nations, along with many smaller *non-government organizations* (NGOs), are keenly interested in digital library technology. Advances in digital library technology are radically lowering the bar for the design and production of richly-organized, coherent, focused collections of information.

Now, anyone with access to sufficient source material can use public-domain software to build large, fullysearchable, collections the size of traditional personal or institutional libraries—in minutes. Let the minutes stretch to hours and the collection can be polished, organized, branded, distributed.

It can include fully-illustrated text, images, video, music. It can present attractively-designed pages with consistent use of icons. Keywords, key phrases, even acronyms and their definitions, can be extracted—automatically—and used to underpin novel means of access.

Let the hours stretch to days and metadata can be manually added that permits further levels of organization. Given access to programming skills, creative new facilities that stretch the imagination can be rapidly integrated into the system.

All this, one might say, can be done with ordinary Web sites: there is no need for digital library technology. However, bitter experience has shown that all but the most rudimentary sites do require significant institutional support—for organization and maintenance.

The Web is littered with incomplete, unfinished, unmaintained, outdated, inconsistently-organized, useless information collections. Just as traditional library cataloging procedures integrate new works into existing collections with minimal overhead so that they immediately become first-class members of the collection, so digital libraries allow new documents to be added completely automatically.

In the case of traditional libraries this is done through the small but nonnegligible overhead of generating a new catalog entry. With ordinary Web sites it requires inserting links manually into index pages and the like, and may involve adding links not only into the new document but also into existing ones that ought to reference it—it's like rewriting the book, and maybe revising all other books in the library too! In contrast, digital libraries bring access structures instantly and effortlessly up to date whenever new documents are added.

The challenge for HCI is to design and build digital library systems that fulfil the potential of digital libraries as a "killer app" for computers in developing countries, which will bring concomitant benefits in almost every other sphere of application. For the information consumer we need access to information that is guaranteed across space, time, and culture.

We need flexible distribution mechanisms for documents, and for information objects of all types, that can be accessed on all computer platforms—including the lowliest. We need a choice of distribution over the Web or on removable media such as CD-ROM or DVD. Digital libraries can incorporate flexible presentation that caters to individual differences, such as large-font displays or spoken output for the visually impaired.

Libraries are places where information is preserved, not rendered obsolete, and digital libraries must instill confidence that information prepared today can be accessed next week, next decade, next century—regardless of technological changes.

An important aspect of digital libraries is their ability to work in local languages, promoting pluralism and reducing the risks of homogeneity. Because language is the vehicle of thought, communication, and cultural identity, this will encourage diversity and strengthen individual cultures. But there is a long way to go: even Unicode is woefully incomplete in certain areas, such as African languages.

Naturally, today's digital library systems focus principally on the reader: the consumer of the material stored in the library's treasure-house. But digital libraries make a more radical, and perhaps ultimately more important, contribution by empowering ordinary users to conceive, assemble, build, and disseminate new information collections themselves and principle, modest computing resources are quite sufficient to enable users to build new collections by gathering together material in local files or on the Web; augmenting it with appropriate metadata that supports convenient search and browsing operations; incorporating advanced features like key-phrase extraction, document summarization, and metadata extraction; designing an attractive and functional interface; and publishing the collection on a variety of different media that are suitable for the intended readership.

The HCI challenge is to realise this potential for users—such as most librarians—who have a strong understanding of information and its organization, but no more interest in computers than they have in papermaking technology, last millennium's vehicle for information dissemination.

UNIVERSAL ACCESS

Universal access to digital libraries presents huge challenges to software engineers and HCI practitioners. The Greenstone digital library software allows us to glimpse some of the issues, although it certainly does not yet effectively address them all.

Most digital libraries are accessed over the web, using any web browser. However, in many environments, particularly in developing countries, web access is insufficient and the system must run locally.

And if people are to build and control their own libraries, a centralized solution is inadequate: the software must run on their own computers. Thus digital library systems intended for broad access should run on a wide variety of computer systems, particularly low-end ones. Developed under Linux, the Greenstone server runs on any Windows, Unix, or MacOS/X system. All versions of Windows are supported, from 3.1 up.

Supporting primitive platforms poses substantial challenges of a rather mundane nature: for example, Microsoft compilers no longer support Windows 3.1 and it is necessary to acquire obsolete versions. Under Windows, pre-built collections can be viewed on any system with at least 8 Mb RAM, but collections cannot be built under Windows 3.1/3.11—for this at least a Pentium processor is generally required, except for very small collections.

The fact that Greenstone does not run on early Macintosh systems is a serious drawback in certain environments. In an international cooperative effort established in August 2000 with UNESCO and the Belgium-based Human Info NGO, Greenstone is being distributed widely in developing countries with the aim of empowering users, particularly in universities, libraries, and other public service institutions, to build their own digital libraries.

UNESCO recognizes that digital libraries are radically reforming how information is acquired and disseminated in its partner communities and institutions in the fields of education, science and culture around the world, and particularly in developing countries.

Their hope is that this software will encourage the effective deployment of digital libraries to share information and place it in the public domain. The UNESCO distribution of Greenstone is a CD-ROM that contains the full source code and executable binaries for Windows and Linux, along with all necessary associated software.

Full documentation and five demonstration collections are included. The current CD-ROM is trilingual, with complete interfaces, instructions, and documentation in English, French and Spanish. For those with Web access, the same package is also available for download from the Greenstone Web site, often in a form that is slightly ahead of the CD-ROM version—for example, many other language interfaces are included and full documentation is available in Russian and Kazakh too. Providing accessibility in different languages is more difficult than one might at first realise.

As well as the manuals, installation instructions and installation prompts, the licensing agreement, and the readme files have to be translated too. Greenstone collections like the Humanity Development Library can be published as standalone collections on removable media such as CD-ROM, or presented on the Web. CD-ROM is a very practical format in developing countries.

Any Greenstone collection can be converted into a self-contained Windows CD-ROM that includes the Greenstone server software itself and an integrated installation package. The installation procedure has been thoroughly honed to ensure that only the most basic of computer skills are needed to install and run a collection under Windows.

Even standalone Greenstone users interact through a Web browser: Netscape is supplied on each CD-ROM for those who do not already have a browser. In standalone mode the software runs locally but incorporates a Web server so that if the system happens to be connected to a network—say a hospital or school intranet—information is available to other machines that may not possess CD drives.

This happens automatically: no special configuration is necessary. Another difficult engineering challenge is checking for the existence of a network. While installed network software is easily detected, it is hard to determine non-intrusively whether it is operational.

Incorrectly installed or configured software is endemic in developing countries, because computers there are often cast-offs whose software is inappropriate to their present environment, yet system support to rectify the problems is unavailable.

It is essential for universal access that such problems are addressed properly and solved satisfactorily without involving the user, even though they are mundane and timeconsuming. Greenstone provides some support for the visually impaired by incorporating a "textual" mode of access that replaces all images by textual prompts.

This output is suitable for users with speech synthesizers or other specialized access devices. However, the facility is not well advanced: in particular, we have not yet refined it through usability testing and interface improvement.

HISTORICAL DEVELOPMENT OF LIBRARY

GROWTH AND DEVELOPMENT OF ORIENTAL LIBRARIES IN INDIA

Libraries have always had a pivotal role in the storage, processing, and dissemination of information. Some may serve general needs, but special libraries serve the needs of a particular community of users. Among special libraries, Oriental libraries hold an important place because they preserve the cultural heritage of a nation or a civilization.

Oriental Libraries

"Oriental Libraries" are those libraries that have literature pertaining to

Oriental studies and languages. "Oriental" in this context refers to the ancient Near East, including India, Persia, and ancient Arabia, among other places, and the languages and literatures of those places and peoples.

Growth and Development

India is a vast repository of different cultures, both because it was invaded by a number of foreign countries and peoples, and because of its contacts with people from the East. The languages from those Eastern countries are part of Indian literature. The literature in those Eastern languages created India's Oriental libraries.

Their history can be traced back to the Vedic period, when the written literature was kept in Ashrams or Gurukuls. Gurukuls were mostly located peaceful forest environments. With the passage of time, Gurukuls were also established in cities.

Jain and Buddhist Era

Taxila was one of the famous educational centres where students came from different parts of the country. Varanasi also distinguished itself by having a large number of Gurukulas. During this period, the literature was preserved in the Sutra style of composition.

Buddhist and Jain Monastries acted as repositories of knowledge, for religious literature as well as other types. Monastic Oriental Libraries were also called Viharas. Over time, these Viharas developed into institutions of higher learning. A federation of Viharas constituted a Mahavihara, which was a larger educational institutional institution.

Nalanda Mahavihara is the best example. Fa-Hien, a Chinese traveller, also found a number of monastaries in India. Kanyakubja, Sravasti, Kusunagara, Vaisali, and Patliputra were centres of Oriental literature according to Fa-Hien. Hiuen-Tsang, another Chinese traveller, visited India during 629-645 A.D.

He left a detailed account of his visit, which gives us significant information about Buddhist educational institutions possessing a rich variety of Eastern literature. Taxila was a center of learning in Ancient India and a large number of people from all over the world and the subcontinent itself visited this place to gain knowledge.

Literature related to medicine and archery enriched the library at Taxila. Rahula Sankrityayana, Angiris set up a seminary with a Granthakuti attached to it at Taxila, which later flourished in to an academy or university. Nalanda University is the best known of ancient India 's universities. It has been called the treasure house of information by European archeologists. The information there helped locate Buddhist shrines in India.

It is believed that King Kumara Gupta built the first monastery at Nalanda to train Buddhist monks. Nalanda University was an expansion of this seminary. King Buddha Gupta, Jagatha Gupta, Baladitya, and Vijra made additions and expansions to the building.

There were three large libraries with vast amount of literature in Oriental languages on subjects such as science, medicine, astrology, fine arts, literature. The University of Valabhi was built by the Maitraka Kings during the years 475-775 A.D. Its library had a variety of Eastern literature. This great university and its library lasted until the 12th century, when they were completely destroyed by Arab invaders.

Odantapuri University was founded by King Gopala and was a well-known center of learning. It had a library that was rich in Brahmanical and Buddhist works. Mohammad Bakhtiyar Khilji destroyed this monastic university along with its library. Somapuri also possessed a wealth of Oriental literature, but it was destroyed by fire in the middle of the 11th century.

Vikramasila monastery, built by King Dharmapala, had a variety of literature on metaphysics, tantras, grammar, ritualism, and logic. The library fulfilled the demands of outsiders, especially those from Tibet, by providing them copies of manuscripts in a most liberal way. Another University with a significant Oriental collection, especially in Tantric Buddhism, was Jagaddala, founded by King Ramapala.

Another monastery with a rich wealth on different aspects of Oriental literature was Kanheri University, built during the reign of Amoghavarsha. By the 10th century, the corpus of Jain literature had increased many times, and Jain monks had contributed substantially to nearly all branches of knowledge known at that time. The Jayendra monastery of Kashmir had a good library where the Chinese traveller Hiuen–Tsang spent two years copying manuscripts.

Similarly, he spent fourteen months at the Chinapati monastery. Several Hindu kings and their ministers, who flourished between 10th and 12th centuries AD, are credited with establishing libraries and supporting the library movement. Among them was King Bhoja of Dhara, who flourished in the 11th century, and was a distinguished scholar with a rich library. King Kumarapaladeva of the Chaulakyas is said to have established 21 Jain Libraries. He kept a copy of Kalpasutra written in golden ink in each one of them.

Mughal Empire

When the Muslims established their rule in India at the beginning of the 13th century, Muslim emperors paid special attention to libraries, taking care to establish libraries in educational institutions. They constructed no separate library buildings; rather, books were deposited and preserved in educational institutions, mosques, and Khangahs.

Many Muslim rulers were from the East, and they helped enrich libraries with Oriental literature. Paper began be used as a writing material in the 12th century, and this helped book production in this periods. Mughal sovereigns and their courtiers were educated and accomplished, and some maintained personal libraries.

The Muslim sovereigns collected and preserve the Vedas, the Ramayana, and other Hindu religious books. They also translated a variety of books in

Hindi in to Persian and Arabic, and helped disseminate Hindu art and culture. After the establishment of Sultans of Delhi in 1202, a new period in the history of Oriental libraries came in to existence. These minor Muslim rulers and nobles encouraged Islamic learning and established *maktabs* (primary schools), *madrasas* (schools of higher learning), libraries, and mosques.

They encouraged Arabic and Persian literatures in all branches of learning, and enriched Oriental literature in the libraries. They gave shelter and protection to scholars, who brought literature from other parts of the world to India. The Library of Khwajah Nizam-ud-din Auliya was an important Oriental library.

It was the property of the *Waqf* (religious board) and was open to every man of letters. During the reign of the Khilji dynasty the number of Oriental libraries increased. Jala-ud-din Khiljee established the Imperial Library at Delhi and appointed Amir Khusru as its librarian.

The Tughluq Dynasty opened a new chapter in the history of Oriental libraries in India. Mohammad Tughluq built one thousand madrasas, each with a library with collections in Arabic and Persian. Humayun ascended the throne in 1530 and a library known as Khan-i-Tilism.

Humayun's library played a significant role in Mughal history. Akbar, the greatest of Mughal emperors maintained a very rich library. He added a sizable number of books, obtained from his conquest, from libraries in Gujrat, Jaunpur, Kashmir, Bihar, Bengal, and the Deccan.

His library was unique in its collection of rare books, among which was the Persian *Divan of Human Shah*. By the time of Akbar's grandson, Shah Jahan, the library was a complex organization with a large staff, and headed by Nazim, a noble of the court. In Kashmir, a picture of the first library is found in the Shrine of Hazrat Bulbul Shah, which was established by Muslims.

A magnificient monastery and mosque were constructed by the emperor of Kashmir, Sultan Sadruddin, for Hazrat Bulbul Shah. A library was attached to this mosque. Amir Kabir Syed Hamdani, a theologian and scholar had a well established personal library that contained Oriental literature. He established a number of libraries in Kashmir which added to the wealth of the Indian Oriental libraries.

The Sultans of Kashmir had given funds to establish madrasas and libraries. Each madrasa had a library. Sultan Zain-ul-Abedin-ul constructed a library which historians tell was one of the best in the world. Among the other libraries built by Budshah, Darul-ul-Uloom Nausherah was the best.

Another library, by the name of Madrasa-i-Sher, was built by Budshah near modern Islamabad. During the Chak Sultanate many libraries thrived and brought Oriental literature to the limelight. Akbar conquered Kashmir in 1587 and established many madrasas and libraries there. In Gujrat and Malwa, a number of libraries were introduced by Ahmad Shah I and Dilawar Khan.

Shah Jahan, like his predecessors, patronized learning and education and built a library with a rich collection of Arabic and Persian manuscripts.

Dara Shikkoh, Aurangzeb, and Bahadur Shah Zafar also contributed to the development of Oriental libraries. Mughal rule was a period of literary excellence. Most of the emperors were themselves scholars, and also extended their patronage to scholarship and learning.

Other Kingdoms

There were kingdoms in other parts of India that also had libraries enriched by Oriental literature. The kingdoms of Bahmani and Deccan had independent kings who reigned for 340 years, and who were patrons of learning, as were the Bahmani kings, who continued their rule up to 1526 AD and had an empire that stretched from coast to coast.

They founded many colleges and libraries. Ahmad Shah built a magnificient college near Gulbarga. Muhammad Shah Bahmani II built another imposing college at Bidar that is one of the many beautiful remains of the grandeur of the Bahmanis. All these colleges had libraries that possessed an enormous amount of Oriental literature.

Arabian and Iranian literature brought by visitors and travellers were added to the libraries of Bahmanis. The Urdu language was at its zenith during the reign of Firoz Shah Bahmani, and a vast amount of Urdu literature enriched the Bahmani Libraries.

The library of Gesudaraj was distinguished among the libraries of Deccan. Books on Sufism and religion were available in this library. The emperors of Qutub Shahi also established a good number of libraries during their reign, and a vast amount of literature in Persian was included. Tipu Sultan, son of Haider Ali and emperor of Mysore established a number of libraries.

"Zaimul-Umoor" was the great university of Seringa Patnam in his reign. He collected books from many countries including Europe. The library had a copy of the Holy Quran which was written by the hand of Aurangzeb Alamgir. It is estimated that the library had nearly 2,000 volumes of Persian, Arabic, and Hindi manuscripts from all branches of Islamic literature.

After the downfall of the Mughals, and with the invasion of Ahmad Shah Abdali, the literary wealth of the Indian libraries was looted away. In 1857, after the Sepoy mutiny, thousands of books were destroyed and thousands of important, valuable, and rare books were siphoned to England.

British and other Europeans

The growth and development of Oriental libraries was regenerated again during European and British rule. The interest shown by the British and European scholars in Oriental Learning and Indology, along with the social, cultural and religious movements spearheaded by eminent Indians, resulted in new Oriental libraries. These institutions established libraries for Oriental scholarship. The result of this renaissance is a number of special libraries devoted to Oriental and Indological collections in various parts of the country.

Rampur Raza Library, very rich in Indo-Islamic studies and arts, was created by Nawab Faizullah Khan in 1794, and has tremendous manuscript wealth. One can find manuscripts in Arabic, Persian, Urdu, Sanskrit, Sinhali, Tamil, Kannada, and other Oriental languages.

The Asiatic Society Library, Kolkatta, a premier and leading oriental institutions of the country was established in 1784 by Sir William Jones. Colonel Mackenzie, an Englishman and an engineer by profession established an Oriental Library by the name of " *Government Oriental Manuscript Library* (GOML) " in Chennai.

Contemporary Libraries

Khuda Baksh Oriental Library was founded in 1842 by Maulvi Khuda Baksh Khan, who donated his entire personal collection. Since 1977 it has been issuing regularly a multi-lingual research quarterly *Khuda Baksh Library Journal.* The library has been recognized as a research center by seven Indian universities. The collection has a rich repository of Persian and Arabic manuscripts. Maulana Azad Library, Aligarh Muslim University was initially founded as "Anglo Oriental College (MAOC) at Aligarh in 1875 and raised to the status of a university in 1920.

The personal collection of Maulana Azad also enriches the library. The library has a total collection of over 1 million volumes and 14,571 manuscripts. The Maulana Azad Library has the largest collection of Urdu books in the Indian subcontinent, which is perhaps largest in the world as well.

The collection includes:

- Urdu
- Arabic
- Persian
- Sanskrit
- Hindi
- Sir Syed Collection
- Gandhian Collection
- Aligarh Collection
- Thesis Collection
- Archives
- Microfiche
- Manuscripts

Hakim Mohammad Syed Library, Jamia Hamdard, New Delhi is a leading university founded in 1906.

It has a well known Oriental library, which has a number of special collections:

- Nazaria Collection
- Abdul Sattar Siddiqui Collection
- Maulana Abdul Salam Niazi Collection
- Jaffri Collection
- Shafi Ahmad Collection

- Dr Tanveer Alvi Collection

The library has 4,500 rare manuscripts. Osmania University Library was established in 1918 and is considered seventh oldest in India, the third oldest in South India, and the first to be established in state of Hyderabad.

The library has a collection of rare books and manuscripts including Palm Leaf manuscripts. The National Library of India, which came in to existence in 1948, is the largest library in India. Previously it was known as the Imperial Library which was formed in 1891 by combining a number of Secretariat libraries.

It has a wide range of collections in a variety of national and international languages. A good number of Arabic and Persian documents are also available here. The Oriental library initiative that took place in ancient India reached its zenith in the period when the British and other Europeans came to India. The Mughals also contributed a great deal to the development of Oriental libraries. Eventually, their extravagant ways caused the libraries to deteriorate, but social and political conditions eventually led to better libraries with larger collections.

ACADEMIC LIBRARIES IN INDIA: A HISTORICAL STUDY

Research in library history in India has remained largely neglected area which has resulted into availability of very limited and scanty literature. Commenting on the status of library history in India, Donald G. Davis, Jr. of the University of Texas at Austin, writes that "although a core literature on Indian library history exists, it has many imbalances and gaps. The scholars are very dispersed in their interests and their geographical location. With one person rarely contributing more than one work. There is little pattern to existing research efforts."

In this context, the role of historian happens to be much more crucial and significant to make an assessment of the growth and development of libraries in India, the factors responsible for their development and the impact of those factors on the library progress. Rajgopalan, in his 1987 presidential address to the Indian Library Association rightly said, "it is generally acknowledged that our libraries are underutilized in relation to investments being made in them.

Non-use and low-use of libraries amount to wastage of facilities being made available. Maybe the literacy rate, lack of reading habits, etc., are the causes for low use from the side of patrons... User education programmes must be organized by libraries in a way that libraries are fully utilized." He further remarked that, "if library historians would address the roots and trends of library issues, they would provide a valuable service to the profession and society."

The Father of Library and Information Science in India,Padmashri Dr. S.R. Ranganathan while giving a radio talk in April 1956 said, "an account of the libraries in the first four periods must necessarily depend upon the historical research. This has not yet been done. The library profession is too small in India to spare a person to fill up this antiquarian gap. Those trained in the scientific method of tracing history are too preoccupied with dynastic and political history to spare sufficient time for cultural history in general and library history in particular."

Thus, an historical study of the growth and development of academic libraries in India, is a desideratum, the fulfillment of which should go a long way in removing the imbalances and gaps. Such a study becomes significant not only in view of the tremendous activity concerning the growth and development of libraries in India, but also because their growth has been shaped in the first phase by the phenomena that have shaped the historical course of this period and, secondly, the rise of library as an important instrument in the advancement of knowledge and socio-economic transformation.

Source Material for Writing History of Libraries

For the purpose of scientific writing of history of libraries, an understanding of the nature of existing source material and knowing the art of using it is essential. The sources for writing the history are available in Pali, Sanskrit, Chinese, Arabic, Persian and European Languages and most of them have been translated into English. These exist in various formats, such as Manuscripts, inscriptions, copper plates etc.

They are either indigenous or foreign. The contribution of foreign travelogues such as Tibetan, Chinese, Muslim, Portuguese, English and other Europeans is highly useful. Some noteworthy foreign travelogues are Itsing, Fahien, Hieun Tsang, Alberuni, Ibn Batuta, Minhaj, Firishta, Badauni, Afif, bernier, mandelso, Manrique de Lara, Martin, Count Noer.

In addition to the contribution of the travelogues, the contribution of historians like Henry M. Eliot, John Dawson, Stanley Lane-Pool, Ishwari Prasad, R.C. Majumdar, Jadunath Sarkar, V.D. Mahajan, Mohammed Muhammed Zubair, J.S. Sarma and N.N. Law etc. is also significant.

Though scanty, yet there are articles written by the library professionals on history of libraries. A few efforts have also been made for conduct of research in the area of history of libraries and such like works have been consulted for the purpose of writing this chapter.

University Libraries in Ancient India

In the Vedic age instructions were imparted "orally, without the medium of books." Taxila from 700 B.C. to 300 A.D. was considered to be the most respected seat of higher learning and education in India but still there is no evidence found so far in the archaeological excavations at Taxila that there had been a good library system in the Taxila University.

Fa-Hien noticed such libraries at Jetavana monastery at Sravasti. In 400 A.D., there came into being one of the biggest known universities, the Nalanda

University, which by 450 A.D. became a renowned seat of learning, its fame spreading beyond the boundaries of India.

Nalanda near Patna grew to be the foremost Buddhist monastery and an educational centre. Most of what we know of the Nalanda University during the 6th and the 7th centuries A.D. is due to the accounts left by Hiuen-tsang, who lived in the institution for three years in the first half of the 7th century, and I-tsing who also stayed there for ten years towards the latter part of the same century.

Information on the Nalanda University Library is also found in the Tibetan accounts, from which we understand that the library was situated in a special area known by the poetical name the Dharmaganja, which comprised three huge buildings, called the Ratnasagara, the Ratnodadhi and the Ratnaranjaka of which the Ratnasagara was a ninestoried building and housed the collection of manuscripts and rare sacred works like Prajnaparamita Sutra etc.

The library at Nalanda had a rich stock of manuscripts on philosophy and religion and contained texts relating to grammar, logic, literature, the Vedas, the Vedanta, and the Samkhya philosophy, the Dharmasastras, the Puranas, Astronomy, Astrology and Medicine. The University of Nalanda and its library flourished down to the 12th century A.D. until Bakhtiyar Khalji sacked it in 1197-1203 A.D.7 and set fire to the establish-ment of Nalanda.

The world famous universities, such as, the Vikramasila, the Vallabhi and the Kanchi were coming up in other parts of the country during the period from the 5th century A.D. to the 8th century A.D. All these universities possessed rich libraries and in the hall containing such books there used to be an image of the goddess Saraswati with a book in her hand.

The Nalanda and the Vikramshila universities were under the control of the king Dharmapala. He founded the Vikramshila monastery in the 8th century A.D. It had a rich collection of texts in the Sanskrit, the Prakrit and the Tibetan languages.

Regarding the library of the university, the *Tabaqat-i-Nasiri* informs us that there were great number of books on the religion of Hindus there; and when all these books came under the observation of the Mussalamans, they summoned, a number of Hindus that they might give them information regarding the import of these books; but the whole of the Hindu community was killed in the war.

Muslim vandalism caused the disappearance of the excellent collection at Vikramashila. The Jaggadal Vihara in Varendra-bhumi was also an important centre of learning with considerable collection of the reading material. It was established by the king Kampala, who ruled from 1084 to 1130 A.D.

The provision of facilities for reading, writing, editing and translating manuscripts shows that this library was in no way less than its contemporary libraries in importance. Though not as large as the library of Nalanda, it abounded in private collection of texts.

Likewise Mithila had been famous for its scholars since the days of Rajrishi Janaka and had a rich collection of various commentaries on the different branches of the Hindu *Shastras.* The library of its university played an important role in teaching and learning. A needle *(Shalaka)* was pierced through the manuscript on the subject of the student's specialization and he was expected to explain the last page pierced.

In this way the student's all-round mastery of the subject was tested. Mithila continued to enjoy its all India importance in the field of learning till the end of the 15th century AD. The university at Sompuri, like that of Vikramshila, occupied a significant position since the days of Dharampala.

Like Nalanda, this university also had its own library. Atisa Dipankar, a noted scholar, lived there. He with the help of other scholars, translated into the Tibetan the *Madhyamkaratnapradipa* of Bhavaviveka. This university was destroyed by fire in the middle of the 11th century A.D. Efforts were made by the monk Vipulsrimitra to renovate the university but it could not regain its past glory.

At a time when Nalanda was famous for its *Mahayana* courses of study, the Maitrakakings provided their patronage to the Mahavihara of Vallabhi. This university was famous for its *Hinayana* studies. The fact that this university had a good library is supported by a reference in a grant of Guhasena, dated 559 A.D., wherein a provision was made out of the royal grant for the purchase of books for the library.

This important seat of learning at Kanheri, on the West Coast, flourished during the reign of Amoghavarsha in the 9th century A.D. The library occupied a significant position within the establishment, and the donors provided money to buy books for the library.

The last of the famous seats of learning in Eastern India was Navadwipa in Bengal. It reached its height of glory from 1083 to 1106 A.D. as a centre of intellectual excellence as well as its rich library facilities, when Lakshman Sen, a king of Gauda, made it his capital. However, this library was also destroyed along with the centre by Bakhtiyar Khalji.

Situated in South India at Amaravati, on the banks of the Krishna, the Nagarjuna Vidyapeeth flourished in about 7th century A.D. Its library housed in the top floor of the five storyed building of the university had an enormous collection on the Buddhist philosophy, particularly of the *Mahayana* school that Nagarjuna had founded, science and medicine.

There is enough archaeological evidence that supports the existence of this 7th century university and its library. The enormity of the collection in this library is borne out by the fact that it not only had works on the Buddhist literature and the *Tripitakas,* but also works on several branches of scientific knowledge, such as, Botany, Geography, Mineralogy and Medicine. It was a great attraction for scholars from the different parts of India and from countries, like, China, Burma and Ceylon.

University Libraries in Medieval India

The existence of academic libraries during the medieval period of Indian history is not known, though the Muslim rulers did patronize libraries in their own palaces. A lone exception, however, was a library attached to a college at Bidar, having a collection of 3000 books on different subjects. Aurangzeb got this Library transferred to Delhi to merge it with his palace library. During the medieval period, due to Muslim invasions and political troubles, the powerful empires and kingdoms of Indian rulers fell one by one. This affected higher education and the development of academic libraries as well.

Libraries in Modern India

During the British rule in India, number of academic institutions were established by the East India Company, and by the Christan missionaries. Some of the worth mentioning events which led to the growth and development of higher education in India during this period were the establishment of the Calcutta College in 1781, Jonathan Duncan, then a British agent, founded the Benaras Sanskrit College in 1792. The Calcutta Fort William College was founded in 1800. All these colleges were having their own libraries.

The Charter Act of 1813, the foundation of Fort William and Serampore Colleges, Calcutta, Madras and Bombay universities and their libraries, Hunter, Raleigh and Calcutta University Commissions, library training programmes, the establishment of Inter University Board, Sargent Report and appointment of the University Grants Committee, the establishment of Madras University, University of Bombay, University of Calcutta and their libraries, the constitution of Inter-University Board, the appointment of Hartog Committee, the Montague-Chelmsford reforms of 1919, the Government of India Act of 1935, and the Sargent Committee Report etc. laid foundation for establishment of libraries in various parts of the country.

The Fort William College was founded in Calcutta on 18th August 1800 by the Marquis of Welleselay, the Governor-General of India during 1798-1805. Reverend David Brown, Provost of the college was instrumental in setting up the library which had a well rounded collection of Eastern manuscripts.

In the absence of adequate financial support, the library could not survive for long and in 1835 it was decided to close the library and its valuable collection was transferred to the Asiatic Society Library in Calcutta between 1835-39. The Charter Act of 1813 passed by the British Parliament gave the East India Company complete responsibility for educating Indians.

The establishment of C.M.S. College in Kottayam, Hindu college in Calcutta in 1816 and Raven Shaw College in Cuttack in 1816 was the immediate result of the Charter Act 1813. These and other colleges came into existence thereafter had their own libraries the day they were established. Serampore

College during this period was founded by the Danes in 1818 and the King of Denmark in 1927 agreed to give this college an academic status by providing equivalence to the Danish Universities with power to confer degrees.

The library of this college too was established along with its foundation and at a later stage the college was given affiliation to the University of Burdwan for the purpose of conferring degrees. The 7th March 1835 decision of the British Indian Government to promote English literature and sciences in India was resulted into the spread of number of colleges in India and by 1839 there were over forty colleges with attached libraries in the British territory in India.

For their establishment, lots of money was made available by the Indians in the form of donations. In 1840 Presidency College was founded in Madras, followed by a medical college in Bombay in 1845. This progress in education was instrumental in establishing universities in India.

The Charles Wood dispatch of 1854 popularly known as the 'Magna Carta of English Education' in India also paved the way for the establishment of the universities in the presidency towns. Sir John Colville introduced the Bill to establish universities in India and it was passed by the Governor General of India Lord Dalhousie on 24th January 1857, paved the way for the foundation of three universities based on the London Universities Model in the Presidency towns of Calcutta, Madras and Bombay.

Indian Education Commission, popularly known as Hunter Commission was appointed by the British Indian Government in 1882 to study the progress of education under the new policy adopted in 1854 by the East India Company and transferred to the Crown and accepted by the Secretary of State in 1859. Sir William W. Hunter in his report had clearly stated that the conditions of the libraries was in a very poor state and declared them "hardly creditable." The Commission paid special attention to the colleges and their libraries and other facilities.

The direct result of the Commission was the establishment of Panjab University, Lahore and Allahabad University in 1882 and 1887 respectively but still the condition of the education and libraries remained in a poor state.

The Raleigh Commission 1902 appointed by Lord Curzon to investigate the conditions and prospects of the Indian universities and to recommend measures to improve their constitution and working and standards of teaching also paid special attention to the academic libraries and found that, "the library is little used by graduates and hardly at all by other students." Further, the Commission commented, "In a college where library is inadequate or ill arranged, the students have no opportunity of forming the habit of independent and intelligent reading."

Thus, the Commission specifically recommended that reference services must be made an integral part of all libraries in colleges and universities, and that one of the prerequisite conditions for the grant of university affiliation to a college be the accessibility of students to the library of the institution.

The recommendations of the Raleigh Commission were included in the Universities Act of 1904 and provided the power to all universities to require that all colleges applying for affiliation maintain proper libraries, equipment, library building, and lend books to all students but the situation and the status of libraries could not be improved much simply because the recommendations made by the Commission and the provisions made in the act could not be implemented properly.

The Calcutta University Commission popularly known as Sadler Commission was appointed by the government in 1917 to study the situation and the status of education in the country and to make recommendations to solve the existing problems.

The Commission noticed that "one of the greatest weak-nesses of the existing system is the extraordinarily unimportant part which is played by the library" and found that "in some colleges the library is regarded not as an essential part of teaching equipment but merely as a more or less useless conventional accessory." The Commission made the recommendations regarding the libraries that college libraries be strengthened and that training should be given to the students and occasionally to the teachers about use of the library.

One of the immediate result of the Calcutta University Commission was the establishment of a few new teaching-cum-residential universities at Patna in 1917, Osmania in Hyderabad in 1918, Dacca, Aligarh, and Lucknow in 1921, Delhi in 1922 and Nagpur in 1923 and all of them were established along with the establishment of libraries as an integral part of the university system.

As stated earlier, the impact of the Commission could very well be seen in the establishment of several universities along with their libraries. This was the period when in the libraries scenario, a person appeared who at a later stage turned the entire scene and become the father of library science in India.

The man was none other than Dr. S.R. Ranganathan. The University of Madras appointed Dr. S.R. Ranganathan as its Librarian in 1924. He was trained at the University of London Library School before joining his duties at Madras. Things did change rapidly after his joining. For example, he introduced the lending and reference services at the Madras University Library and extended the library hours for the benefit of the readers.

Whereas the hours had previously been 7 a.m. to 4 p.m., they were changed to 7 a.m. to 6 p.m. He delivered a series of lectures to about two thousand teachers at the conference of the South Indian Teachers' Union in 1929 regarding the use and importance of the library services.

The Madras Library Association started a summer course in librarianship and the lectures for this course were mainly delivered by Dr. Ranganathan. The main objective of the course in its beginning was to spread the ideas of the value of good library services and modern library methods among potential users of the library. The budget of the university library of Madras had been very poor from the beginning and it was really a difficult task to manage, run and administer the library effectively within it.

Ranganathan brought this poor financial position to the notice of the then Chief Minister, Dr. P. Subbaroyan, when he delivered a speech during an educational conference held at Madras in 1926. In his speech, Ranganathan "gave a graphic account of the library network in Europe and the United States of America and compared it with the poor, appalling facilities existing in India.... added that paucity of funds prevented him developing his library."

The Chief Minister was highly impressed by Ranganathan's speech and promised to give more State help to the University Library. Its immediate result was a grant of rupees 6,000 which was added to the annual grant from the State, and, in addition, rupees 100,000 in lump sum were sanctioned by the Madras State Government in the same year to buy books and periodicals in pure sciences, humanities, and social sciences.

Provision was also made for additional grants to the library, as and when new departments of study and research were established. In the words of Ranganathan, "This was the first time when such a forward financial step in the history of the university libraries in India was taken in the second quarter of the 20th century."

The University of Madras library made a good start under Ranganathan's effective leadership and administration. In 1930, the library had five well-trained reference librarians to help the readers, and they "carried the work to a high pitch of efficiency."

This was the first time in the history of Indian libraries that a special reference service was introduced in a university library. The library collection increased to 93,000 volumes in 1935 and on September 3, 1936, the library was shifted to its first new and permanent functional building. By 1944, when Ranganathan resigned from the position of the Librarian, to become the University Librarian at the *Banaras Hindu University* (BHU), the collection of the Madras University Library had augmented to 1,20,000 volumes.

The contribution of Dr. Ranganathan to the growth and development of libraries in general and the Madras University Library in particular is undoubtedly tremendous and unforgettable. It will not be wrong to say that the Library School of Madras and the Madras University Library were the laboratories of Ranganathan to propound his ideas in library science and to test them practically.

Some of the important and major ideas of Ranganathan were the Five Laws of Library Science which were enunciated by him in 1924, and their formulation and publication in 1929 and 1931 respectively. These laws are still considered a unifying theory for all library practices and services, and set of guidelines for the dynamic development and study of library science as a whole.

The University of Bombay Library received a special grant of rupees 50,000 from the Central Government in 1939 to strengthen its collection for graduate studies. During the period from 1931 to 1939, a few more special grants were given to the library for its collection development. A very special grant of rupees 10,000 was given by Kikabhai and Maniklal, sons of the late Premchand Roychand, in 1931 to replace the electric clock of the library tower.

The collection, which stood at 4,504 volumes in 1900, rose to 70,000 in 1939 and 73,582 in 1947. Though higher education and academic libraries made some progress during the first quarter of the present century, yet their growth and development was not very well organized.

Academic institutions and their growth after 1916 created a few problems also and the general feeling was that the "quality of Education was being sacrificed for quantity." While such a situation prevailed, the Indian Statutory Commission, popularly known as the Simon Commission, was appointed by the Government in 1927 to study the conditions prevailing in India.

The Simon Commission appointed an Auxiliary Committee to look into the growth of education in India. Sir Philip Hartog, a former member of the Calcutta University Commission, and a former Vice-Chancellor of the University of Dacca, was appointed its Chairman.

In its report, submitted in 1929, the Committee stated that "the dispersal of resources for university teaching among a number of colleges had made it difficult to build up university libraries of the type required for advanced work both at the Honours and the research stage majority of the university libraries were inadequate and all needed great additions."

In addition to want of books, libraries also lacked good current periodicals in their collections. The Committee also made a special note of the low academic standards in many colleges and universities and the "unhealthy competition for candidates between neighbouring universities".

This report, however, did not offer any comprehensive, detailed, and realistic solutions to the problems. In 1935, Ministry of Education was formed in each province, as per the provisions of the dyarchy in the Montague-Chelmsford Reforms of 1919, supplemented by those of the new Government of India Act of 1935.

The Ministry of Education in India requested the Central Advisory Board of Education in 1944 to survey the educational conditions in the country. The Board's report, known as the Sargeant Report, after its Chairman, Sir Sargeant, the Educational Advisor to the Government of India, came up with a master-plan for the development of education in the post-World War II India. Its terms of reference covered education at all levels-primary, secondary, and higher.

The Indian universities, as they existed then, despite many admirable features, did not fully satisfy the requirements of a national system of education. During the British rule, several committees and commissions set up periodically, paved way for the foundation of several colleges and the establishment of many universities and in many cases the libraries were also established along with them.

It is also true that as compared to the first two decades the development of university libraries after 1924 did make better progress but the college libraries were still neglected and were struggling to get their recognition.

There were only 12 universities in India in 1924 and their number swelled to 18 by the time India got freedom in 1947. In fact, the academic libraries during the British rule had no significance in the academic life of the institutions of higher education and the pivotal role that can be played by the academic libraries in the life of the institutions could very well be seen in the policy statement of higher education of the free India and the fact was also proven when at the time of national reconstruction, the importance of libraries in teaching and research was recognized, and libraries received the early attention of the Government of India.

Academic Libraries in India after Independence

The actual process for the development of university libraries in India can be said to have been set in motion with the appointment of the University Education Commission presided over by Dr. S. Radhakrishnan and its recommendations, such as, annual grants, open access system, working hours, organization of the library, staff, steps to make students book conscious and the need to give grants to teachers to buy books.

The section on libraries of the report opens with a powerful statement on the importance of libraries in university education and states, "teaching is a cooperative enterprise. Teachers must have the necessary tools for teaching purposes in the shape of libraries and laboratories as also the right type of students."

The Commission in the course of its study of the academic libraries, found that "libraries were hopelessly inadequate to serve the curricular needs of a modern university. They were ill-housed, illstocked, and ill-staffed and were totally lacking in standard literary and scientific journals. Service was in the hands of personnel that had hardly any notion of the objectives of university education. The annual appropriation for book purchase seldom exceeded the ten thousand mark."

In addition, the annual grant for these libraries were not sufficient. Therefore, the Commission recommended that at least six per cent of the total budget of each academic institution should be set aside for the library. Only then will the condition of these libraries improve.

It added that if institutions were not willing to allocate six per cent of their budget to libraries, they should spend ₹40 per student enrolled. The Commission also suggested that greater attention should be paid to improve the reference services in the university libraries. Therefore, "documentation and biblio-graphical services must be developed in order to promote research among the faculty and students, make libraries proper centres for research activities, and to raise the standards of services."

As far as the library staff is concerned, the Commission was of the view that it is very important to have well-qualified staff, including the Director, in order to provide excellent service in any library. The Director's qualifications must include Ph.D. in Library Science and he must have the rank and salary of a professor, capabilities of organization and management, and should have full powers of an administrator to run the library effectively.

University Education Commission. There is no doubt that the recommendations of the Commission "were based on the needs of the modern library services in universities for the promotion of research and creative learning." It was for the first time that such detailed attention was paid to the library matters by a commission on university education in India.

Ranganathan Committee (1957)

The most comprehensive and significant document on the university and college libraries is the Report of the UGC library committee, chaired by Ranganathan. The Report was published by the University Grants Commission in 1959 entitled 'University and College Libraries.' It was perhaps the first attempt by any Library Committee in India to systematically survey the academic libraries on a national basis, and it was also the first time that the government of India had decided to seek advice from a professional librarian regarding academic libraries. The committee was to advice the UGC on the standards of libraries, building, pay scales, and library training.

After the survey the library committee invited all academic librarians to a seminar on "Work flow in university and college libraries," at Delhi from March 4 to 7, 1959 to keep them informed about the progress the committee had made surveying the academic libraries. It wanted to discuss its recommendations with them. Some of the recommendations of the Committee included the provision that the UGC and the State Government should help the college and the university libraries in the collection development of both books and periodicals.

The formula suggested by the committee was that funds be given "at the rate of ₹15 per enrolled student and ₹200 per teacher and research fellow. There should also be special initial library grants in the case of a new university and of a new department in an existing university, a similar scale should be followed for the college libraries. In order to promote co-operation among libraries, a Union Catalogue of books and a Union List of periodicals to be prepared.

The Committee strongly recommended that an open access system be introduced in every academic library. Committee also stressed "that reference service is the essential human process of establishing contact between the right reader and the right book by personal service. Reference service is vital in promotion of reading habit in student each library should provide an adequate number of reference librarians to function as library hosts and human converters."

Other recommendations included building up a microfilm collection, copying facilities for microfilms and book material, appointment of a committee to look into the standards of teaching, examination and research in the library schools, and appointment of full-time teaching faculty members rather than asking librarians to teach part time in the library schools.

The Committee added that "the status and the salary of the library staff should be the same as that of the teaching and research staff', *i.e.*, Professor, Reader, and Lecturer etc." The recommendations of the committee had a farreaching effect on the development of the university libraries later.

They had not only provided a framework to the UGC to implement its grants-in-aid programmes but also given to the university authorities important guidelines. Particular mention, in this connection, may be made of the recommendations concerning the library finances which had helped libraries to secure enough finances by way of annual grants from the universities themselves and of development grants from the UGC.

The recommendations on the library personnel and staff strength have given to the library staff status and salaries equivalent to the academic staff and ensure provision for adequate staff for various library operations. The Committee submitted its report to the UGC with the hope that it will provide a blueprint for the systematic development of university libraries in the country.

Hence, in-spite of many hurdles like education being a state subject in the Indian Constitution, considerable development in the university libraries has taken place and as such the condition of these libraries in 1953 was much better than in the 1940's and even the early 1950's.

Kothari Commission

The Education Commission under the chairmanship of Dr. D. S. Kothari marked another important stage in the history of university libraries in India.

The Commission devoted considerable attention to the develop-ment of the university libraries and made suitable recommendations on the following points:

- Norms for financial support;
- Long range planning for library development;
- The need for the establishment of a well equipped library before the starting of a university, college, or department;
- Suitable phasing over of the library grants;
- Encouraging the students in the use of books;
- Interdisciplinary communication; and
- Documentation service in libraries etc.

The Education Commission had also addressed itself to the role of libraries in adult education and recommended establish-ment of a network of public libraries. It wanted the school libraries to be integrated with public libraries for purposes of the adult education programmes. The Report, submitted by Dr. D. S. Kothari, on June 29, 1966, emphatically pointed out that "nothing can be more damaging than to ignore its library and to give it a low priority. No new college, university or department should be opened unless adequate number of books in the library are provided."

The Commission was shocked to note that the recommen-dations of the Radhakrishnan Commission had not been fully implemented, for only four universities in India has spent five per cent or more of their budget on books and periodicals acquisitions, though the 1948's Commission has suggested that six per cent of the total budget be spent on libraries. Other universities had spent less than five per cent of their budget on libraries, "Surprisingly enough there are five universities which spent even less than one per cent of the total budget on the libraries."

It was clear proof that the university libraries in India were not functioning properly to fulfill the needs of higher education. The Kothari Commission recommended that a long range plan for library development should be drawn up for each academic institution taking into consideration anticipated increase in enrollment, introduction of new subjects and research needs etc., and documentation service be encouraged in libraries, and documentation experts be appointed to help researchers and do indexing and abstracting.

It was further recommended that "the book selection should be oriented towards supporting instruction and research." The library should "provide resources necessary for research in fields of special interest to the university; provide library facilities and services necessary for the success of all formal programmes of instruction."

Monetary guidelines were also suggested by the Commission. "As a norm, a university should spend each year about ₹.25 per student registered and ₹300 per teacher depending on the stage of development of each university library." It was also suggested that "the foreign exchange needed for university and college libraries should be allowed separately to the UGC."

The Wheat Loan Programme

During the 1950's and early 1960's the Indian academic libraries received huge grants from the UGC amounting up to ₹100,000 for books, buildings, equipment and even for additional staff. At the same time many libraries got additional grants from a special US fund called the 'Wheat Loan Programme.' The American Congress passed a special Act, in 1951 known as the 'Public Law 480' to loan India $ 19,000,000 to buy much needed wheat from the US. Under the agreement of the loan, India had to buy American books, periodicals and scientific equipment worth $ 50,000 to be used for research purposes in the Indian libraries.

This, money India had to pay as interest on the loan. Part of the money was to be spent on the exchange of scholars, including librarians, between the two countries. The United States authorities bought some educational material and equipment from India for research purposes and higher education in the American Universities.

During 1951-1961 Indian libraries spent US $ 1,400,000 of the purchase of American books, US dollar 160,000 on libraries, US $ 40,000 on the travel and study grants for thirty three Indian librarians to visit the United States and US $ 75,000 on the travel and study grants of the five Americans.

College Libraries

The College libraries in India have a significant role to play in higher education. Majority of the undergraduate students, *i.e.*, 88.5 per cent and graduate students, *i.e.*, 53 per cent, attend these colleges. When India attained Independence many among the 533 affiliated colleges did not have their own libraries, but at present, every college in the country has a library.

Majority of the college libraries do not have proper facilities to meet the needs of their users. Their collections are not up-to-date, budgets are their very inadequate and limited, and a large number of them are single libraries. In many colleges, there is neither a library hall nor a sufficient big room, not to think of a separate building for the library.

Any unused room, quite often somewhere out of sight, would be considered adequate to house a few shelves of books. And in most college libraries there is complete darkness even during the day time, as the windows are closed out of a fear that the books may be stolen.. Different studies, conducted by scholars and Srivastva have explicitly established that the condition of the college libraries in India are far from satisfactory.

The college libraries are open only six to eight hours a day. Many do not have any qualified librarian on their staff and have closed stacks only. The several commissions and committees, like the Radhakrishnan Commission of 1948, did not stress the importance of the college libraries in their reports. However, the University Grants Commission gives more importance to the college libraries.

As the quality of higher education and research, especially at the graduate level, depends upon, among other things, the standard of the college libraries and their services. Therefore, the UGC has played a significant role in the growth and development of college libraries since 1953 by giving grants for books, equipment, staff and library buildings and has done a remarkable job in salary improvement of the college librarians.

The UGC's contribution to the college libraries is at the rate of ₹15 per student with a maximum of ₹10,000 with some additional and special grants for text books, when a new subject is introduced in the Curriculum.

On the other hand, the colleges and the state governments have failed to provide their equal share. The total Expenditure on the college libraries according to the recommendation of the Education Commission should be 6.25 per cent of the total budgets of the colleges, but in most cases it has remained between 1.5 per cent and 2.3 per cent.

Sardana Collection development of the college libraries are done without taking into consideration the actual needs of the faculty and the students of the colleges as sixty per cent of them consist of text books and 20 per cent cover fiction.

Even this small inadequate collection, in depth and content, is not used effectively due to the closed stacks system and lack of staff and facilities for instruction concerning their use. The net result is that the utility factor of the college libraries comes practically to nothing.

In most college libraries, books are neither properly classified nor catalogued. In several libraries no systematic classification is followed for collection arrangements. The only service the college library renders to its clientele is book-lending. There are colleges where students are not even allowed inside the library.

The UGC is aware of the slow progress of the college libraries. In addition to providing financial help for development, it has also from time to time organized seminars to keep the college librarians aware of the new developments in the field. But these seminars have made only a limited effect on the progress of the college libraries. The condition of the college libraries in the country should be a cause for alarm among the academic community.

In the interests of the development of higher education in the country along proper lines, it is important to make a detailed study of the style of functioning of the college libraries and of the utilization of the library resources and facilities by the students and teachers. This will help in the preparation of more realistic and operational policies and programmes for ensuring the proper functioning, utilization and development of the college libraries. The college library has to be made the intellectual hub of the institution, serving equally, both the students and teachers.

This is all the more necessary because about 90 per cent of the students in higher education in India pursue their studies in colleges and they have only very small and substandard college library resources to fall back upon. Although, owing to various efforts of the UGC as well as other forces, the traditional concept that the college library is a custodian of books has changed, yet there is evidence enough to show that the condition of the college libraries is generally poor, their development is rather slow and that the position of the college libraries and their librarians in India, with a few exceptions, is pitiable.

University Libraries

University libraries all over the world have their own place of importance in the scheme of higher learning. Libraries are not only repositories of knowledge but also dispensers of such knowledge. There is no doubt that where libraries of universities and institutions of higher learning are ignored or not given due recognition, the country as a whole suffers because the standards of study, teaching and research very heavily depend upon the qualitative and quantitative service rendered by the university libraries.

The Radhakrishnan Commission expressed that "the library is the heart of all the university's work, directly so, as regards its research work and indirectly as regards its educational work, which derives its life from research. Scientific research needs the library as well as its laboratories while for humanistic research the library is both library and the laboratory in one. Both for humanistic and scientific studies, a first class library is essential in a university."

The growth of university libraries since Independence can be seen in respect of the initiatives taken by the Central Government considering the vital importance of higher education and role of libraries in the educational development, commitment to fulfill the demand of higher education, and the foundation of the UGC in 1953 by an Act of Parliament. The Radhakrishnan Commission recognized the value and importance of a well equipped and organized library system and its role in higher education.

It had found many drawbacks and pitfalls in the university libraries and had made many recommendations for the improvement of library facilities. The Ranganathan Committee, appointed by the UGC in 1957, made some outstanding recommendations, which included standards for library building, collection development, staff and services and furniture etc. These recommendations were accepted by the UGC and forwarded for implementation.

The Kothari Commission also made valuable recommen-dations for this purpose, but the role of the University Grants Commission deserves special mention, because it has played a vital role by "regularly providing appropriate grants and funds to all universities for development of libraries, to purchase books and journals...., construction of new library buildings and for library equipment and furniture."

Dr. D. S. Kothari, the Chairman of University Grants Commission, said, "Libraries play a vital role in the development of institutions of higher learning. The University Grants Commission attaches great importance to the strengthening of library facilities in the universities and colleges and their efficient administration. The commission has also been giving grants to institutions for books and journals construction of library building and appointment of library staff."

One of the most remarkable and identifiable development in the history of higher education and libraries was the foundation of the INFLIBNET in 1991. Information and Library Network Centre is an autonomous Inter-University Centre of the UGC of India. It is a major National Programme initiated by the UGC in 1991 with its Head Quarters at Gujarat University Campus, Ahmedabad. Initially started as a project under the IUCAA, it became an independent Inter-University Centre in 1966.

Its objectives are:

- To promote and establish communication facilities to improve capability in information transfer and access, that provides support to scholarship, learning, research and academic pursuit through cooperation and involvement of agencies concerned.

- *To establish Inflibnet*: Information and Library Network a computer communication network for linking libraries and information centres in universities, deemed to be universities, colleges, UGC information centres, institutions of national importance and R&D institutions, etc. avoiding duplication of efforts.

Inflibnet performs following major activities:

- Provides grants to universities to automate the libraries, establishing the network facilities and create an information technology environment.
- Developed and distributed Software for University Libraries (Soul) which is an integrated userfriendly library management software. The latest version of the software is 2.0 which is competent to operate with the latest technologies and international standards such as MARC21, Unicode based and NCIP 2.0 based protocols for electronic surveillance and control.
- Indian Catalogue of University Libraries in India (IndCat) is Online Library Catalogue of books, theses and journals available in major university libraries in India which provides bibliographic description, location of the material in all subjects available in more than 112 university libraries. Thus, IndCat has over 10 million bibliographical records of books from more than 113 universities. In addition, the database of theses, expert databases, project databases and Sewakoffline database access facilities are also extended to the libraries of higher learning institutions.
- To enhance the skills of university library staff for implementation of Inflibnet programme, it conducts training programme for library staff, onsite training for member library staff, training on SOUL software, holding Calibre convention every year and workshops for senior level staff of the university libraries are conducted.
- It has brought out a document entitled 'Inflibnet Standards and Guideline for Data Capturing' prepared by a task force of experts based on Common Communication Format (CCF).

Another very important and significant landmark in the history of higher education and development of libraries in India is the establishment of "Ugcinfonet Digial Library Consortium" by the UGC on the concluding day of its Golden jubilee celebrations by his Excellency the then President of India, Dr. A.P.J Abdul Kalam at Vigyan Bhawan on 28th December 2003. UGC-Infonet is an innovative project launched by UGC to facilitate scholarly e-resources to Indian academies through joint partnership of UGC, Inflibnet and Ernet.

This includes interlinking of universities and colleges in the country electronically with a view to achieve maximum efficiency through Internet enabled teaching, learning and governance. The UGC-Infonet is overlaid on Ernet infrastructure in a manner so as to provide assured quality of service and optimum utilization of bandwidth resources. The network will be run and managed by Ernet India.

The project is funded by UGC with 100 per cent capital investment and up to 90 per cent of recurring costs. UGC and Ernet India have signed the necessary MoU for this purpose. A joint technical and tariff committee, has been setup to guide and monitor the design, implementation and operations of Ugcinfonet. Information for Library Network (Inflibnet) an autonomous Inter-University Centre of UGC, is the nodal agency for coordination and facilitation of the linkage between Ernet and the Universities.

Under this programme, information and communication technologies (ICT) and internet will be used to transform learning environment from a monodimensional one to a multidimensional one. This was created to help and benefit more than 310 universities and about 14,000 colleges affiliated with these universities and approximately 10 million students with the e-journals, thus, is a boon to higher education system in many ways.

The UGC-Infonet digital Library consortium has the following objectives: Bhatt,

- To subscribe electronic resources for the members of the consortium at highly discounted rates of subscription and with the best terms and conditions.
- Promote the rational use of funds.
- Guarantee local storage of the information acquired for continuous use by present and future users.
- To impart training to the users, librarians, research scholars and faculty members of the institutions on the electronic resources with an aim to optimize the usage of the electronic resources.
- To have more interaction amongst the member libraries.
- To increase the research productivity of the institutions in terms of quality and quantity of publications
- Strategic alliance with institutions that have common interests resulting reduced information cost and improved resource sharing.

National Knowledge Commission

The National Knowledge Commission was set up by the Government of India on 13th June 2005 with a time-frame of three years, from 2nd October 2005 to 2nd October 2008. As a high-level advisory body to the Prime Minister of India, the National Knowledge Commission was given a mandate to guide policy and direct reforms, focusing on certain key areas such as education, science and technology, agriculture, industry, e-governance etc. Easy access to knowledge, creation and preservation of knowledge systems, dissemination of knowledge and better knowledge services are core concerns of the Commission.

The Commission envisaged the future road map for the growth and development of academic libraries by imbibing core issues such as, set up a national commission on libraries, prepare a national census of all libraries, revamp LIS education, training and research facilities, re-assess staffing of libraries, set up a central library fund, modernize library management, encourage greater community participation in library management, promote information communication technology applications in all libraries, facilitate donation and maintenance of private collections, and encourage public private partnerships in LIS development, etc.

SARASWATHI MAHAL LIBRARY

Saraswathi Mahal Library is located in Thanjavur, Tamil Nadu, India. It is one of the oldest libraries in Asia, and has on display a rare collection of Palm leaf manuscripts and paper written in Tamil, Hindi, English, Telugu, Marathi, and a few other languages indigenous to India.

The collection comprises well over 60,000 volumes, though only a tiny fraction of these are on display. The library has a complete catalogue of holdings, which is being made available online. Some rare holdings can be viewed on site by prior arrangement.

HISTORY

The Saraswathi Mahal library started as a Royal Library for the private pleasure of the Nayak Kings of Thanjavur who ruled 1535-1675 AD. The Maratha rulers who captured Thanjavur in 1675 patronised local culture and further developed the Royal Palace Library until 1855. Most notable among the Maratha Kings was Serfoji II, who was an eminent scholar in many branches of learning and the arts.

In his early age Serfoji studied under the influence of the Dutch Reverend Schwartz, and learned many languages including English, French, Italian and Latin. He enthusiastically took special interest in the enrichment of the Library, employing many Pandits to collect, buy and copy a vast number of works from all renowned Centres of Sanskrit learning in Northern India and other far-flung areas.

Since 1918 the Saraswathi Mahal Library has been a possession of the state of Tamil Nadu. Its official name of the Library was changed to "The Thanjavur Maharaja Serfoji's Sarasvati Mahal Library" in honour of the great royal Marathan patron.

EFFORTS

The library is open to the public; it also supports efforts to publish rare manuscripts from the collection, as well as ensuring all volumes are preserved on microfilm. The Library has installed computers in 1998 for the Computerisation of Library activities. As a first phase, the Library catalogues are being stored in the Computer for easy information retrieval. It is also proposed to digitalise the manuscripts of this Library shortly.

THE COLLECTION

The bulk of the manuscripts (39,300) are in Sanskrit, written in scripts such as Grantha, Devanagari, Nandinagari, Telugu. Tamil manuscripts number over 3500, comprising titles in literature, music and medicine. The Library has a collection of 3076 Marathi manuscripts from the South Indian Maharastrian of the 17th, 18th, and 19th centuries; this includes the hierarchy of the Saints of Maharashtra belonging to Sri Ramadasi and Dattatreya Mutts. The Marathi manuscripts are mostly on paper but a few were written in Telugu script on palm-leaf. There are 846 Telugu manuscripts in the holdings, mostly on palm leaf. There are 22 Persian and Urdu manuscripts mostly of 19th century also within the collection.

Apart from these manuscripts there are 1342 bundles of Maratha Raj records available at the Library. The Raj records were written in the Modi script of the Marathi language. These records encompass the information of the political, cultural and social administration of the Maratha kings of Thanjavur.

SOME OF THE RARE BOOKS AND MANUSCRIPTS

- Dr. Samuel Johnson's dictionary published in 1784
- The pictorial Bible printed in Amsterdam in the year 1791
- The Madras Alamnac printed in 1807
- Lavoisier's *Traité Élémentaire de Chimie* ("Elements of Chemistry")
- The notes of Bishop Heber on Raja Serfoji II
- The correspondence letters of William Torin of London who purchased a lot of books for Raja Serfoji II and the Saraswathi Mahal Library
- The Globe used by the raja.
- Ancient maps of the world
- Town planning documents of Thanjavur including the underground drainage system, the fresh water supply ducting system
- Pictorial charts of the theory of evolution of man as evinced by Charles Le Brun

LIBRARY MUSEUM

A Museum is located in the Library building to reveal the importance of the Library to the Public. This Museum is small but organised into sections highlighting ancient Manuscripts, Illustrated Manuscripts, Printed copies of the Original Drawings, Atlases, Thanjavur-style Paper Paintings, Canvass Paintings, Wooden Paintings, Glass paintings, Portraits of the Thanjavur Maratha kings, and the Physiognomy charts of Charles Le-Brun. These materials give an idea of the total variety in the vast collection within the Library.

The Saraswati Library is situated within the campus of the Thanjavur Palace. Visitors can have a glimpse of preserved books and can sit and read in the library premises. Better preservation of books and facilities like air-conditioning with dehumidifiers, redesigning of space for comfortable reading, online catalogue facility should be taken up to preserve this internationally renowned treasure trove of books and palm-leaf manuscripts ! Efforts were made to microfilm and catalogue the contents way back in 1965 when Indira Gandhi was Information and Broadcasting Minister, Government of India who sanctioned the fund for the library's development. Since then no efforts were made to scan the documents and computerise the same using present day technology. It is also a designated 'Manuscript Conservation Centre' (MCC) under the National Mission for Manuscripts established in 2003.

KHUDA BAKHSH ORIENTAL LIBRARY

Khuda Bakhsh Oriental Library is one of the national libraries of India. It was opened to public in October, 1891 by Khan Bahadur Khuda Bakhsh with 4,000 manuscripts, of which he inherited 1,400 from his father Maulvi Mohammed Bakhsh.

It is an autonomous organization under Ministry of Culture, Government of India, and is governed by a Board with the Governor of Bihar as its ex-officio Chairman. known for its rare collection of Persian and Arabic manuscripts. It also hosts paintings made during the Rajput and Mughal eras of India. It is also a designated 'Manuscript Conservation Centre' (MCC) under the National Mission for Manuscripts.

HISTORY

The library finds its origin in private collection of a bibliophile Mohammad Bakhsh and expanded by his son Khuda Bakhsh, who inherited 1,400 manuscripts and continued to add to the collection and eventually converted it into a private library by 1880. The library was opened to public upon its inauguration by Sir Charles Elliot, Governor of Bengal on 5th October, 1891.

In 1969 through a Federal Legislation, an Act of Parliament, namely 'Khuda Bakhsh Oriental Public Library Act (1969), the Government of India declared Khuda Bakhsh Oriental Public Library a centre of national importance and government took over the funding, maintenance and development of the library. Today it continues to attract scholars from all over the world.

Past directors of the library have been Dr. Abid Reza Bedar, who after remaining with the Raza Library, came as Director to the institution in 1972, and did some important work towards reviving the library along with his successor Habibur Rehman Chighani, at present the Director of the library is the Dr. Imtiaz Ahmad, since February, 2004.

COLLECTION

Some of the notable manuscripts are *Timur Nama* (*Khandan—Timuria*), *Shah Nama, Padshah Nama, Diwan-e-Hafiz* and *Safinatul Auliya,* carrying the autograph of Mughal Emperors and princes and the book of Military

Accounts of Maharaja Ranjit Singh. Apart of it the library also has specimens of Mughal paintings, calligraphy and book decoration and Arabic and Urdu manu-scripts, including a page of Quran written on deer skin.

BHANDARKAR ORIENTAL RESEARCH INSTITUTE

The Bhandarkar Oriental Research Institute (BORI) is located in Pune, Maharashtra, India. It was founded on July 6, 1917 to honour the life and work of Dr. Ramakrishna Gopal Bhandarkar (1837–1925), long regarded as the founder of Indology (Orientalism) in India. The institute is well known for its collection of old Sanskrit and Prakrit manuscripts.

THE INSTITUTE

This institute is of a public trust registered under Act XXI of 1860. Initially, the institute received an annual grant of 3000 Rupees from the Government of Bombay. Presently, it is partially supported by annual grants from the Government of Maharashtra. The Institute also receives grants from the Government of India and the University Grants Commission for specific research projects.

The institute has one of the largest collections of rare books and manuscripts in South Asia, consisting of over 1,25,000 books and 29,510 manuscripts. The institute publishes a journal, *Annals of the Bhandarkar Oriental Research Institute* four times a year. The Institute also hosts the Manuscripts Resource and Conservation Centre under the auspices of the National Mission for Manuscripts, a project of the Ministry of Culture, Government of India. In 2007, the Rigveda manuscripts preserved at the Institute were included in UNESCO's Memory of the World Register.

THE MANUSCRIPT COLLECTION

The Government of Bombay, in 1866, started a pan Indian Manuscript Collection project. Noted scholars like George Bühler, F. Kielhorn, Peter Peterson, Ramkrishna Gopal Bhandarkar, S. R. Bhandarkar, Kathavate and Ghate collected more than 17,000 important manuscripts under this project. This collection was first deposited at Elphinstone College in Bombay.

Then it was transferred to Deccan College (Pune) for better preservation. After the Bhandarkar Oriental Research Institute was founded in 1917, the BORI founders proposed to offer even better preservation and research.

Hence Lord Willingdon, the then Governor of the Bombay Presidency and the first president of BORI, transferred the valuable Government collection of manuscripts to the BORI on April 1, 1918. The first curator, P.K. Gode took active initiatives to enhance this collection. Presently, the Institute has over 29,000 manuscripts.

The largest part of the collection (17,877 Manuscripts) is part of the "Government Manuscript Library", while there is an additional collection of 11,633 manuscripts also. The most prized collections include a paper manuscript of the Cikitsâsâra-sangraha dated 1320 and a palmleaf manuscript of the Upamiti-bhavapra-pañcakathâ dated 906. Among the several scholars referring to the works at BORI, the most well-known person arguably is the Bharat Ratna awardee, Pt. Pandurang Vaman Kane.

THE CRITICAL EDITION OF THE MAHABHARATA

A long term project under the auspices of BORI, started on April 1, 1919, was the preparation of a Critical Edition of the Mahabharata. V.S. Sukhtankar was appointed general editor of the project on August 1, 1925 and he continued until his death on January 21, 1943.

After his death, S.K. Belvalkar was appointed general editor on April 1, 1943. On April 1, 1961 P. L. Vaidya appointed as General Editor of the project on the retirement of S. K. Belvalkar. R. N. Dandekar appointed as the joint general editor on July 6, 1957. To widespread acclaim, the completion for publication was announced on September 22, 1966, by Dr. Sarvapalli Radhakrishnan, then President of India, at a special function held at the institute.

The Critical Edition was collated from 1,259 manuscripts. This edition in 19 volumes (more than 15000 demi-quarto size pages) comprised the critically constituted text of the 18 *Parvas* of the Mahabharata consisting of more than 89000 verses, an elaborate Critical Apparatus and a Prolegomena on the material and methodology.

Further work since the initial publication has produced a Critical Edition of the Harivamsa, a Pratika Index, a Bibliography of ancillary materials, and a Cultural Index. The project of preparing a critical edition of the Harivamsa was inaugurated by the President of India, Rajendra Prasad on November 19, 1954. The publication was completed in November, 1971.

The critical edition in two volumes consists the 4 *Parvan*s of the Harivamsa. The Pratika Index in 6 volumes consists 360000 verse quarters with appendices. Two volumes of the Cultural Index have been published so far. The constituted text of the critical edition has also been made available on the CD-ROM.

VANDALISM IN 2003

The institute was vandalized in December 2003 by a mob made up of members of an extremist self styled Maratha youth squad, calling themselves the Sambhaji Brigade, named after Shivaji's elder son. They claimed to be angered by the help provided by the institute's staff (in translating manuscripts) to a Western writer, Dr. James Laine, who discussed the telling and retelling of stories about Shivaji's parentage and life in his book on narrations of the Shivaji story.

The mob also damaged thousands of manuscripts and attacked Shrikant Bahulkar, a Sanskrit scholar who had only explained some Sanskrit references to Laine. The incident provoked widespread reaction and historian Gajanan Mehendale to destroy parts of his in-progress biography of Shivaji.

The vandalism and a ban on the book were denounced by historians who put their signatures to the statement include R.S. Sharma, R.C. Thakran, Suraj Bhan, Irfan Habib, D.N. Jha, Shireen Moosvi and K. M. Shrimali. Oxford University Press-publisher of James Laine's, 'Shivaji: Hindu king in Islamic India', withdrew the book after protests from Ninad Bedekar and other right-wing politicians as it contained allegedly objectionable statements about Shivaji.

ASIATIC SOCIETY LIBRARY

At present, the library of the Asiatic Society has a collection of about 1,17,000 books and 79,000 journals printed in almost all the major languages of the world. It has also a collection of 293 maps, microfische of 48,000 works, microfilm of 387,003 pages, 182 paintings, 2500 pamphlets and 2150 photographs.

The earliest printed book preserved in this library is Juli Firmici's *Astronomicorum Libri* published in 1499. It has in its possession a large number of books printed in India in the late 18th and early 19th centuries. The library also possesses many rare and scarcely available books. The library has a rich collection of about 47,000 manuscripts in 26 scripts. The most notable amongst them are an illustrated manuscript of the *Qur'an,* a manuscript of the *Gulistan* text, and a manuscript of *Padshah Nama* bearing the signature of Emperor Shahjahan. The number of journals in thepossession of the library is about 80,000 at present.

The early collection of this library was enriched by the contributions it received from its members. On March 25, 1784 the library received seven Persian manuscripts from Henri Richardson. The next contribution came from William Marsden, who donated his book, *History of Island of Sumatra* (1783) on November 10, 1784. Robert Home, the first Library-in-Charge (1804) donated his small but valuable collection of works on art.

The first accession of importance was a gift from the Seringapatam Committee on February 3, 1808 consisting of a collection from the Palace Library of Tipu Sultan. The library received the Surveyor-General Colonel Mackenzie's collection of manuscripts and drawings in December 1822.

MANUSCRIPT COLLECTION

Manuscript Collection of the society is varied and rich, and covers most of the Indian languages and scripts and even several Asian ones, *e.g.,,* Assamese, Bengali, Gujarati, Gurumukhi, Kanarese, Urdu, Marathi, Modi, Nagari, Newari, Oriya, Rajasthani, Sarada, Armenian, Sinhalese, Arabic, Persian, Pushto, Javanese, Turki, Burmese, Chinese, Siamese, Tibetan etc. The materials used for the manuscripts are also varied: palm and palmyra leaves, barks of different trees, papers of various grades.

Sanskritic Manuscripts

The manuscripts cover the period from 7th c. A.D. down to the 19th century. These are useful source materials to illustrate the development of the Indian scripts (especially Bengali, Nagari etc.). The colophons and post-colophons contain information relating to socio-economic conditions of the people.

Besides, they help us to fix the chronology of the Royal dynasties of India. Where the inscriptions fail to ascertain dates and chronology, the manuscripts may throw some light, provided a thorough critical study of these and their colophons and postcolophons were made.

Some of the rare Sanskrit manuscripts may be mentioned here:

- Brihati,
- Amrita Vindu,
- Kiranavali,
- Charucharya,
- Nartaka Nirnaya,
- Parasika-prakasa,
- Sanskrita-ratnakara,
- Lalitavistara,
- Horoscope of a Muslim of the Mughal Court (1640 A.D.) A Deed of Mortgage (1639),
- Ramayana (Bengali) of Ramananda Yati,
- Vajrayana text (11th c.),
- A text on Buddhist Nyaya,
- Rigveda Padapatha,
- Laghu-Kalachakra-tika,
- Kalachakravetara,
- Kuttanimatam,
- Vajravalinama mannadalopayika,
- Ramacharita of Sandhyakar Nandi,
- Bhattikavyatika of Srinivasa, and
- Paragali Mahabharata.

The manuscript of Kubjikamatam is of the 7th Century A.D. The manuscript of Rigveda Padapatha, copied in 1362 A.D., is perhaps "the oldest manuscript of the Rigveda."

Islamic Section

Of the many Islamic Manuscripts there are some which are extremely rare and unique.

Of these only a few may be mentioned:

- Tahdhib Sharh As-Sab' at Mullaqat (early 12th c. Arabic),
- Qalaid al-Iquian wa Mahasin al-Ayan (12th c.),
- Kharidat al-Qasr (12th c.),
- Al-Jam Baynas as-Sahihin abridged version with autograph, (13th c.),
- A-Madkhul(13th c.),
- Tafsir-i-Quran (Persian, 13th c., important also for calligraphy),
- Tuhfat al-Ahbar fi usul at Hadith wa'l Akhbar (15th c.),

- Kitab al-I'lan (18th c.),
- Saha' if-i-Shara' if or Duraral Mansur (Persian, 19th c., an autographed copy), and
- Adab-i-Alamgiri (18th c.).

There are large numbers of illuminated and illustrated manu-scripts of different schools, many of which are unique for their calligraphy, delicacy of their lines, and elegance of composition and charming colour schemes.

These miniatures still afford glimpses of India's past achievements, Of these unique manuscripts (earliest belonging to the 10th Century A.D.) mention may be made of a few:

- Astasahasrika Prajnaparamita,
- Aparimitayurnama Mahayana sutra,
- Pancharaksha,
- Paramarthanama Sangati,
- Devimahatmya,
- Viveka Panchamrita,
- Bhagavatgita,
- Shahnama,
- Kullayat-i-Saadi,
- Suwaru'l aqalim,
- Farang-i-Aurang Shahi,
- Ain-i-Akbari,
- Diwan-i-Makhfi,
- Qissa-i-Nush-Afarin,
- Jamiut-Twarikh,
- Amir nama Tutinama,
- Iyar-i-Danesh,
- Bihar-i-Danesh,
- Tarjuma Mahabharata,
- Tafribul-Imarah (by Silchand, dedicated to J. H. Lushington), and
- Imaratut-Akbar (by Chitarmal for James Duncan).

Many scholars are using the collection for editing their texts and for translation in modern languages.

English Manuscripts

In the Library there are preserved a large number of old letters some of which date back to1784, just after the Society was founded. These letters were received by the Society from persons belonging to different walks of life, requesting information on such subjects as old and rare manuscripts, ancient monuments, coins etc.

Some among the writers of these letters were persons well known for their literary, scientific and other cultural accomp-lishments. These old files constitute important documents relating to the history of the Society, as also of many other scientific and humanistic organisations that were established in India either in the 19th or in the 20th century.

Urdu Manuscripts

The Society has a fine collection of about 234 Urdu manu-scripts many of which were received as a gift from the Fort William College.

Sino-Tibetan and Burmese Manuscripts

The Society has a complete set of Kanjur and Tanjur texts of the Buddhist scriptures and some extra-canonical works. These were collected by B. H. Hodgson and A. Csoma de koros. A section of the collection has been catalogued. There are over one hundred titles of Chinese books, some of which are rare and valuable for Chinese studies.

These cover almost all the subjects relating to Chinese Culture, Civilization and Science and Buddhism. Subjects covered include Classical Literature, Language. History, Geography, Topography, Philosophy, Religion, manners and customs, biography of scholars, sciences (Botanical, Astronimical, Zoological).

The Society has a valuable collection of about 162 Burmese manuscript written on parabaikes and palm leaf. The manuscripts deal with Buddhistic texts, Religion, History of the world and also of Burmja and Arakan, works on Gramour (including that of kaccayana) and Rhetoric, Buddhist cosmography, Astrology, Medicine etc.

Bengali Manuscripts

Other than Sanskrit, a few Bengali manuscripts have been found written by Bengali Brahmins residing in Varanasi. Parageli Mahabharat, Chuti Khan's Asvamedha Parva, and many other important manuscripts were purchased. Mss. donated by Justice Ramaprosad Mukherjee and Sri A Roy enriched the collection. The society has 703 Bengali and 12 Assamese manuscripts in the collection. It comprises Asiatic Society's own collection, Government collection, Indian Museum collection and donors' collection.

At present, the collection of Bengali manuscripts in the possession of Asiatic Society is rich in respect of number and rarity. The Society has manuscripts on Ramayana, Mahabharata, Srimadbhagavat, Mangala Kavyas, treatises on Vaisnava faith and its allied subjects. Folk literature, erotic verses and Vaisnaba Sahajiya Cult etc.

Rajasthani Manuscripts

The Society possesses very rare, valuable and important Rajasthani Manuscripts which date the pre-middle and middle years. The Society prepared and brought out a descriptive catalogue of Rajasthani manuscripts comprising 636 manuscripts.

RARE BOOK DIVISION

In 1978 the Council decided to open a Rare Book Division. The preliminarhy screening of the collection has since been started.

Among the earliest printed books mention may be made of the following:

- Julii Firmici Astronomicorum libri octo integri (Venice 1499),
- Kitabal-Qanum (Arabic/Romae 1595),
- Kripar Sstrer Arthabhed (Bengali in Roman Character, Kisbon 1743);
- S. Purchas's Purchas: His Pilgrimage (London, 1 61 4),
- N. Halhed's Grammar of the Bengal Language, (Hooghly, 1778),
- Malabar and English Dictionary, (Madras, 1779),
- Rasamanjari (Sanskrit, Banaras, 1791),
- Ram Ram Bose's Lipimala (Bengali, Serampore, 1802),
- The Ramayana 3 vols, (Bengali, Serampore, 1803),
- Hitopadesa (Sanskrit, Serampore, 1804),
- Colebrooke's Grammar of the Sanskrit language vol. 1 (Serampore, 1805).

KINDS OF LIBRARIES

PUBLIC LIBRARY

A public library is a library that is accessible by the public and is generally funded from public sources and operated by civil servants. There are five fundamental characteristics shared by public libraries. The first is that they are supported by taxes; they are governed by a board to serve the public interest; they are open to all and every community member can access the collection; they are entirely voluntary in that no one is ever forced to use the services provided; and public libraries provide basic services without charge.

Public libraries exist in many countries across the world and are often considered an essential part of having an educated and literate population. Public libraries are distinct from research libraries, school libraries, and other special libraries in that their mandate is to serve the general public's information needs.

Public Libraries also provide free services such as preschool story times to encourage early literacy, quiet study and work areas for students and professionals, or book clubs to encourage appreciation of literature in adults. Public libraries typically allow users to take books and other materials off the premises temporarily; they also have non-circulating reference collections and provide computer and Internet access to patrons.

SERVICES OFFERED

In addition to print books and periodicals, most public libraries today have a wide array of other media including audiobooks, e-books, CDs, cassettes, videotapes, DVDs, and video games, as well as facilities to access the Internet and inter-library loans. Readers' advisory is a fundamental public library service that involves suggesting fiction and nonfiction titles.

Public libraries may also provide other services, such as community meeting rooms, storytelling sessions for infants, toddlers, preschool children, or after-school programmes, all with an intention of developing early literacy skills and a love of books. In person and on-line programmes for reader development, language learning, homework help, free lectures and cultural performances, and other community service programmes are common offerings.

One of the most popular programmes offered in public libraries are summer reading programmes for children, families, and adults. In rural areas, the local public library may have, in addition to its main branch, a mobile library service, consisting of one or more buses furnished as a small public library, serving the countryside according to a regular schedule.

Public libraries also provide materials for children, often housed in a special section. Child oriented web sites with on-line educational games and programmes specifically designed for younger library users are becoming increasingly popular. Services may be provided for other groups, such as large print or Braille materials, Books on tape, young adult literature and other materials for teenagers, or materials in other than the national language.

California and Nevada now offer a new service called Link+. This new programme links county libraries across the two states, allowing patrons access to books their library may not have in their collection.

Librarians at most public libraries provide reference and research help to the general public, usually at a reference desk but can often be done by telephone interview. As online discussion and social networking allow for remote access, reference is becoming available virtually through the use of the Internet and e-mail.

Depending on the size of the library, there may be more than one desk; at some smaller libraries all transactions may occur at one desk, while large urban public libraries may employ subject-specialist librarians with the ability to staff multiple reference or information desks to answer queries about particular topics at any time during regular operating hours. Often the children's section in a public library has its own reference desk.

Public libraries are also increasingly making use of web 2.0 services, including the use of online social networks by libraries. Public libraries in some countries pay authors when their books are borrowed from libraries. These are known as Public Lending Right programme.

DIGITAL DIVIDE

As more commercial and governmental services are being provided online, public libraries increasingly provide Internet access for users who otherwise would not be able to connect to these services.

Part of the public library mission has become attempting to help bridge the digital divide. A study conducted in 2006 found that "72.5 per cent of library branches report that they are the only provider of free public computer and Internet access in their communities". A 2008 study found that "100 per cent of rural, high poverty outlets provide public Internet access, a significant increase from 85.7 per cent last year".

The *American Library Association* (ALA), addresses this role of libraries as part of "access to information" and "equity of access"; part of the profession's ethical commitment that "no one should be denied information because he or she cannot afford the cost of a book or periodical, have access to the internet or information in any of its various formats."

In addition to access, many public libraries offer training and support to computer users. Once access has been achieved, there still remains a large gap in people's online abilities and skills. For many communities, the public library is the only agency offering free computer classes and information technology learning.

As of 2008, 73.4 per cent of public libraries offered information technology training of some form, including information literacy skills and homework assignment help. A significant service provided by public libraries is assisting people with e-government access and use of federal, state and local government information, forms and services.

Internationally, public libraries offer *information and communication technology* (ICT) services, giving "access to information and knowledge" the "highest priority." While different countries and areas of the world have their own requirements, general services offered include free connection to the Internet, training in using the Internet, and relevant content in appropriate languages. In addition to typical public library financing, *non-governmental organizations* (NGOs) and business fund services that assist public libraries in combating the digital divide.

ORIGINS AS A SOCIAL INSTITUTION

The culmination of centuries of advances in the printing press, moveable type, paper, ink, publishing, and distribution, combined with an ever growing middle class, increased commercial activity and consumption, new radical ideas, massive population growth and higher literacy rates forged the public library into the form that it is today. Public libraries are not a new idea; Romans made scrolls in dry rooms available to patrons of the baths, and tried with some success to establish libraries within the empire.

Naturally, only those few that could afford an education would be able to use the library, where those less than rich or without control of money; women, children and slaves could not. In the middle of the 19th century, the push for truly public libraries, paid for by taxes and run by the state gained force after numerous depressions, droughts, wars and revolutions in Europe, felt mostly by the working class.

Matthew Battles states that:

- "It was in these years of class conflict and economic terror that the public library movement swept through Britain, as the nation's progressive elite recognized that the light of cultural and intellectual energy was lacking in the lives of commoners".

Libraries had often been started with a donation, an endowment or were bequeathed to various, parishes, churches, schools or towns, and these social and institutional libraries formed the base of many academic and public library collections of today.

Andrew Carnegie had the biggest influence in financing libraries in the United States of America, from the east to west coast. From just 1900 to 1917, almost 1,700 libraries were constructed by Carnegie's foundation, insisting that local communities first guarantee tax support of each library built.

The establishment of circulating libraries by booksellers and publishers provided a means of gaining profit and creating social centers within the community. The circulating libraries not only provided a place to sell books, but also a place to lend books for a price. These circulating libraries provided a variety of materials including the increasingly popular novels.

Although the circulating libraries filled an important role in society, members of the middle and upper classes often looked down upon these libraries that regularly sold material from their collections and provided materials that were less sophisticated. Circulating libraries also charged a subscription fee, however the fees were set to entice their patrons, providing subscriptions on a yearly, quarterly or monthly basis, without expecting the subscribers to purchase a share in the circulating library.

Circulating libraries were not exclusively lending institutions and often provided a place for other forms of commercial activity, which may or may not be related to print. This was necessary because the circulating libraries did not generate enough funds through subscription fees collected from its borrowers. As a commerce venture, it was important to consider the contributing factors such as other goods or services available to the subscribers.

Many claims have been made for the title of "first public library" for various libraries in various countries, with at least some of the confusion arising from differing interpretations of what should be considered a true "public library". Diffi-culties in establishing what policies were in effect at different times in the history of particular libraries also add to the confusion.

The first libraries open to the public were the collections of Greek and Latin scrolls which were available in the dry sections of the many buildings that made up the huge Roman baths of the Roman empire. However, they were not lending libraries.

The "halls of science" run by different Islamic sects in many cities of North Africa and the Middle East in the 9th century were open to the public. Some of them had written lending policies, but they were very restrictive. Most patrons were expected to consult the books on site. The later European university libraries were not open to the general public, but accessible by scholars.

PUBLIC LIBRARIES IN INDIA

Public library is largely regarded as the People's University. It has tremendous developments in India from the early period to till date at various stages. Most of the Indian states now have free public library services to develop the people of India at different levels.

ANCIENT PERIOD

- "The history of the development of the public library may be said to be as old as that of education in India". During Vedic times, the pupils stayed in the *guru-gruha* for several years for education. Since ancient times, India is being very much pertinent in search of knowledge and wisdom. Oral communication was the best means amongst the people of India and writing was not available. "The earliest written and recorded materials found in India are the inscriptions on stone pillars of King Asoka; these inscriptions could be called the first outside open libraries". Later, *Ashrams* came into existence in India and students study under the supervision of well-known teachers. They kept many manuscripts for use of the teachers and students as well as for the visitors. Many students joined ashrams and such big ashrams were known as *vidyapeeth*, where numbers of teachers are engaged to teach the students. These educational institutions collected many different manuscripts and other materials which can help in their teaching and daily routine. They kept and preserved carefully. "The reading materials, of course, related to many subjects formed the source material for transmitting knowledge in different streams of education and culture. The collections might be likened to modern libraries since they were carefully maintained and extensively used by students and teachers alike". Such *ashrams* or *vidyapeeths,* where manuscripts and other reading materials were reserved, may be regarded as a kind of library as they serve information and knowledge to the students and community in different ways. Pandey S K Sharma stated that; "In India, since the ancient times libraries have been functioning as light houses for those who wanted to read and to extend the boundaries of various disciplines. References are available to prove that Nalanda University had its own multistoried library in 600 AD with massive collection of manuscripts. The collection of the library was housed in three buildings, each having nine floors and three hundred rooms. This library was opened by the then Emperor of India, King Davapal. The library was open for any body that was known scholar and took interest in reading, interpreting and even copying the documents kept in the library. Chinese traveller Whuen Sang is known to have consulted this library in the seventh century and to have taken from here hundreds of treatises to China and Japan. This library was completely destroyed by Bakhtiar Khilaji, who invaded India in 1205 AD. And burnt the library. The library kept on burning for about six months".

Libraries in ancient India also developed at other famous centers of learning, such as *Vikramshila* and *Odantapuri.* Universities of ancient India, like Taxila and Vikramshala also have valuable collection on *tantras* and manuscripts in their libraries.

MEDIEVAL PERIOD

Muslims mostly rule the Medieval Period of India. Historically, it is also known as Mughal Period. There were great changes not only in social and political, but also on education and library system during this period. The Muslim rulers made great contributions to Indian culture and libraries played a significant role in the sociocultural development of the nation. "The period of Mughal is considered as the golden period of Indian history for its educational, literary, and library activities". Babur, king of Kabul invaded India and annexed Delhi to his kingdom. "He established the first Mughal Imperial Library in 1526".

Babur inherited manuscripts from his father and kept in his library and also collected books from different sources of his kingdom. Babur died in 1530 and was succeeded by his son Humayun. Humayun much lived in Agra and established library in his palace. He set up a library at Agra Fort, which was managed by Lal Beg.

In his library, he kept books, gilded pen cases, portfolios, picture books and beautiful works of calligraphy. After the death of Humayun, his son, Akbar, succeeded him in 1356. Akbar is regarded as one of the greatest Mughal king. Akbar improved the management of library with some technical works. He appointed Sheik Faizi to manage and control library services.

Akbar was very interest in manuscripts and appointed calligraphers to copy good manuscripts. He established a separate library for women at Fatehpur Sikri and made great improvement to the library. At the time of his death in 1605, the Imperial Library has twenty-four thousand books.

Jahangir, another rule of Mughal period, made a law that when a wealthy man died heirless, the property should be used for building and repairing schools, monasteries, libraries, and other institutions. Some wealthy and scholars, like Abdul Rahim Khan-i-Khanan, Shaik Faizi, Gulbadan Begum and ruler of Mysore and Jaipur also have their private libraries.

Some Hindu learning centers also have libraries. "The libraries of these centers contain huge collections of manuscripts on religion and philosophy as well as other subjects like medicine, science and history". Christian missionaries have also contributed for the libraries since the coming of Vasco da Gama in India.

During the Mughal period, library technical works, *viz.*, Accessioning, Classification and Cataloguing were also carried out in some ways. The head librarian was known as *"Nizam"* and the assistant librarian *as "Muhatin"* or *"Darogha"*. Other staff of libraries during Mughal period is Scribes, Book Illustrators, Calligraphers, Copyists, Translators, Bookbinders and Gilders.

THE BRITISH PERIOD

The Britishers came to India primarily to establish trade and commerce. Some of them were very interested for the upliftment of rich cultural heritage of India. "A number of Academic institutions were established during the British period by the East India Company and by the Christian missionaries".

The University of Calcutta was established in 1857 and its library was opened in 1873. Other Universities, University of Bombay and University of Madras were established in 1879 and 1907 respectively. There were only nineteen Universities in India before 1947. Universities were equipped with libraries in accordance with the Indian University Act of 1904.

The Bengal Royal Asiatic Society set up library in 1784, Bombay Royal Asiatic Society in 1804 and Calcutta Public Library in 1835. Establishment of these libraries enlightened the community and may be regarded as the foundation of the concept of public libraries to the Indian people.

Some of the important libraries set up in 19th. Century in India are Andrews Library, Surat in 1850, Gaya Public Library, Gaya in 1855, Long Library, Rajkot in 1856, Connemara Public Library, Madras in 1860, Government Library, Janagarh in 1867, Adyar Library, Adyar in 1886 and Dahi Laxmi Library, Nadiad in 1892.

Apart from these, other libraries, like Gujarat Vernacular Society along with a library, in Ahmedabad 1848 and Barton Library, Bhavnagar in 1882 were also established. Some of the Indian states also established public libraries.

Such as Baroda established Baroda State Library in Baroda in 1877, Cochin established Public Library and Reading Room in Trichur in 1873, Dhar established Victoria General Library in Dhar in 1856, Indore established General Library in Indore in 1852, Jaipur established Maharajah's Public Library in Jaipur in 1899. Others states also established such kind of libraries, *viz.*, Jammu and Kashmir in 1879, Kahtiawar, in 1886, Kolhapur in 1850, Nizam's Dominion in 1891 and Travancore in 1829.

The first significant date in the development of public libraries in India is 1808 when the Bombay Government initiated a proposal to register libraries, which were to be given copies of books published from the 'Funds for the Encouragement of Literature'.

The contributions of His Highness the Maharaja Sayajirao III, Gaekwar of Baroda towards library movement in India cannot be overlooked. He is remembered today as the Father of Library Movement in India. At the age of 18, in 1881, he was entrusted with full power of the government of Baroda in the Gujarat speaking region of the Bombay Presidency and the Peninsula of Kathiawar.

Baroda's population was predominantly rural, the main occupation was agriculture. The people in general were economically poor and socially backward. Education was the foundation to reconstruct a new social and economic life and education should be the right of the humblest villager.

He introduced free and compulsory education in his princely states. Baroda became the first territory not only among the native states but also in British India to have compulsory free primary education. He opined that primary education was to be the very base and decided to preserve it by means of libraries, which were the only agencies for perpetual universal self-education.

He decided to establish library as an experiment in one of the towns of a *taluka* and in order to implement his idea immediately; he issued orders to his ministers. "In conformity to his ruler's instructions, the Minister of Education prepared a detailed plan to open Circulating Libraries in the State, which was approved in March, 1907. Every public library instituted through the State's financial assistance was to be named as Circulating Library".

In 1906, he went to America as "an observer, a student desirous of acquiring all the knowledge and experience that could enable him to make his own State a model one in India". He was very much impressed by the library services of America for the development of the people in their social, economic and educational life. He then invited an American, William Alanson Borden, a pupil-assistant of Charles A Cutter, who is working as Librarian of the Young Men's Institute, New Haven, Connecticut to come and established library services in India.

In response to his invitation, Borden reached Baroda on November 6, 1910, and became the Director of State Libraries. It can be traced back that public library movement started since 1910 in India. Borden makes a survey of libraries in Baroda and concludes that there were over 241 libraries, holding a little over 100000 volumes. But he did not find any of those libraries adequately housed, nor did he find them shelved in such a manner as to make them most attractive to readers or convenient to those in charge.

He then make proposal for the best services of libraries in the State as:

- Should Your Highness feel disposed to grant me the necessary authority, I propose to organize a Department of Public Libraries, to rank with the other Departments of Your State, with the necessary equipments of officers and clerks, etc. and to bring all the libraries under its control and management;
- To unify all the collections of books in Baroda City into one Central library;
- To add to this Central library, general and technical books;
- To erect a suitable library building of fireproof construction, with

reading grooms, study rooms, Women's Library, Children's library, Lecture hall, Library school, and executive offices;

- To make that library to be Free Public Library of Baroda City, and also the main storehouse for all the valuable historical documents and papers now in private hands in the State, but which the owners would probably be glad to have stored in a safe place;
- To make it also the center from which traveling libraries should start and from which the books, new and old, could be distributed to the various branch libraries in the different towns, cities, and villages of the State.

The Maharaja apparently accepted Borden's proposals, and ordered that the whole scheme might be implemented in parts. The Library Department was created under Order No.9/19, January 30, 1911, for organizing libraries in Baroda.

As the Director of state libraries, he planned a network of free public libraries consisting a state central library, four district or divisional libraries, forty-five town libraries, and more than a thousand village libraries-all integrated into one chain system.

Borden played a leading role for the establishment, management and organization of public libraries in India. As a result of system, within two decades 85% of the Baroda urban and rural population had access to libraries.. Borden developed library classification scheme to suit Indian libraries.

Another great contribution of Borden was the establishment of the first library school in India, in which he trained his own assistants and successors. Borden conducted the first formal library-training programme in India at Baroda in 1911. He was instrumental in the foundation of the Baroda Library Club and its journal, "Library Miscellany", published quarterly in three languages between 1912 and 1919.

University of Madras created the post of University Librarian in 1923 and Dr. S R Ranganathan joined the post on 4 January 1924. Ranganathan published his Five Laws of Library Science in 1931, Colon Classification in 1933 and Classified Catalog Code in 1934.

He also prepared Model Public Library Bill and drives to legislate library bill in Indian states. He made a tremendous contribution for the development of libraries in India. Scholars, educationists and people of library bent of mind founded Calcutta Public Library in 1835 and the same was opened on 21 March 1836 for the public.

In 1944, Calcutta Public Library was shifted to a new and spacious building, constructed in honour of the Governor-General of India, Lord Metcalf. Indian War of Independence broke out in 1857 resulted in to Europeans of Calcutta withdrew their support for the library management in 1899. Consequently, the management and establishment of the library were gradually waning and by the end of the century, the activities of the library came into standstill.

Lord Curzon, the then Viceroy and Governor-General of India visited Calcutta in 1899 and found a miserable condition of Calcutta Public Library. He bought the rights of the Library from the proprietors and later merged it with the Official imperial Library consisting of government departmental libraries of the East India Company. He then declared open of a new Imperial Library of India on 30 January 1903 in the Metcalf Hall. In 1948, one year after the independence of India, Imperial Library was transformed into National library of India and was housed to the Viceroy's Palace in Calcutta, namely, the Belvedere Palace.

POST-INDEPENDENCE PERIOD

Public libraries in India made a tremendous growth after the independence of India in 1947. The central and the state governments took a number of steps forward for the development of the nation from the point of education and considered library as essential part of it.

The programmes executed by provincial and central governments since 1910 for the social and adult education of the populace paved the way for the enactment of library laws and rules for grants-in-aid in the country. Hence public library became part of the education budget.

To enhance the level of literacy of 16% in 1941, the government undertook some programmes such as extension services, continuing education, social education, non-formal education and adult education. The government further initiated steps for the development of community and organized some projects in this regard. Libraries were considered to be an essential part of the Community Development Project that was launched during the first plan period.

In order to accelerate the pace of socioeconomic development, the government considered public libraries to be an integral part of development projects.. The Connemara Public Library in Madras became the State Central Library in 1950 under the provision of Madras Public Libraries Act 1948, and became one of the three depository libraries in 1955.

Delhi Public Library was established in 1951 as the first UNESCO Public Library Pilot Project under the joint auspices of UNESCO and Government of India to adopt "Modern Techniques to Indian Conditions" and to serve as a model public library for Asia.. In 1954, the Delivery of Book Act was passed to include newspaper.

The act obligated every publisher in India to deposit one copy each of its publications to the National Library in Calcutta, the Asiatic Society Library in Bombay, Connemara Public Library in Madras, and Delhi Public Library in New Delhi The Advisory Committee for Libraries as constituted in 1957 by the Government of India, with K P Sinha as the Chairman.

The Committee submitted its report in 1959 with a drafted Model Library Bill. The Planning Commission constituted a Working Group on Public Libraries in 1964 and the Commission submitted its report in 1965 with a

Model Public Libraries Act. The model bill was sent to all the states/UTs, which do not have Public Libraries Act.

In 1972, the Government of India, Planning Commission constituted Working Group on Development of Public Libraries to make recommendations for library development. Raja Rammohun Roy Library Foundation, an autonomous body under the Department of Culture, Ministry of Education, was established in 1972.

The main objective of the Foundation was to assist state library services in developmental works. In 1979, a library section was established in the Department of Culture under the Ministry of Education, which section was under the charge of an Under Secretary. The objective was to promote the development of public libraries in India.

A Working Group on Modernization of Library Services and Informatics was appointed by the Planning Commission in 1983 and submitted its report in 1984 with the formulation of National Policy on Library Services and Informatics. Delhi Public Library became a copyright library in 1982.

National Literacy Mission was adopted in 1986, which emphasized education for women and also establishment of rural libraries. Library networks and systems were strengthened at the national level institutions in the development of literature in neo-literates. Fourteen states namely, Tamil Nadu, Andhra Pradesh, Karnataka, Maharashtra, West Bengal, Manipur, Kerala, Haryana, Mizoram, Goa, Orissa, Gujarat, Uttaranchal and Rajasthan have enacted Public Libraries Bills during 1948 to 2006.

The Government of India, Department of Culture, appointed a Committee on National Policy on Library and Information System in 1985. The National Policy on Education, 1986 states that a nationwide movement for improvement of existing libraries and the establishment of new ones will be taken up, provision will be made in all educational institutions for library facilities, and the status of librarianship improved.

The National Book Policy, 1986 also had an impact on libraries, as:

- Provision of reading material for children by all the agencies involved;
- That 10 per cent of the annual education budget of the governments be used to purchase books for libraries.

These goals are to be achieved by using formal, non-formal, and open channels of learning.. Rural libraries should become the focal point for postliteracy and continuing educational programmes. Publishers, voluntary organizations, and school library programmes undertaken as part of the "Operation Blackboard Scheme" of the National Education Policy on Education, 1986 were given assistance. The following five libraries were regarded as national importance and may be stated in a very brief manner.

National Library, Kolkata

National Library, Kolkata was established in 1836 in the name of Calcutta

Public Library. It was not a Government institution running on a proprietary basis. The then Governor General, Lord Metcalf transferred 4,675 volumes from the library of the College of Fort William to the Calcutta Public Library.

This and donations of books from individuals formed the nucleus of the library. Prince Dwarkanath Tagore was the first proprietor of the Calcutta Public Library. Both the Indian and foreign books, especially from Britain, were purchased for the library. In the report of 1850 we find that the library started collecting books in Gujarati, Marathi, Pali, Ceylonese and Punjabi.

The Government of Bengal and North Western Provinces regularly made by individuals as well as donations. The Calcutta Public Library had a unique position as the first public library in this part of the country. Such a well-organized and efficiently run library was rare even in Europe during the first half of the 19th century. Because of the efforts of the Calcutta Public Library, the National Library has developed rare books and journals in its collection.

The Imperial Library was formed in 1891 by combining a number of Secretariat libraries. Of these, the most important and interesting was the library of the Home Department, which contained many books formerly belonging to the library of East India College, Fort William and the library of the East India Board in London.

But the use of the library was restricted to the superior officers of the Government. Lord Curzon, the then Governor General of India, was the person who conceived the idea of opening a library for the use of the public. He noticed both the libraries, Imperial Library and Calcutta Public Library, were under-utilized for the want of facilities or restrictions. So, he decided to amalgamate the rich collection of both of these libraries.

He was successful in effecting the amalgamation of Calcutta Public Library with the then Imperial Library under certain terms. The library, called Imperial Library, was formally opened to the public on 30th January 1903 at Metcalf Hall, Kolkata.

The aims and objectives of the Imperial Library, well defined in a Notification in the 'Gazette of India' *as ' It is intended* that it should be a library of reference, a working place for students and a repository of material for the future historians of India, in which, so far as possible, every work written about India, at any time, can be seen and read. John Macfarlane, the Asst.

Librarian of the British Museum, London, was appointed as the first Librarian of the Imperial Library. After his death, the famous scholar and linguist Harinath De took over the charge of the library. After his death J. A. Chapman became the librarian. Mr. Chapman showed keen interest in the affairs of the library and worked hard to improve its status. After his retirement, Khan Bahadur M.A. Asadulla was appointed as the librarian and he continued as the librarian till July 1947.

The policy of acquisition broadly adhered to by the Imperial Library was enunciated by Lord Curzon in his speech at the opening ceremony of the library, "The general idea of the whole Library is that it should contain all the books that have been written about India in popular tongues, with such additions as are required to make it a good all-round library of standard works of reference."

After the independence the Government of India changed the name of the Imperial Library as the National Library, with an enactment of the Imperial Library Act 1948 and the collection was shifted from the Esplanade to the present Belvedere Estate. On 1st February 1953 the National Library was opened to the public, inaugurated by Maulana Abul Kalam Azad. Sri B.S. Kesavan was appointed as the first librarian of the National Library.

The reviewing Committee in its report of 1969 suggested that the following should be the basic features of the National Library; Acquisition and conservation of all significant printed materials produced in the country to the exclusion of ephemera:

- Collection of printed materials concerning the country wherever published and also acquisition of photographic record of such materials that are not available within the country;
- Acquisition and conservation of manuscripts having national importance;
- Planned acquisition of foreign materials required by the country;
- Rendering of bibliographical and documentation service of retrospective materials, both general and specialized;
- Acting as a referral centre purveying full and accurate knowledge of all sources of bibliographical activities;
- Provision of photocopying and reprographic services; and
- Acting as the centre for international book exchange and international loan..

Khuda Bakhsh Oriental Public Library, Patna

Khuda Bakhsh Oriental Public Library, Patna was open for the public in October 1891 with 4000 Oriental manuscripts. Maulvi Khuda Bakhsh donated his entire collection to the nation by a deed of trust.

Acknowledging the immense historical and intellectual value of its rich and valued collection, the Govt. of India declared the Library as Institution of National Importance by an act of Parliament in 1969. The Library is now fully funded by the Ministry of Culture. This autonomous institution is being governed by a Board with the Governor of Bihar as its ex-officio Chairman and Director is carrying the responsibility of dayto-day management of Library affairs.

Rampur Raza Library, Rampur

Rampur Raza Library, Rampur was founded by Nawab Faizullah Khan in 1774 AD. It was brought under the management of a Trust till the Government of India took over the library on 1 July 1975 under the Act of Parliament, which declared it as an institution of National importance.

It contains very rare and valuable collection of manuscripts, historical documents, specimens of Islamic calligraphy, miniature paintings, astronomical instruments and rare illustrated works in Arabic and Persian languages besides 80,000 printed books. Nawab Faizullah Khan who ruled the state of Rampur, from 1774 to 1794, established the library with his personal modest collection kept in the Tosha Khana of his Palace.

Now the Library occupies the position of an autonomous institution of national importance under Department of Culture, Government of India and is fully funded by Central Government. The Library has now attained an International status of higher studies.

Thanjavur Maharaja Serfoji's Sarasvati Mahal Library, Thanjavur

Thanjavur Maharaja Serfoji's Sarasvati Mahal Library, Thanjavur is one among a few medieval libraries existing in the world. It contains very rare and valuable collections of manuscripts, books, maps and paintings on all aspects of Art, Culture and Literature.

The Encyclopaedia Britannica in its survey of the Libraries of the world mentions this as "the most remarkable Library in India". The Library houses a rich and rare collection of manuscripts on art, culture and literature. Conceived and christened as the Royal Palace Library by the Nayak Kings of Thanjavur. And the Maratha rulers nourished it for intellectual enrichment.

In 1918 this Library was made as a public Library. A body constituted by the Government and financed by the Central and State Governments now administers the library. During the reign of Nayaks of Thanjavur, "Sarasvati Bhandar" was formed and developed. The Maratha rulers who captured Thanjavur in 1675 A.D. patronized the culture of Thanjavur and developed the Royal Palace Library till 1855 A.D.

The Sarasvati Bhandar was situated within the Palace campus and the Manuscripts used for the purpose of reading by the Royal personages. Among the Maratha Kings, King Serfoji II, was an eminent scholar in many branches of learning and with great enthusiasm he took special steps for the enrichment of the Library.

It is a fitting tribute to the great collector Serfoji that the Library is named after him. Till the survival of the last Maratha Queen, the Library was the Palace property. After that, the Library together with the Palace properties formed the subject of litigation in Civil Courts.

The Royal Family members voluntarily came forward to delete this Library from the suit properties formed an Endowment and dedicated this Library to the public with one lakh rupees for its maintenance and upkeep. The Government of Madras in their G.O. Ms. No.1306 Home dated 5th October 1918, took possession of the Library under the Charitable Endowment Act and framed scheme for the Library management.

In 1983, the Library was declared as an Institution of National Importance. The Government of Tamil Nadu abolished the Five Member

Committee of administration and made it as a Registered Society as per G.O. 209 (EST) dated 1-2-83. The Society was constituted and got registration on 9-7-1986 under the Tamil Nadu Registered Societies Act of 1975.

The Society consists of ex-officio members of Central and State Governments, nominated Scholars, Member from the Royal family and the Director of the Library. The Hon'ble Education Minister of the Government of Tamil Nadu is the ex-officio Chairman of this society.

Harekrushna Mahtab State Library, Bhubaneswar

Harekrushna Mahtab State Library, Bhubaneswar was conceived during 1st Five Year Plan under the advice of Government of India and was completed in 1959, enshrined within a beautiful land of 3 acres in a prime location of Capital City of Bhubaneswar.

In 1967, it was named as Gandhi Bhawan commemorating birth centenary of Mahatma Gandhi, the father of the nation. In 1987 it was renovated and entire space of the four storied building was utilized for the functioning of two Libraries *i.e.* State Library for the entire State of Orissa and another Public Library for Bhubaneswar City.

In 1987, Government decided to rename the State Library and the Public Library as Harekrushna Mahtab State Library and the Bhubaneswar Public Library respectively. The former is a Reference Library and lending of books is not permitted whereas the latter is a Lending Library for the public of Bhubaneswar City. These two Libraries have managed to function over the limited space. Total readers seats available are about 350 against the present demands of 600-700 readers per day.

LIBRARY LEGISLATION IN INDIA

Since the beginning, the public libraries served as the local information centers making the source of knowledge readily available to the public. The local community from the local fund or individual munificence could not achieve the services of a public library. Public leaders, scholars and learned societies have realised that the only way to establish and develop a public library system is through legislation.

The UNESCO Public Library Manifesto, 1972 stated that, "The public library should be established under the clear mandate of law", which is substantiated by the IFLA/UNESCO Public Library Manifesto 1994 as;

- "The public library shall in principle be free of charge. The public library is the responsibility of local and national authorities. It must be supported by specific legislation and financed by national and local government. It has to be an essential component of any long-term strategy for culture, information provision, literacy and education".

Libraries are recorded under the Article 246 of Indian Constitution, Seventh Schedule List II of State List No.12 and the Indian Constitution Act,

1956, *"Libraries, museums and other similar institutions controlled or financed by the State; ancient and historical monuments and records other than those to be of national importance."*

Provision of public library service is the responsibility of the State Government as the subject matter of libraries is relatable to entry 12 of the State List in the Seventh Schedule to the Constitution of India.

Dr. S R Ranganathan regarded as the pioneer of library legislation in India. "The concept of legislation for libraries is a contribution of S R Ranganathan to Indian public libraries". He made library legislation obligatory for the implementation of the second law of library science, "Every reader his/her book". Ranganathan the second law can be properly carried out only by legislation.

Dr. S R Ranganathan strived a lot for library legislation and prepared different library bills for the Indian Union and constituent states; such as;

- Model Library Act for constituent states of India;
- Bengal;
- Bombay;
- Central Province and Berar;
- Old Madras state which later became Act in 1948;
- United Province;
- Cochin;
- Travancore;
- Union Government;
- Madhya Pradesh;
- Union and Constituent States;
- Constituent States;
- Union;
- West Bengal;
- Kerala;
- Uttar Pradesh;
- Mysore which became Act in 1965;
- Assam;
- Gujarat and Model Library Bill.

Public libraries also considered as community information centers providing access at local level to a wide range of knowledge and information for the benefit of the individual and society as a whole. To ensure sustained development and information network services public libraries should be based on legislation.

"Public library legislation may be in various forms depending upon the government structure. It can be simple, allowing the establishment of public libraries but leaving standards of service to the level of government directly responsible for the library, or more complex, with specific detail on what services should be provided and to what standard".

But no British Government passed library Act for creation of public library system in Indian states.. There have been different efforts to work out library legislation models in India. In the pre-independent and post-independent of India, there have been five models of public library bills suggested by experts and national level professional associations and organizations.

MODEL PUBLIC LIBRARIES ACT OF DR. S R RANGANATHAN

The first Model Public Libraries Acts was prepared by Dr. S R Ranganathan in 1930 and revised in 1957 and 1972. It was discussed at the First All Asia Educational Conference held at Banaras during 26-30 December 1930. It was introduced in West Bengal Legislature in 1931 and in Madras Legislature in 1933. The Bill could not be passed due to financial clauses on library grant, library cess etc.

Salient features of final version are:

- Establishment of public libraries in city, rural and other areas;
- Constitution of State Library Authority *i.e.* Minister of Education;
- Constitution of State Library Committee as an advisory body of the State Library Authority;
- Constitution of Local Library Authority for each city and one for each district;
- State Library Authority, Government and Local Library Authority may determine library rate in such a manner and may determine collection of library cess from time to time.

MODEL PUBLIC LIBRARIES BILL OF MINISTRY OF EDUCATION

The Government of India, Ministry of Education appointed an Advisory Committee for Libraries in 1957, under the Chairmanship of Shri K P Sinha, former Director of Public Instruction, Bihar. This committee recommended the need for library legislation for each state. As a follow-up action of the Advisory Committee, the Ministry of Education, Government of India appointed a committee under the Chairmanship of Dr. M D Sen. The Committee drafted Model Public Libraries Bill in the year 1963.

The salient components of this Bill are:

- Constitution of State Library Authority as an apex body to advise the Government in the matter of library developments;
- Constitution of State Library Directorate for direction and controlling of library services;
- Constitution of District Library Committee in each district;
- Treatment of employees as government servant;
- Collection of library cess at the rate of 6 paise per rupee on house tax and property tax.

MODEL PUBLIC LIBRARIES BILL OF THE PLANNING COMMISSION

The Planning Commission, Government of India, constituted a 'Working

Group on Libraries' in 1964 to plan and advice on the development of Libraries during the Fourth Five Year Plan. The Working Group recommended a Library Development Scheme to be implemented during the Fourth Plan period with a financial commitment of ₹.309 million, which was appended by Model Public Libraries Bill and submitted its report in 1965. Bill was not considered even by a single state.

The Bill included the following features:

- Establish, maintain, develop and integrated adequate public library service in the state;
- Constitution of Committee of Experts to prescribe the standards of service;
- Constitution of State Library Council to advise the government for the promotion and development of library service;
- Establishment of State Library Directorate to control, direct and supervise library system in the state;
- Establishment of State Central Library, State Regional Libraries and District Libraries;
- Treatment of employees in the system of State Government Servants
- Government shall be the financial source and shall maintain the public library system in the state.

MODEL PUBLIC LIBRARIES BILL OF INDIAN LIBRARY ASSOCIATION

The Indian Library Association (ILA) formed in 1933, has keen interest in library legislation. The ILA discussed library legislation at its various seminars organized in 1964, 1978 and 1981. Consequently, ILA Council at its meeting held on 23 June 1989, keeping in view of the developments and experiences gain from the existing Acts, resolved to prepare a Model Library Bill.

Accordingly, as asked by ILA, Dr. Velaga Venkatappaiah, Chairman, Central Sectional Committee on Public Libraries of the ILA prepared a Model Public Library Bill. ILA accepted the draft Bill with minor changes at its National Seminar on Public Library Legislation in 1990 at the final product of the Model Public Libraries Bill was published in 1991.

The Bill was circulated to all the states and union territories but few states reacted favourably to the Bill. This Model Bill was again discussed in a National Seminar on Library Legislation and revised as the Model State Public Library and Information Service Act in 1995. In view of emergence of Information Technology at all levels, the model act was again revised in 2000.

The important components of this Bill are:

- State Library and Information Service, based on a State Policy;
- Constitution of State Library Authority at the apex level with Minister of Libraries as Chairman as policy making and executive body;

- Establishment of Directorate of Public Libraries for directing, controlling and supervising;
- Constitution of City, District Library Authority for rendering service from district to village level;
- Provision for network of Public Library and Information Services from state to village level;
- Constitution of State Library and Information Service;
- Collection of Library cess on house tax and property tax, entertainment tax, professional tax, vehicle tax, etc.;
- Constitution of State Boards for education, book production, co-ordination, etc.;
- Accountability of public expenditure and services.

MODEL UNION LIBRARY ACT

The Government of India appointed a committee to explore the possibilities to establish a National Central Library at New Delhi in 1948. Dr. S R Ranganathan, a member of the committee drafted a Library Development plan in 1950 with a 30-year programme and a draft Library Bill for the states and Union Public Library Act.

This was revised in 1959 and again in 1972. However, libraries falls under the state list of the constitution and it may not be possible to pass Bill as a Union Act, unless and until the constitution is suitably amended for this purpose.

The main features of this model Act are:

- Constitution of a National Library Authority;
- Establishment of national central libraries;
- Constitution of National Library Committee as an advisory body to the National library Authority;
- Constitution of National library fund;
- Amendment to the delivery of Books and Newspaper Act, 1954.

The IFLA/UNESCO Public Library Manifesto 1994 reads that, "The public library is the local center of information, making all kinds of knowledge and information readily available to its users". Public libraries, to become an enthusiastic source of information and knowledge for the local community, needs certain forms of developments in terms of infrastructure, collection and the trinity of library as well. It cannot survive by the local contributions and dedication alone, but through the support of government.

"The pubic library, as a democratic institution operated by the people for the people, should be established and maintained under the clear authority of law; supported wholly or mainly from public funds; open for free use on equal terms to all members of the community regardless of occupation, creed, class or race". Efforts have been going on well under the initiatives of professional associations and learned societies in this context. "In India, the post independence era was favourable to the establishment of public libraries based on legal basis"..

STATES WITH LIBRARY LEGISLATION

During the last six decades, 14 Public Library Bills were enacted in different states of India, such as:

- *Tamil Nadu:* The Tamil Nadu Public Libraries Act 1948;
- *Andhra Pradesh*: The Andhra Pradesh Public Libraries Act 1960;
- *Karnataka:* The Karnataka Public Libraries Act 1965;
- *Maharashtra*: The Maharastra Public Libraries Act 1967;
- *West Bengal:* The West Bengal Public Libraries Act 1979;
- *Manipur:* The Manipur Public Libraries Act 1988;
- *Kerala*: The Kerala Public Libraries Act 1989;
- *Haryana:* The Haryana Public Libraries Act 1989;
- *Mizoram:* The Mizoram Public Libraries Act 1993;
- *Goa:* The Goa Public Libraries Act 1993;
- *Orissa*: Orissa Public Libraries Act, 2001;
- *Gujarat:* Gujarat Public Libraries Act, 2001;
- *Uttaranchal:* Uttaranchal Public Libraries Act, 2005.
- *Rajasthan:* Rajasthan Public Libraries Act, 2006

Tamil Nadu

Tamil Nadu is the first state that enacted Public Libraries Act in independent India. It came into force with effect from 1 April 1950. The objectives of the Act are contained in its Preamble as, 'An act to provide for the establishment of public libraries in the province of Tamil Nadu and the organization of comprehensive rural and urban Library Service therein". It has 19 sections.

The salient features of this Act are given below:

- This Act facilitates establishment of Public Libraries in the State.
- Constitution of State Library Committee for the purpose of advising the government on such matters relating to libraries.
- Provision for appointment of Director of Public Libraries to control, direct and supervise public libraries.
- Constitution of Local Library Authorities, one for the City of Madras and one for each district.
- Every Local Library Authority shall levy in the area a library cess in the form of a surcharge on property tax or house tax at the rate of six paise per rupee.
- The Government shall contribute Library Fund to each of the Local Library Authority, except the City of Madras, to the amount of library cess collected.
- The Act amended Sec.9 of the Press and Registration of Books Act, 1867, Central Act XXV of 1867 to the effect that every printer shall

deliver five copies of each book to the State Government out of which four will be deposited in the State Central Library, Madras.

Tamil Nadu was very rich in public libraries. The Connemara Public Library was opened for the public in 1896 and became the State Central Library from 1 April 1950. There is a tremendous growth and development of public libraries since an enactment of Tamil Nadu Public Libraries Act 1948 being the first state in India with Library Legislation.

As on March 1998, the state has public library service units, as–1 State Central Library, 29 District Central Libraries, 1548 Branch Libraries, 506 Village Libraries, 649 Part-time Libraries, and 8 Mobile Libraries. The Department of Public Libraries has been offering extension services, like–Mobile Library Service, Home Delivery Service, Library Service for Children, Library Service for Police Personnel, Library Service for state workers and remote settlers in the hills, Hospital Library Service, Rural Library Service, Part-time Library Service, Library Service for Students, Library Service for research scholars and Library Service for competitions for various civil services.

Andhra Pradesh

The state of Andhra Pradesh was formed in 1956, comprising Andhra areas of composite Madras state and Telengana area of Hyderabad area, whereas Madras Public Libraries Act in force in Andhra area. To solve administrative problems on two acts in operational in one state; both the acts were amalgamated, modified and up-to-date as Andhra Pradesh Public Libraries Act 1960.

It received the Governor assent on 18th. February 1960. Andhra Pradesh is the second state that has enacted Public Libraries Act in independent India. Its Preamble reads that, *"An Act to* consolidate and amend the laws relating to the establishment and maintenance of Public Libraries in the State of Andhra Pradesh and matters connected therewith".

It has seven chapters. Important features of this Act are as below:

- Constitution of 'The Andhra Pradesh Granthalaya Parishad', as a corporate body, having perpetual succession and power to the provisions of this Act.
- Constitution of Directorate of Public Libraries to direct, supervise and control Public Library System.
- Constitution of Zilla Granthalaya Samastha, one for the City of Hyderabad, one for the district of Hyderabad and one for each districts.
- Provision to collect library cess by every Zilla Granthalaya Samstha in its area as surcharge on property tax or house tax up to eight paise per rupee.
- The accounts of Zilla Granthalaya Samstha shall be open to inspection.
- Provision of Government Grant-in-aid to private libraries.
- Provision for constitution of a Library Service for the Zilla

Granthalaya Samstha for the appointment of Librarians.

Andhra Pradesh is one of the leading states in India for the promotion of library services in India. It is the second in India with Public Libraries Act in 1960.

The structure of public library services can be classified into three categories consisting of:

- *Government Libraries:* 1 State Central Library, 6 Regional Libraries, and 1 Mobile Library,
- *Zila Grandhalaya Samstha Libraries:* 23 District/City Central Libraries, 1448 Branch Libraries, 355 Village Libraries, 3 Mobile Libraries, and 576 Book Deposit Centers,
- *Aided Libraries:* 1238 Gram Panchayat Libraries, 37 Cooperative Society Libraries, and 680 Private Libraries.

Karnataka

Karnataka is the third state in an independent India that have enacted Public Libraries Act. The objective of this Act can be seen in its Preamble that reads, '*An* Act to provide for the establishment and maintenance of Public Libraries and the organization of a comprehensive rural and urban library service in the State of *Karnataka* '.

Important features of this Act are given below:

- Constitution of State Library Authority to meet twice in a year, Minister of Public Libraries as its Chairman and State Librarian as *ex-officio* Secretary.
- Provision for creation of an independent Department of Public Libraries with a profession as its head, to supervise, direct and control library services.
- Provision for the establishment of State Library as apex of public library system in the state.
- Constitution of Local Library Authority, City Library Authority and District Library Authority.
- Provision for setting up of Advisory Library Committee for Branch and Village Library Services.
- Collection of library cess on tax on lands and buildings.
- Additional sections in State Central Library
- State Bureau of Copyright Collection
- State Library for the Blind
- State Bureau of Inter Library Loan
- State Bibliographical Bureau
- State Bureau of Technical Service.

Karnataka is the third state in India that enacted Public Library Bill in 1965. The Belgaum Native General Library, established in 1848 by M.J.D.Invararity, was regarded as the first library started in Karnataka state. There were other seven libraries or reading rooms in Belgaum, namely, Library at Chikkodi established in 1886, Nippani Library in 1875, Gokak Library in

1865, Athani Library in 1865, Sampagaon Library in 1866, Khanapur Library in 1868, and Saundatti Library in 1870.

The existing public libraries in Karnataka are-1 State Central Library, 1 Indira Priyadarshini Chidren's Library, 1 Public Technical Library, 27 District Central Library, 19 City Central Library, 14 Mobile Libraries, 490 Branch Libraries, 107 Service Stations, 31 Reading Rooms, 5766 Gram Panchayat Libraries, 21 Aided Libraries, 200 Slum Libraries and 600 Reading Rooms in Slum Areas.

Maharashtra

Consequent upon the constitution of Maharashtra state, The Maharashtra Public Libraries Act, 1967 succeed Kolhapur Public Libraries Act 1945. The fourth state in an independent India that has enacted Public Libraries Act is Maharashtra state. Preamble of the Act read that, "To provide for the establishment, maintenance, organization and development of public libraries in the state of Maharashtra".

Important features of this Act are:

- Constitution of State Library Council. Minister for Education shall be the ex-officio President of the Council. The Council will advise the State Government on all matters connected with the administration of this Act.
- Constitution of a separate department of Libraries and the appointment of a professional Director;
- Establishment of Maharashtra State Library Service;
- Establishment of State Central library and a Divisional Library for each Division;
- Constitution of District Library Committee in each of the district. Chairman of the Education Committee of a Zilla Parishad in the district shall be ex-officio President of the Committee.
- Constitution of Library Fund by the State Government for carrying out the purpose of this Act. The State Government will contribute not less than a sum of twenty-five lakhs to the Library Fund every year.

The Birtishers started public libraries in Maharashtra after defeating Marathas in 1818 but no Indians were allowed membership of these libraries till 1830. Pioneer libraries estab-lished by Indian in Maharashtra were at Ahmednagar in 1838, Bombay in 1845, and Poona in 1848. In 1939, the government constituted a Library Development Committee to prepare a plan for public library development in the state of Bombay.

The report was implemented from 1955 to 1967. After an enactment of Maharashtra Public Libraries Act 1967, public library system was developed through voluntary organizations with grants from the government. As on 1998, Maharashtra has different categories of public libraries as–1 State Central Library, 6 Divisional Libraries, 31 District Libraries, 63 Taluka Grade A

Libraries, 144 Taluka Grade B Libraries, 58 Taluka Grade C Libraries, and 3842 Recognized Libraries.

West Bengal

The West Bengal Legislature passed this Act and assent of the President was first published in the Calcutta Gazette, Extraordinary on the 7th January 1980. West Bengal enacted the Public Libraries Act in 1979 to become the fifth state of India with library legislation. Its preamble stated that, *"An Act to provide for the* establishment of Public libraries in the State of West Bengal and to regulate, guide, central, supervise and to grant recognition to the existing libraries in the State as also to provide for a comprehensive rural and urban library service in the State of *west Bengal".*

Some of the important salient features of this Act are:

- Constitution of State Library Council for the purpose of advising the Government on the matters of public library services. Minister-in-Charge of Library Services shall be the Chairman of the Council;
- Constitution of the Department of Libraries to supervise and direct the maintenance of Public Libraries;
- Constitution of Local Library Authority for each district. The District Magistrate shall be the Chairman of the Local Library Authority. Provision for constitution of Executive Committee for Local Library Authority;
- The Government is empowered to appoint District Library Officers and District Librarians in districts. The Government, in consultation with the Local Library Authority may place a person in charge of a District Library to be called as District Librarian;
- Financial management of local libraries rests upon the Local Library Authority. Means of augmenting funds are:
- Contributions, gifts and income form endowments;
- Grants from the government
- Collection of Local Library Authority under the Act.

In 1780, Mr. John Andrews run a commercial library in Fort William and the first public library; Calcutta Public Library was established during the British period in 1836, which is now known as National Library. By 1900, there were 50 public libraries in Bengal.

The state government took up a seven tier library development scheme, which envisaged setting up of public libraries at different levels-State Central Library; District Library; Sub-Division/Area Library; Rural Library; Village Library; and Delivery Stations/Book Deposit Centers. By 1996, West Bengal has one State Central Library, 22 District Libraries, 120 Sub-Divisional/Town Libraries, and 2276 Rural/Area/Primary Unit Libraries. There are also around 3000 non-governmental/non-sponsored public libraries. West Bengal is the fifth state in India with Library Legislation in 1979.

Manipur

Manipur is the sixth state in an independent India that has enacted Public Libraries Act in 1988. The preamble stated the objectives of this Acts as, "An Act to provide the establishment and maintenance of Public Libraries in the State of Manipur and matters connected therewith".

Salient features of this Act are given hereunder:

- Constitution of a State Library Committee, to advise the State Government on all matters arising under this Act and to exercise and perform such other powers and duties as may be prescribed.
- Constitution of a separate Department of Public Libraries under the Director, as its head.
- Constitution of District Library Authority for each district to supervise library services in the area of its jurisdiction.
- Provision to constitute Executive Committee and Sub-Committees of District Library Authority to enquire into and report or advice on any matters, which it may refer to them.
- Constitution of Library fund formed mainly with the contribution of the State Government.

Manipur is the sixth state in India with Public Library Acts in 1988. Manipur Club established in 1927 was changed over into Manipur Book Club/Manipur Club Library and again changed into Jubabati Memorial Library in 1933. But the library had a setback during the Second World War.

Imphal Public Library, also known as Khwai Public Library was established in 1938 but was functioning till 1960 and later it was demolished in 1994. District Library and Children's Library-cum-Museun were merged on 26 August 1970 and came to be known as State Central library.. There are 9 District Libraries, 1 State Central Library, and 215 Libraries organized by Voluntary Organizations..

Kerala

Kerala Public Libraries Act, 1989 is also known as Kerala Granthasala Sanghom, 1989. Kerala enacted its pubic Libraries Act in 1989 to become the seventh state in India with library legislation. Preamble of this Act stated its objectives as, "*An Act* to consolidate and unify the library laws in the State and to provide for the recognition in the entire library system in the State of Kerala with a view to the development and maintenance of comprehensive rural and urban library service and for matters connected therewith or incidental hereto".

Important features of the Act are:

- Constitution of Kerala State Library Council with Executive Committee to advise the government on all matters connected with this Act and to supervise and direct all maters relating to library service in the state;

- Secretary of the State Library Council shall be the Chief Executive Authority of the State Library Council;
- Constitution of District Library Council to supervise, co-ordinate and control the Library service under its jurisdiction and to promote co-operation between libraries and cultural and educational institutions in the country;
- Constitution of Taluk Library Union, with the power to supervise, coordinate and control the library services in the Taluk and to give directions and advise to affiliated libraries in regard to their day to day function and management;
- The Government may make every year a grant to the State library council with a maximum of one per cent of the education budget of the State.
- The State Library Council shall maintain a fund called State Library fund. Library cess collected and grants of State and Central Government will be credited to the State Library fund.
- Transfer of Kerala Granthaala Sangham with its staff, assets, and liabilities to the State Library Council.
- Collection of Library Cess in the form of a surcharge on the building tax or the property tax at the rate of 5 paise for the whole rupee.

Christian missionaries started libraries in Kerala during the 19th century. The history of public library movement in Kerala started in 1829 with the establishment of Trivandrum Public Library. There are more than 5000 public libraries in Kerala now, one in every 8 square kilometers.

Public libraries can be grouped into four categories, as–Libraries directly run by the Government, Libraries run by the local bodies, Grant-in-Aid libraries affiliated to the Kerala Grandhasala Sangham, and Libraries run by the Local Library Authorities.

The Kerala Grandhasala Sangham was established in 1947 and was registered under Section 9 of the Travancore Company Act, 1939 and in 1948 the Government approved it as the Central Agency of the Libraries. It plays an incredible role for the promotion, development and encouraging the people of the state through library services. Kerala enacted Public Library Bill in 1989 to become the seventh state in India with Library Legislation.

Haryana

Haryana is the eighth state in India with library legislation. The preamble stated its objectives as, "An Act to provide for the establishment, maintenance and development of Public Libraries in the State of Haryana and for matters ancillary *thereto.*"

Some of the important features of this Act are:

- Constitution of State Library Authority to advise the Government on all matters for the promotion of library services in the State. Minister-in-charge of libraries will be the Chairman;

- Establishment of State Library Directorate to execute the programmes approved by the State Library Authority;
- Establishment of State Central library;
- Constitution of District Library in each district and Municipal/City/ Town library; Block library; Village library; and Smaller book deposit centers;
- Provision for three types of library funds, such as State Library Fund, District Library Fund, and City/Town/Block/Village Library Fund;
- Levy of Library cess in the form of surcharge on property tax and house tax as decided by the government from time to time;
- Provision to recognize state library associations, and co-operative institutions by the State Library Authority.

Before the creation of this separate state, some public libraries were already established, Guru Gobind Singh Municipal Library in 1926, Shri Parmeshwari Yuvak Librray in 1927, and Sri Bal Amar Samiti Library in 1932. A State Central Library was started in 1967 by th4 Government of Haryana. Besides it has started 12 District Libraries, 11 Sub-Divisional Libraries and 11 Municipal Libraries.

Many philanthropic trusts and local bodies/organizations had also established public libraries, which took active role in the promotion of reading habits and library services in the state. The Haryana Library Association was founded in 1967. The Haryana Public Libraries Bill was passed in 1989 and independent Directorate of Libraries was established in January 1993.

Mobile library services to reach the interior of the remote villages with reading facilities were started and the people are very much encouraged for the development of libraries at villages and panchayat levels as a social education center and community information center as well.

Mizoram

Mizoram is the ninth state of India to have library legislation. Preamble of this Act stated its objective as, "An Act to provide for the establishment, maintenance and development of comprehensive public libraries system in the State of Mizoram".

Important features of this Act are:

- Constitution of State Library Council to advise the Government on all matters relating to libraries and also in regard to promotion and development of libraries in the State;
- Constitution of the Department of Public Libraries to control and supervise the public library system in the State;
- Constitution of State Library, District Library, Sub-Divisional Library and Village Libraries;
- Provision of grant-in-aid to recognized libraries;

- No library cess. All expenses shall be made from the Government funds.

Goa

Goa is the tenth state to have library legislation in India. Preamble of this Act stated that, "An Act to provide for the establishment, maintenance and development of Public Libraries in the State of Goa and for the matters ancillary hereto".

Important salient features of this Act are:

- Constitution of State Library Council with the Minister-in-charge a the Chairman to advise the Government on all matters arising under the Act;
- Constitution of State Library Directorate for controlling and directing the public library system in the State;
- Organization of State Library, District Library, Taluk Library, and Village library;
- Creation of Public Library employees similar to the employees of State Government;
- Recognition of one State Library Association as co-operating institution;
- State library fund from different sources, *viz.*, Government contribution, Government Grants, and any other contribution from the public;
- Levy of Library Cess in the form of a surcharge on Indian Made Foreign Liquor at the rate of 50 paise per bulk litre of beer.

Under the order of the Viceroy, *Dom Manuel de Portugal e Castro*, a public library, *Publica Livraria* was opened and attached to *Academia Militar* in 1832 and it was named as *Bibliotheca Nacional de Goa* in 1959 and came under the administration of Education and Health Services department. The Government of Goa constituted a State Level Expert Committee in 1978 and State Library Advisory Board in 1983 for the development of library services in the state. The public libraries of Goa can be categorized into five levels, as State Library, Taluka Libraries, Village Libraries, Government Aided Libraries, and Municipal Libraries. Goa is the tenth state in India with Public Library Act in 1993.

Orissa

The establishment of Diamond Jubilee Library at Kendrapara in 1897 and at Baripada in 1898 started the development of public library and followed by establishment of other libraries in the state. Three Government functionaries, Department of Information and Public Relations, Department of Sports and Culture, and Department of Housing and Urban Development operated public libraries in the state for some times.

In 1975, the Department of Cultural Affairs, Government of Orissa took complete charge of Public Libraries from the Department of Education. There is one State Library, 13 District Libraries, 4 Sub-Divisional libraries, 6 Ex. District Board Libraries, and 4 Memorial Hall Libraries.

Gujarat

Objective of Gujarat Public Libraries Act provided in its preamble is to provide for the promotion and development of public libraries in the State of Gujarat and for that purpose to constitute State Library development Council and for the matters connected therewith or incidental thereto.

Important features of this act are:

- Constitution of State Library Council with Minister–in-charge of Libraries as its Chairman;
- Establishment of Public Library Department with Director as its head of office;
- Establishment of District and Taluka Libraries at the headquarters of taluka;
- Constitution of District and Taluka Library Advisory Committee;
- Formation of State Library Development Fund;
- Recognition of libraries run by voluntary organi-zations.

The first considered public library in Gujarat was called, "Himabhai Institute of Library" established in 1849 in Ahmedabad. Other pioneer public libraries are Andrews Library established in 1850, Lang Library in 1857, Lakhajirao Pusthakalaya in 1868, Bhagavatsihji Library in 1884, State Library in 1865, Barton Library in 1882, Takhsinhi Library in 1877, and Victoria Jubilee Library in 1891.

There are 2 State Central libraries, 18 District Libraries in all the districts, 45 Taluka Libraries, 129 Mahila Libraries run by voluntary organizations, more than 300 Book Service Centers and Mobile Library service.

Uttaranchal

Uttaranchal is the 27th state of Indian Union, separated from Uttar Pradesh and coming into existence on 9.11.2000. The state comprises ten districts, namely Uttarkashi, Dehradun, Tehri Garhwal, Chamoli, Pithoragarh, Nainital, Uddam Singh Nagar, Pauri Garhwal and Hardwar. Public Libraries within these districts were automatically came under the Uttaranchal administration.

The state literacy rate is 72.28%. The state government is very interested to serve the people through public libraries and the Uttaranchal Public Libraries Bill was enacted in 2005 to become the thirteenth state in India with Library legislation. Some of the well established libraries by the state government of Uttar Pradesh were taken over while coming up into existence.

Rajasthan

Libraries were established in Rajasthan as early as 14th. Century and maintained in the form of *Pothi-Khanas* consisting rich collections of manuscripts on different disciplines. Rana Kumbha's Saraswati Bhandar Library was established in 1448. Raja Man Singh established library, *Pothi-Khana* in 1592 by keeping rare and important manuscripts.

Pioneer Public Libraries were established in Bharatpur in 1907, Sikar in 1908, Kota in 1910, Fatehpur in 1910, and Jodhpur in 1915. There are 5 Divisional libraries, 24 District Libraries, and 8 Tehsil Libraries with 600 Book Deposit Centers on 15 August 1956. Mobile van was also provided to Division Libraries to supervise library services in the state.

STATES/UTS WITHOUT LIBRARY LEGISLATION

Public library systems and services of Indian states and Union Territories are highlighted hereunder.

Arunachal Pradesh

Arunachal Pradesh, formerly known as North East Frontier Agency, introduced library service since 1950s. During the Seventh Five Year Plan period, the state government took up the scheme of developing libraries in the state and set up a number of libraries at block and circle levels. Mobile library system was introduced in the state capital. The state has six categories of library, such as–1 State Library, 2 Branch Libraries, 13 District Libraries, 2 Sub-Divisional Libraries, 20 Block Libraries, and 45 Circle Libraries.

Assam

In 1865, George Williamson, a tea-planter of Golaghat bequeathed 10,000 pounds for the purpose of educational and set up of libraries in Assam and the government taken up as an experiment measure to established public libraries at the initiatives of British government in 1902-1903 at Dhubri, Guwahati, Nagaon, Jorhat, Tezpur, Shillong, Sibsagar, Goalpara, Dibrugarh, Hailakandi, etc. and then handed over to the Local Boards.

The people were awakened and established rural libraries in some areas. The Assam Library Association came into existence in 1938 and extended all possible help to established public libraries in different areas. The Central Library, established in 1954 at Shillong and the Assam Government Public Library established in 1903 was amalgamated in 1956 and renamed as the State Central Library.

In 1955, seven District Libraries were set up at Guwahati, Nagaon, Jorhat, Dibrugarh, Tezpur, Dhubri and Silchar. Book Mobile Service along with 70 Deposit Centers for Circulation of Books was organized to villages in 1959. Assam is running 1 State Library, 1 Branch Library, 22 District Libraries, 14 Sub-Divisional Libraries, and 1 Children Library.

Bihar

The ancient Educational and Cultural Centers like Nalanda, Vikramshala,

Pataliputra and Taxila had magnificent libraries and Bihar Library Association was founded on 15 October 1936. The Association popularized importance of libraries and in 1937 prepared a Draft Scheme for the development of libraries in Bihar.

There is one State Central Library at Patna, having seven wings, *viz.*, State Reference Library, State Lending Library, State Library for Blind, State Bureau of Inter-Library Loan, State Bibliographical Bureau, State Bureau of Technical Service, and State Institute of Library Training and Research.

At present, there is 1 State Central Library, 6 Divisional Libraries, 7 Special Libraries, 17 District Central Libraries, 2 State Libraries, 11 Sub-Divisional Libraries, 328 Block Libraries, and 4422 Village Libraries in Bihar. The Library service is at the government level is under the control and supervision of the Commissioner of Education. In the state of Jharkhand area, there are 5 District Libraries, 4 Sub-Divisional Libraries and other Village Libraries are under the public library sector. The state of Jharkhand came into existence on 15 November 2000 by separating some areas of Bihar state.

Himachal Pradesh

Under the scheme of Integrated Library Service formulated by the Union Ministry of Education, a small library system was introduced in 1952. A State Central Library was established in Solan in 1959, and within two years sic District Libraries were opened. The State Central Library created four departments, namely, reference, Lending, Periodicals, and Children Section for the benefit of the readers.

Membership registration is free of charge to all the residents of Himachal Pradesh. It has 1 State Central Library, 11 District Libraries, 15 Community Central Public Libraries, and 101 Senior Secondary School Libraries in the state. The School Libraries are also used as public libraries after the school hours. Two Mobile units are set up in 1961 to cater the needs of the community particularly in the rural areas of the state.

Jharkhand

The state of Jharkhand, separated from Bihar, is having 18 public libraries established by the state government.

These public libraries may be classified into four groups as below:

- Three State Public Libraries, one each at Ranchi, Chaibasa, Dhanbad and Dumka.
- One Divisional Library at Hazaribagh;
- Five District Libraries, one each at Gumla, Lohardaga, Daltonganj and Godda; and
- Eight Sub-Divisional Libraries, one each at Garhwa, Lahetar, Pakur, Simdega, Chatra, Sahebganj, Saraikela, and Khunti..

The library building are, generally, not functional to cater more readers at a time. Furniture is inadequate and water supply system is poor. No electricity connection was available to some of them due to non-payment of bills. Collection and subscription of periodicals/newspapers are not adequate to serve the library users as well.

Jammu and Kashmir

The state is divided into 14 districts. The Christian missinaries started education. Until 1947, the state has only two public libraries, namely, Sri Pratap Singh Library in 1893 in the city of Srinagar and Sri Ranbir Singh Library in Jammu.

The state government establishes the department of public Libraries in 1961 for the establishment and promotion of public library services in the state. The state has 2 Central Libraries, one each in the province of Jammu and Kashmir, 14 District Libraries, 51 Tehsil Libraries, and 18 Block Libraries.

Madhya Pradesh and Chhattisgarh

The state of Madhya Pradesh including Chhattisgarh lies in the heart of the country came into existence on 1 November 1956. Madhya Pradesh was divided into two states, *viz.*, Madhya Pradesh and Chhatisgarh on 1 November 2000; hence the state of Chhattisgarh came into existence. It has 5 Regional Libraries in Bhopal, Gwalior, Jabalpur, Rewa, and Indore, 42 District Libraries, 6 Information Centers, 80 Private Public Libraries, and 15800 Gram Panchayat Libraries. The Madhya Pradesh Library Association was formed in 1957.

Meghalaya

Meghalaya has taken up the State Library of Assam established in Shillong in 1903 as its State Central Library. It has one State Central Library, four District Libraries, and Libraries run by voluntary organizations in different localities. The Meghalaya Library Association was established in 1994.

Nagaland

Nagaland has established a State Central Library at Kohima in 1981 functioning under the Directorate of Art and Culture. It offers computer facilities and reprographic services to its readers. There are eight District Libraries and four of them have completed computerization. 330 Rural libraries are registered under the department of Art and Culture.

Punjab

The first public library in Punjab, known as Punjab Public Library was established at Lahore in 1884. Other pioneer libraries are Dyal Singh Public Library was established at Lahore in 1896 through a trust created in the name of Dyal Singh, Sir Ganga Commercial Public Library established in 1923, and Dwarka Das Public Library at Lahore in 1921.

Pioneer Municipality Libraries in the state were established in Ludhiana in 1878, Lahore in 1884, Patiala in 1897, Amritsar in 1900,

Kapurthala in 1904, and Sangrur in 1912. There are 2 State Central Libraries at Chandigarh and Patiala, 14 District Libraries, and 97 Municipal Libraries. Dr. A.C.Wooner founded the Punjab Library Association in 1915 at Lahore. The Association organize training, seminar, conferences and also publish some library literatures.

Sikkim

Sikkim public libraries came into existence under the influence of academic libraries in the state. After 1975 the Government of Sikkim realised the importance of public libraries and has started a few libraries but public libraries have not made much progress in a systematic way. All the four districts have a separate District Library at the district headquarters. These libraries were controlled, supervise and administered by the Cultural Department of the Government of Sikkim.

Tripura

From the nucleus of "Ujjayanta Palace Library", the then Maharaja Birchandra Manikya established a library in the Royal Palace in the year 1896 in Agartala was called as "Birchandra Library" and declared open to the public. This library was taken over by the government in 1953 and named as Birchandra Public Library and from 1977; it was designated as a State Central Library and renamed as Birchandra State Central Library.

Libraries are look after by the Government of Higher and Technical Education and at present the position of public library in Tripura is–1 State Central Library, 3 District Libraries, 7 Sub-Divisional Libraries, 10 Block Level Public Libraries, 2 Rural Libraries, and 1 Children Library. The departments of Social Education and Panchayat Raj also run some public libraries in the state.

Uttar Pradesh

Uttaranchal state came into existence on 9 November 2000 separating some areas from the state of Uttar Pradesh. Some libraries were established in the early days, such as, Raza Library, Rampur in 1750, Allahabad Public Library, Allahabad in 1763, Maulana Azad Library, Aligarh in 1877, Bharati Bhawan Library, Allahabad in 1889 and Lyall Library, Aligarh in 1899. The state has a State Central Library at Allhabad, 69 District level libraries, 62 other prominent public libraries run by voluntary organizations..

Andaman and Nicobar Island

Andaman and Nicobar Island, one of the Union Territories of India, have never experienced the services of libraries until a small library was set up in the cellular jail in the early 1930s. The prisoners were allowed to read books, newspapers and magazines in this library. The Government took initiatives in establishing school libraries. In 1957 an Information Centre was set up at Port Blair.

In 1964, this Information Centre was converted into District Library and later on considering the public interest the District Library was enlarged and reorganized into the State Library in 1977. Library service is under the Department of Education and financed by the Andaman and Nicobar Administration and the department came forward with an idea of spreading education through the libraries. At present, there is 1 State Central library, 1 State Library, 2 District Libraries, 12 Zonal Libraries, and 3 Public Libraries..

Dadra and Nagar Haveli

In the Union Territory of Dadra and Nagar Haveli, there is a State Central Library at the capital city Silvasa and Public Library, known as Central Libariy at Naroli, Kanvel, Randha, Kilvani, Dapido, Amoli, Dushni and Mandoni. The Central Library at Silvasa and Naroli were established in 1954 and 1965 respectively.

Central Libraries at Silvasa, Dadra and Kanvel are functio-ning in their own buildings whereas the remaining libraries were in a rented building and primary schools. There are no public libraries run by voluntary organizations in this Union Territory. The library services were under the control and supervision of the Director of Education..

Daman and Diu

The Assistant Director of Education under the control of the Department of Education supervises library services in the Union Territory of Daman and Diu. There are 3 Municipal Libraries at Moti Daman, Nani Daman, and Diu. Establishment of a Central library, 2 District libraries, and 1 Mobile Library is under consideration..

Lakshadweep

There was no library service in this Union Territory before independence. The first public library was established at Karavati in 1951. However, the island has the apex library of this Union Territory established in 1958 as Freedom Fighters Central Library, which was subsequently named as Lakshadweep Central Library.

It has well organized public library system in which Lakshadweep Central Library serves as the State Central Library and each of the ten constituent inhabited islands Androtti, Amini, Agatti, Bitta, Chetlat, Kadmat, Kalpeni, Karavatti, Kilton, and Minicoy is provided with a public library by the Administration of Lakshadweep. These libraries were earlier known as Reading Room-cum-Library.

Library services are looked after by a Library Development Officer who performs the supervision function under the overall control of the Director of Social Welfare and Culture. To develop and sustain library movement, the administration has constituted a state level committee known as 'Lakshadweep State Library Committee' in 1994 comprising 10 members including Library Development..

Pondicherry

The history of Library in Pondicherry began with the establishment of a *'Bibliotheque Publique'* in 1827 with a modest stock of books collected from several Government establishments functioning in this region. The British Indian Government also donated some books to this library from time to time.

It was renamed as *'Romain Rolland Library'* in 1967 after the French scholar Romain Rolland. The General Assembly, in 1892, authorized the opening of the library at Karaikal and constituted a Commission to advise the administration on measures to be taken for the development of the Library.

The Library was originally named as *'Bibliotheque Coloniale'*. This library was renamed as *'Bibliotheque Publique'* in 1952 and subsequently categorized as Regional Library and called as Government Public Library. The first library was actually started by the 'Association of Old Students' in 1918 at Mahe.

The Old Boys Association donated all the books and furniture of Mahe Public Library. In 1964, the Union Territory Administration has evolved a policy of opening Branch Libraries at rural areas of the territory and the number of Branch Libraries opened in four regions are, 46 in Pondicherry region, 14 in Karaikal region, 3 in Mahe region, and 2 in Yanam region.

The Director of Education from 1954 to 1991 controlled the library services. Since 1991, Director of Art and Culture is the head of the Library services. There are three Assistant Library and Information Officers to look after the library services under the Director of Art and Culture.

National Capital Territory of New Delhi

Before the independence, Delhi was very poor in library services, particularly in public libraries, due to political structures, lack of educational facilities, and attitude of the authorities. Harding Library was established in 1862 and housed in a portion of the Town Hall.

In 1942, Delhi Municipal Committee changed the name of the library to the Harding Municipal Public Library, which was further rechristened in 1970 as the Hardayal Municipal Public Library after the famous freedom fighter and intellectual Lala Hardayal.

The British Council Library and American Information resource Centre are also being developed for the public and function with the latest technology which enrich public library services in Delhi. Marwari Seth Kedar Nath Goenka in the Chandi Chawk area of Delhi set up the Marwari Library, the first of any type founded through community awareness in Modern India, in 1915.

Under the UNESCO's Pilot Project, the Ministry of Education, Government of India, founded Delhi Public Library in 1951. It was very much developed and became one of the depository libraries in India. The Delhi Public Library consists of the Central Library, Zonal Libraries, Branch Libraries, and Sub-Branch Libraries in addition to the Community libraries, Resettlement Colonies libraries, Sports libraries, and an adequately good network of Mobile Library Services to link up the remote urban and rural areas spread over the Union Territory of Delhi.

CONTRIBUTION OF RAJA RAMMOHUN ROY LIBRARY FOUNDATION

1972 was a significant year in the history of library movement in India. The country was celebrating the silver jubilee of its independence from the British Administration in 1972. Coincidentally it was an International Book Year with the slogan of 'Books For All' emphasizing promotion of reading habits among the masses. Not only that, it was the auspicious occasion of the bicentennial birth anniversary of an Indian social reformer, who stressed the need of modern education for the development of the nation.

In this august year, Raja Rammohun Roy Library came into being in May 1972. It is the nodal agency of Government of India to support public library services and systems and promote public library movement in the country. Raja Rammohun Roy Library Foundation is an autonomous organization, established and sponsored by the Department of Culture, Government of India.

It is registered under the West Bengal Societies Registration Act, 1961. Its headquarters is located at Kolkata. In view of the expanding activities, the Foundation has opened zonal offices under the Assistant Field Officers for monitoring the impact and implementation of the assistance rendered by the Foundation such as-Eastern Zonal Office at Calcutta; Northern Zonal Office at New Delhi; Southern Zonal Office at Chennai and Western Zonal Office at Mumbai.

Objectives

Raja Rammohun Roy Library Foundation is a national agency for the promotion of library services in general and public library services in particular. The main objective of the Foundation is to promote and support public library movement in the country by providing adequate library services and by developing reading habits all over the country with the active cooperation of State Government and Union Territories and of Voluntary Organizations operating in the filed of library services, cultural activities, adult education and the like.

Objectives of the Foundation may be listed as below:

- To promote library movement in the country;
- To enunciate a national library policy and to help build up a national library system;
- To provide financial and technical assistance to libraries;
- To provide financial assistance to organizations, regional or national engaged in the promotion of library development;
- To publish appropriate literature and to act as a clearing house of ideas and information on library development in India and abroad;

- To promote research in problems of library development;
- To advise the government on all matters pertaining to the library development in the country; and
- To propagate the adoption of library legislation in the country.

Assistance Programme

The Foundation promotes public library services rendering book and financial assistance to the public libraries under different schemes of assistance. The scheme of assistance is of two types, *viz.*, Matching and Non-Matching schemes.

Matching Schemes

Assistance under Matching Scheme is given from the resources shared on matching basis with the States/Union Territory Administrations on the basis of developed states 50;50; developing and lagging states 60;40 and North-Eastern States 90;10. This revised matching scheme is effective from 2005.

The Matching assistance can be given to achieve its main objectives for:

- Assistance towards building up of adequate stock of books and reading materials.
- Assistance towards development of rural book deposit centers and mobile library services.
- Assistance towards organization of seminars, workshops, training courses and book exhibition.
- Assistance towards storage and display of books including reading room furniture.
- Assistance to public libraries below district level for increasing accommodation.
- Assistance to public libraries below State Central Libraries to acquire TVcum-VCP sets for educational purposes/Computer for library application.
- Assistance towards Networking of Public Libraries.

Non-Matching Schemes

The Foundation fully gives assistance under this scheme from his own resources to implement its objectives for:

- Assistance towards building up of adequate stock of books through central selection.
- Assistance to voluntary organizations providing public library Services
- Assistance to children libraries or children's section of general public libraries including women section and senior citizen section.
- Assistance to public libraries towards celebration of 50 years, 100 years and 125 years.
- Assistance towards collection and compilation of library statistics through official and non-official agencies.

- Assistance to centrally sponsored libraries.
- Assistance towards organization of seminars/conferences by national level library organizations.
- Assistance towards establishment of children's corner.

Promotion of District Youth Resource Centres *(DYRCs)*

The development of DYRCs is being made commensurate with the decision of the inter Ministerial Steering Committee constitutes for the purpose with the representative from Ministry of Sports and Youth Affairs, Ministry of Culture, Raja Rammohun Roy Library foundation and Nehru Yuvak Kendra Sanghatana.

The DYRCs are assisted for the following purpose:

- Towards building up adequate stock of books.
- Towards acquiring storage materials and library furniture.
- Towards construction of library building.
- Towards acquisition of computers with accessories.

Promotional Activities

RRRLF has undertaken a number of promotional activities for qualitative improvement of library services. It is associated and interacts with different national and international library professional associations like IFLA, ILA, IASLIC and different state level library associations.

Some of the promotional activities taken up by the Foundation for the qualitative improvement of library services may be given as below:

- It organizes seminars and conferences on the topics related to the development of public libraries in India.
- It plays a major role in the preparation of National Policy on Library and Information Systems and also issued guidelines on public library systems and services.
- It instituted 'RRRLF Fellowship' to eminent men and women in the field of library services who have contributed significantly to the library movement particularly, public library movement in the country through active involvement in the movement, organizational initiative, intellectual leadership or are dedicated to the propagation of the reading habit among the mass. Fellowship carries a cash award of ₹25, 000/-besides a plaque and a citation detailing the services rendered by the Fellow in the country.
- 'RRRLF Best Library Award' for the Best State Central Library in India. The Award carries a Citation and a cash incentive of ₹1 lakh.
- 'RRRLF Best District Library Award' in each of the six regions. The Award carries a Citation and cash incentive of ₹50,000/-.
- The Foundation instituted 'RRRLF Best Rural Library Awards' one for each state since 2005.
- 'Raja Rammohun Roy Award' was introduced annually to the best contributor of an article covering the area of development of Public

Library Systems and Services or suggesting measures for the promotion of reading habits.

Research Cell and Special Library

A research cell along with a special library on Library and Information Science and statistics unit supported by a computer unit are providing necessary input to its various activities. About 5000 important books and journals on Library and Information Science and allied fields have been acquired in the library. Besides carrying on Research Projects on public library or allied subject, the Research Cell renders advisory and consultancy services whenever required. It has prepared and published a report on loss of books in libraries for the Government of India.

Publications

The Foundation has brought out many useful publications for the promotion and development of public library services in the country.

Some of its significant publications are;

- Indian Libraries; Trends and Perspectives
- Raja Rammohun Roy and the New Learning
- Directory of Indian Public Libraries
- RRRLF Newsletter
- Granthana-Indian Journal of Library Studies
- Annual Report
- Books for the Millions at their Doorsteps..

Modernization Programme

The Foundation is taking steps to meet the new technologies of information for the promotion of library services. It has a Computer Section for building-up data bank of Public Libraries for the country. This section is planned to give information storage, retrieval and data processing support for all the application areas. It has keen interest with enthusiasm to computerized state libraries in India. It gave computers to the state and district libraries to carry out Foundations' zeal to computerize such libraries. The work is going on to computerized shortly.

NATIONAL POLICY ON LIBRARY AND INFORMATION SYSTEM

John Martin said, "Policy is a statement of a specific goal or goals which are to be achieved, or to be pursued; a statement of the means by which realization of the goals will be brought about; an assignment of the responsibilities for implementation of the means, and a set of rules or guidelines regulating the activity".

National Policy on Library and Information Science is to "provide a framework for properly planned and co-coordinated development of library and information structure in a country, resulting thereby in an enhanced and user-oriented information services to its user population". The need for the formulation of National Policy on Library and Information Systems was brought to the notice of the Government of India by Indian library profession since 1950s by Dr. S.R.Ranganathan and in the recommendations of the Library Advisory Committee Report, 1958. Afterwards, professional organizations, like RRRLF, NISSAT and National Library urged upon the Government the necessity of enunciating such policy.

The matter was discussed in the annual conference of IASLIC in 1979 at Roorkee and ILA in 1984 at Jaipur. Consequently, Indian Library Association submitted a draft policy statement to the Government in 1985. The Planning Commission Working Group in its report *Modernization of Library Services and Informatics for the 7th Five-Year Plan* emphasized the need of such policy.

The Raja Rammohun Roy Foundation, after nine years of its inception, took up the task in 1981 and after careful deliberations submitted a Draft National policy on Library and Information Systems to the government in July 1984.

On the basis of the draft policy submitted by the Raja Rammohun Roy Library Foundation and Indian Library Association, the Government of India, Ministry of Human resources Development, Department of Culture, set up a Committee in October 1985 under the Chairmanship of Professor D.P.Chattopadhyaya for the formulation of a National Policy on Library and Information Systems and the final report was submitted in May 1986 which includes:

- The Public Library system;
- The Academic Library System;
- Special Libraries and Information Systems;
- The National Library System and the Bibliographical Services;
- Manpower Development and Professional Status; and
- Modernization of Library and Information Systems.

Though the government has not adopted the recommen-dations as the official policy, but it serves as suggestive model for the development of libraries as a whole.

The recommendations under the Public Library System are as follows:

- The most important task before the government is to establish, maintain and strengthen the free public libraries in the country and enable them to work as a system.
- The main thrust in this area should go to the rural public library. A village or a village cluster with an adequate population should have a community library, which will also serve as an information center. Resources of different agencies engaged in the work of public health, adult education, local selfgovernment and such others may be pooled to build up this composite center.
- An important link should be established between the community library of the village and the village primary school. If the school does not have a library of its own, the community library should provide the children with an adequate book-corner.

- The community library should also importantly cater for adult education and make adequate audio-visual aids available to attract the illiterate villagers.
- The district library should serve as an apex library for each district with public libraries at city, town and village levels constituting important components in the district library system. In addition to the usual services to be rendered by it, it should also provide for learning facilities and recreation for the handicapped. Wherever possible, district libraries and comparable city public libraries should provide literature in Braille. The district library and branch libraries should also arrange mobile and circulating library services within its area wherever it is necessary and feasible. Special services should be rendered to hospitals, prisons, and the infirm in their homes.
- Libraries for special groups should be built in areas of tribal concentration or minority communities to develop their distinctive cultures. The government will provide all encouragement for such communities to develop their own libraries through voluntary effort.
- Each public library should have a section for children and, in addition, separate libraries for children with attractive books and audio-visual supporting materials should be established wherever possible.
- The district library will take the leadership in establishing linkages between all other public libraries of the district and work towards resource sharing within the area.
- The key role of public libraries as chief sustaining agencies of distance education should be recognized and they should be adequately equipped with the relevant resources for this purpose.
- All the libraries within a state should form part of a network extending from the community library of the village through intermediary levels to the district and to the State Central Library. This State network should eventually connect with the national level.
- The role of the State Central Library is crucial in networking and the establishment of uniform library procedures within the States. The State Central Library/Directorate of Public Libraries has to perform as the coordinating agency for public libraries in the State.
- To bring about the development of the public libraries in a State it is vital that each State enact its own library legislation. The Central Government should revise the Model Public Library Bill, which it has already prepared, in the light of experience gained in recent years and urge upon the States the importance of enacting such legislation. Finances for library development should be found by each State either from its general revenues or from local taxation.
- The Central Government should assist the State in the development of

public libraries in a larger way than it has done so far. The Raja Rammohun Roy Library Foundation as the national agency for co-coordinating and assisting the development of public libraries be suitably strengthened enabling it to discharge its responsibilities effectively.

NATIONAL KNOWLEDGE COMMISSION

National Knowledge Commission was set up by the Prime Minister of India, Manmohan Singh to prepare a blueprint to tap into the enormous reservoir of our knowledge base so that our people can confidently face challenges of the 21st. Century. The Commission has a designated time frame of three years from 2nd. October 2005 to 2nd. October 2008.

The Commissions' Terms of References are:

- Build excellence in the educational system to meet the knowledge challenges of the 21st. century and increase India's competitive advantage in fields of knowledge.
- Promote creation of knowledge in Science and Technology laboratories.
- Improve the management of institutions engaged in Intellectual Property Rights.
- Promote knowledge applications in Agriculture and Industry.
- Promote the use of knowledge capabilities in making government an effective, transparent and accountable service provider to the citizen and promote widespread sharing of knowledge to maximize public benefit.

The Commission headed by Mr. Sam Pitroda as its Chairman and there are other 5 members, who are renowned persons in different fields of knowledge. It is a high-level advisory body to the Prime Minister of India, with a mandate to guide policy and generate reforms. The Commission is the world's first body of its kind.

The prime focus of the Commission is on five key areas of the knowledge paradigm, such as:

- Access
  - Literacy
  - Language
  - Translation
  - Libraries
  - Networks
  - Portals
- Concepts
  - School Education
  - Vocational Education
  - Higher Education
  - Medical Education
  - Legal Education
  - Management Education

  - Engineering Education
  - Open and Distance Education
- Creation
  - Science and Technology
  - Intellectual Property Rights
  - Innovation
  - Entrepreneurship
- Application
  - Traditional knowledge
  - Agriculture
- Services
  - E-governance

Besides the Working Group on Libraries, other four Committees were set up with specialists and professionals in different areas of Libraries under the Chairmanship of Mrs. Kalpana Dasgupta.

Such Committees are:

- Committee on database creation and networking;
- Committee on private collections;
- Committee to set standards and modalities for collection development, systems and services;
- Committee on staffing pattern and staff requirement of libraries.

Terms of References of the Working Group on Libraries are given below:

- To redefine the objectives of the country's Library and Information Service sector;
- To identify constraints, problems and challenges relating to the sector;
- To recommend changes and reforms to address the problems and challenges to ensure a holistic development of information services in all areas of national activity;
- To take necessary steps to mobilize and upgrade the existing library and information systems and services, taking advantage of the latest advances in Information Community Technology;
- To explore possibilities for innovation and initiate new programmes relevant to our national needs, especially to bridge the gap between the information rich and the information poor within society;
- To suggest means of raising standards and promoting excellence in Library and Information Science education including re-orientation and training of working professionals;
- To assist in setting up facilities to preserve and access to indigenous knowledge and the nation's cultural heritage;
- To set up adequate mechanisms to monitor activities for securing the benefits of acquisition and application of knowledge for the people of India;
- To examine any other issues that may be relevant in this context..

The Notional Knowledge Commission's Working Group on Libraries, after consultations of more than 20 state representatives and NGOs and many more interest groups and professionals in the field, ready its first recommendations for submission to the nation.

Moreover, the Commission submitted its first recommendations to the Prime Minister in December 2006 on the following areas:

- Libraries
- Translation
- Language
- Knowledge Networks
- Right to Education
- Vocational education
- Higher Education
- National Science and Social science Foundation
- E-governance.

The Commission argued Libraries as Gateways to knowledge and continued that a "Library is not a building stacked with books-it is a repository and source of information and ideas, a place for learning and enquiry, and for the generation of thought and the creation of new knowledge.

Public libraries in particular have the potential to bridge the gap between the 'information poor' and the 'information rich' by ensuing that people from all sectors and settings of society and the community across India have easy access to knowledge seek".. The Commission clearly incorporated roadmap for the execution of its recommendations on libraries under different points of consideration. It gave a Library Charter that is incorporated below.

Recognising that the library's objectives are to:

- Disseminate knowledge as widely as possible;
- Serve as a major vehicle to facilitate creation of new knowledge;
- Facilitate optimal use of knowledge by all sectors, such a government, industry, rural sector and civil society;
- Ensure that people from all sectors and all parts of the country have easy access to knowledge relevant to their needs, in their own language.

The library undertakes to:

- Serve as local center of information and a gateway to national and global knowledge providing fair access to knowledge and information to as many as users as possible;
- Offer an inviting and attractive physical space with clean drinking water and toilet facilities;
- Offer proactive services to its user communities;
- Ensure that users are treated with courtesy and respect by library staff;
- Pay attention to the needs of children, women, senior citizens and the physically challenged;

- Optimize its potential to provide access to information and knowledge to all;
- Help users developed information skills to make optimum use of resources;
- Improve its collections and services on continuing basis in consultation with users;
- To work more effectively and efficiently by undertaking every activity in a professional manner;
- To bridge the gap between the information poor and the information rich.

The Commission is organizing discussion forum at different areas for the preparation of its final report, which is expected to be submit to the nation within its stipulated time.

LIBRARY ASSOCIATIONS

The term 'association' is used to denote a group or body of individuals or institutions associated with a common purpose revolving generally for the two main purposes, viz.,:

- Advancement of the service oriented goals of the association, and
- Protection of the interests of the members.

Association may be of different kinds with different objectives and categories, professional or non-professional. However, by considering its nature, Pandey S.K.Sharma defined library associations as 'a group or body of libraries or librarians and users of libraries formed with the common purpose of advancement of library profession including service and also for protection of interests of the members including raising their capabilities to serve more effectively'.

There are more than seventy professional organizations and associations at state level in India. William A Borden went to Baroda in 1910 at the invitation of Maharaja Sayajirao Gaekwar of Baroda and organized the first professional organization of librarians in the country, the Baroda Library Club in 1912. Other professional associations came up afterwards and some of the national level associations worth to be mentioned for their contributions in public library developments in the country.

NATIONAL LIBRARY OF INDIA

The National Library of India at Belvedere, Kolkata, is the largest library in India by volume and India's library of public record. It is under the Department of Culture, Ministry of Tourism and Culture, Government of India. The library is designated to collect, disseminate and preserve the printed material produced in India. The library is situated on the scenic 30 acre Belvedere Estate, in Kolkata. The Library is the largest in India, with a collection in excess of 2.2 million books.

AIMS

- Acquisition and conservation of all significant national production of printed material, excluding ephemera.

- Collection of printed material concerning the country, no matter where it is published, and as a corollary, the acquisition of photographic records of such material that is not available with in the country
- Acquisition and conservation of foreign material required by the country.
- Rendering of bibliographical and documents services of current and retrospective material, both general and specialised.
- Acting as a referral centre purveying full and accurate knowledge.

HISTORY

The Calcutta Public Library

The history of the National Library began with the formation of Calcutta Public Library in 1836. That was a non-governmental institution and was run on a proprietary basis. People contributing ₹300 in subscription became the proprietors. Prince Dwarkanath Tagore was the first proprietor of that Library. ₹300 at that time was a significant amount, so poor students and others were allowed free use the library for some period of time.

Lord Metcalfe, the Governor General at that time, transferred 4,675 volumes from the library of the College of Fort William, Calcutta to the Calcutta Public Library. This and donations of books from individuals formed the nucleus of the library. Both Indian and foreign books, especially British, were purchased for the library. Donations were regularly made by individuals as well as by the government.

The Calcutta Public Library had a unique position as the first public library in this part of the world. Such a well-organized and efficiently run library was rare even in Europe during the first half of the 19th century. Because of the efforts of the Calcutta Public Library, the present National Library has many extremely rare books and journals in its collection.

The Imperial Library

Built after the model of the Town Hall at Ypres. A fine example of the Public Buildings in Calcutta.The Imperial Library was formed in 1891 by combining a number of Secretariat libraries in Calcutta. Of those, the most important and interesting was the library of the Home Department, which contained many books formerly belonging to the library of East India College, Fort William and the library of the East India Board in London. But the use of the library was restricted to the superior officers of the Government.

Amalgamation of the Calcutta Public Library and Imperial Library

In 1903, Lord Curzon, the Governor-General of India, conceived the idea of opening a library for the use of the public. He noticed both the libraries—Imperial Library and Calcutta Public Library were under-utilized because of limited access and lack of amenities. He decided to amalgamate the rich collection of both of these libraries. The new amalgamated library, called Imperial Library, was formally opened to the public on January 30, 1903 at Metcalfe Hall, Kolkata.

Metcalfe Hall had earlier been the residence of the Governor-Generals Wellington, Cornwallis and Warren Hastings:

- "It is intended that it should be a library of reference, a working place for students and a repository of material for the future historians of India, in which, so far as possible, every work written about India, at any time, can be seen and read." —*The Gazette of India*

Declaring the Imperial Library as the National Library

After Independence the Government of India changed the name of the Imperial Library to the National Library, with the enactment of the Imperial Library Act, 1948, and the collection was shifted from the Esplanade to the present Belvedere Estate. On February 1, 1953, the National Library was opened to the public, inaugurated by Maulana Abul Kalam Azad. B. S. Kesavan was appointed the first Librarian of the National Library.

Discovery of Hidden Chamber

In 2010, the Ministry of Culture, the owner of the library, decided to get the library building restored by the *Archaeological Survey of India* (ASI). While taking stock of the library building, the conservation engineers discovered a previously unknown room. The ground-floor room, about 1000 sq. ft. in size, seems to have no opening of any kind. The ASI archaeologists tried to search the first floor area for a trap door, but found nothing.

Since the building is of historical and cultural importance, ASI decided to bore a hole through the wall instead of breaking it. There was speculations about the room being a punishment room used by Warren Hastings and other British officials, or a place to store treasure. After six months of study, it was determined to be not a room at all, but merely "a block stuffed with mud, perhaps constructed by the British architects to strengthen the base of the building."

COLLECTION

Indian Languages Collection

The National Library receives books and periodicals in almost all Indian languages. These are received under the Delivery of Books and Newspapers Act 1954. Language divisions acquire, process and provide reading materials in all major Indian languages. Hindi, Kashmiri, Punjabi, Sindhi, Telugu and Urdu language divisions maintain their own stacks. Other language books are stacked in the Stack division.

Language divisions are also responsible for answering reference queries. The library has separate Indian language divisions for Assamese, Bengali,

Gujarati, Hindi, Kannada, Kashmiri, Malayalam, Marathi, Oriya, Punjabi, Sanskrit, Sindhi, Tamil, Telugu and Urdu. Sanskrit language division also collects and processes Pali and Prakrit books. English books published in India are collected under D.B. Act.

Assamese Language Collection

In1963, a separate division was established in the National Library to collect and process Assamese books. At present the division has 12,000 books. This collection has some works published between 1840 and 1900. Some of the important publications are Asamiya Larar Mitra by Anandaram Dhekiyal Phukan, Larabodh Byakaran by Dharmeswar Goswami, Prakrit Bhugol by Lambodara Datta and several volumes of Sri Sankardev's Kirattan, Gunamala, Srimad Bhagavad, Bargit, Rukmini Haran Nat, and Ankiyanat. Volumes of the periodical Arunodoi are also available in the collection.

Bengali Language Collection

The library has 85,000 books in its Bengali collection. The collection contains very rare and valuable books as well as periodicals published from the last quarter of the 18th century. Early Bengali plays and novels are well represented. The collection has many rare items such as the manuscripts of Sarat Chandra Chattopadhaya, Bibuti Bhushan Bandao-padhaya, Jibanananda Das and Bisnu De.

154 letters of Netaji Subhas Chandra Bose written to his nephew Sri Asok Nath Bose and letters to Sarat Chandra Bose are also available in the collection. The collection has the complete set of Rabindranath Tagore's works, except a few of his early works. This includes 190 first editions of Tagore's works.

Some of the rare and important works in this collection are: A Grammar of the Bengal Language by Nathaniel Brassey Halhed, which is the earliest printed book in Bengali, Henry Forster's A Vocabulary in Two parts, English and Bangalee, William Carrey's Dialogues, Intended to Facilitate the Acquiring of the Bengali Language, Ram Ram Basu's Raja Pratapaditya Charitra, Mrityunjay Vidyalankar's Batris Simhansan, Ramayana translated by Krittibas and published in five volumes, Mahabharat translated by Kashi Ram Das, Chandicharan Munshi's Tota Itihas, Jayanarayan Ghosal's Sri Karunanidhanavilasa, William Carey's Dictionary of the Bengali Language, 2 volumes.

There are 400 titles of Bengali periodicals including many rare 19th century periodicals such as Digdarshan first Bengali monthly and the first issue of Samachar Darpan—the first Bengali weekly.

Gujarati Language Collection

The library has 37,000 Gujarati books. 1100 of them are titles published prior to 1900. This collection also has 30 albums of paintings by Kanu Desai published between 1936 and 1956. Ancient Jaina miniature paintings are well reproduced in Sri Jaina Chitravali, Sri Jaina Chitra Patavali and other valuable books edited by Sarabhai Nawab.

The authentic editions of the poetic works of medieval Gujarati poets such as Narsinh Meheta, Mirabai, Premanand and Symal Bhat are also part of the holdings. The rare titles include Robert Drummond's Illustrations of Grammatical Parts Guzerattee, Maratta and English Languages, translations of Aesop's Fables by Bapushastri Pandya Raykaval, Edalji Patel's Suratani Tavarikh and Jnana Chakra—a Gujarati encyclopaedia in 9 volumes.

Hindi Language Division

Hindi is one of the official languages of India. The collection building of Hindi books has been continuing since the time of the Imperial Library, and a separate division was established in 1960. At present 80,000 Hindi books are in the library collection. The collection has rare works published during the last decades of the 18th Century. Many of the publications published by Lulloo Lal, the first printer, publisher and writer of Kolkata, are represented in this collection.

The following rare books published by Lulloo Lal are in the library: Braja Bhasha Grammar, Lataife Hindi, Rajaniti, and Prem Sagur. In addition, the library has The Oriental Linguist with an Extensive Vocabulary English and Hindoostanee and Hindoostanee and English by John B. Gilchrist, Hindi-Roman Orthoepigraphical Ultimatum by John B. Gilchrist, Rajneeti by Narayana Pandit, Sudamacaritra by Haldhara Dasa, Raga Kalpadruma, Baital Pachisi by Duncan Forbes, Dictionary of Hindee and English by J. T. Thompson, Yavan Bhasa ka Vyakaran by Hooper William, Siva Simha Saroja by Siva Simha Senagar, Hindi Pradipa edited by Balkrishna Bhatt, Brief Account of the Solar System in Hindi, and a microfilm copy of Bal Bodhini—a monthly journal for women edited by Bharatendu Harischandra. There are also about 1200 rare first issues of important journals.

Kannada Language Collection

A separate Kannada division was set up in 1963 in the National Library. In 1960, the library purchased the personal collection of H. Channakeshava Ayyangar. It consists of 1300 books published between the last two decades of the 19th century and the first three decades of the 20th century. An important contribution towards building the collection was the efforts of G. P. Rajaratnam, a noted Kannada author.

Immediately after the enactment of the D.B. Act, Rajaratnam toured the erstwhile Mysore state to create awareness among the publishers about the Act. He collected about 1500 books without any expense to the library. The Kannada collection in the library is particularly useful for the study of the cultural history of Karnataka. At present there are 32,000 Kannada books in the library.

Kashmiri Language Collection

The Kashmiri division was formed in 1983. Currently the library has

500 Kashmiri books. Some of the important items in this collection are Muhammad Yusuf Teng's Shirin Qalm, Wiyur edited by Ghulam Muhammad Rafiq, Ghulam Nabi Khyal's Akah Nandun, Nurnama and compiled by Muhammad Amin Kaim, Fazil and Kashmiri's Krishna Lila.

Malayalam Language Collection

The Malayalam division was established as a separate division in 1963, with around 5000 books. Now the collection has 34,500 books. The earliest printed book, Centum Adagia Malabarica, a Latin translation of Malayalam proverbs, dates back to 1791. The Latin translations are printed alongside the Malayalam originals.

Rare and old books include Robert Drummond's Grammar of the Malabar Language, Dr Gundart's Malayalam-English Dictionary Vartamanapustakam by Parammachkal Govarnno-doracchan, Appu Nedungadi's Kundalata and Chantu Menan's Indulekha. Apart from these, many works representing earlier periods are part of this collection. A few of these are Ramacaritam, works of Niranam, Cerussery's Krishnagatha, Vatakkan Pattukal, Ezuttachan's Adhyatama Ramayana, Ramaprattu Variyar's Kucelavrtam, and Kuncan Nampyar's Tullol.

Marathi Language Collection

The Marathi division was established in 1963 with a collection of 8900 volumes. The division now has 37,000 books in its collection. In 1954 the National Library purchased the library of the Bengal Nagpur Railway Indian Institute, Kharagpur, which had a good number of Marathi books. Sir Jadunath Sarkar collection also has about 350 Marathi books, mostly on the history of the Marathas. The division has many rare and old Marathi publications.

These include William Carey's A Grammar of the Mahratta Language and Dictionary of the Maharatta Language, Simhasana Battisi, Raghuji Bhonsalyaci Vanshavali, Vans Kennedy's A Dictionary of Maratta Language, Nava Karar, A Short Account of Railways by K. Bhatwadekar, Charles Hutton's Bijaganit, Tukaram's Abhangachi Gatha edited by Vishnu Parashuram Pandit and Shankar Pandurang Pandit, Itihasaprisiddha Purushanche va Striyanche Povade edited by H. A. Acworth.

Oriya Language Collection

A separate Oriya division was established in 1973. The Imperial Library had only 133 books; later the collection was increased to 425 books. Currently, the division has 19,500 books. The oldest publication available in the Oriya collection dates back to 1831. It is Rev.

Amos Sutton's Introductory Grammar of Oriya Language. Some of the other rarities in the collection are Jayadeva's Gitagovinda, translated by Dharanidhara, Amos Sutton's An Oriya Dictionary, 3 volumes,

Dharmapustakara Adibhaya, and Purnacandra Odiabhasa Kosh, a lexicon of the Oriya language compiled by Gopalachandra Praharaj.

Punjabi Language Collection

A separate division for the acquisition and processing of Punjabi language books was established in 1974. Most of the works in this collection are of recent origin. There are a few old and rare Punjabi books, such as William Carey's A Grammar of Punjabee Language, Samuel Starkey's A Dictionary of English Punjabee, Geographical Description of the Panjab, Bhai Santosh Singh's Guru Paratap Suraj Granthavali and Gurudas Bhai's Vars.

Sanskrit, Pali and Prakrit Languages Collection

Sanskrit has a rich literature in many fields of knowledge. A separate division in the library collects and processes Sanskrit books. At present the division has over 20,000 Sanskrit books, printed in the Devanagari script. Almost all Indian language divisions possess Sanskrit works printed in their respective language scripts.

The library also has a rich collection of Sanskrit works edited or translated with original scripts, in English and many other foreign languages. The collection attracts scholars from India and abroad. Apart from Sanskrit, books in Pail and Prakrit languages are also collected and processed by this division. At present the library has about 500 books in Pali and a comparable collection of books in Prakrit.

Sindhi Language Collection

Since 1957, the library has been building a collection of Sindhi books. At present the library has 2100 Sindhi books. Shah Abdul Latif's Shah Jo Rasalo and Shah Jo Sher are the rare items in this collection.

Tamil Language Collection

The Tamil division was formed in 1963. The division currently has 57,000 books. Apart from this, the library has 1000 Tamil books and 300 Tamil manuscripts in the Vaiyapuri Pillai collection. There are many rare and old works among the Tamil titles. Early printed Tamil books in the library include the Tamil Bible, John Philip Fabricius's A Malabar and English Dictionary, a Tamil translation of John Bunyan's Piligrim's Progress, and Caldwell's Comparative Grammar of DravidianLlanguages. The collection also includes standard editions of five great Sangam Classics.

Telugu Language Collection

The Telugu division was started in the National Library in 1963. The collection has a good number of old Telugu books published since the earlier decades of the 19th century. Some of the rarities in Telugu available in this collection are William Carey's Grammar of Telugu Language, C.P. Brown's

A Vocabulary of Gentoo and English, Vakyavali, Catalogue of Telugu books in the British Library, London compiled by L. D. Barnett.

Urdu Language Collection

Like Arabic and Persian, the Urdu collection was substantial since the days of Imperial Library. Special collections such as the Buhar Library, Hidayat Husain collection, Zakariya collection and Imambara collection have some Urdu books and manuscripts. In 1968 a separate Urdu division was set up formed in the library. At present it has more than 20,000 books. Some of the oldest are Uklakhi Hindee or Indian Ethics, and Mir Muhamad Taki's Kulliuat-e-Mir.

English Language Collection

The National Library has an invaluable collection of books in the English language, because of the systematic development by Calcutta Public Library and the Imperial Library. Way back in 1848, an attempt was made to acquire journals issued by the foreign learned institutions.

Serious works were purchased in larger numbers than light literature. The same policy has been pursued in recent times. Although the library has English books and other reading materials in almost all subjects, the collection is especially rich in the humanities, British and Indian history and literature

Foreign Languages Collections

One of the aims of the National Library is to collect all the books published on India, anywhere in the world and in any language. At the same time it collects reading materials on other subjects in different languages for the use of the country. The Imperial Library had a good number of Arabic and Persian works and a few other foreign language books. In 1985 the European Languages Division was reorganized and five separate divisions were formed.

These are East Asian Languages Division, Germanic Languages Division, Romance Languages Division, Slavonic Languages Division,West Asian and African Languages Division. The foreign language works are mainly acquired through purchase, gift and exchange. The divisions mentioned are responsible for collection development, collection organisation and information dissemination to the readers in the respective languages. They also maintain their own stacks and provide reading facilities.

East Asian Languages Collection

A separate division collects, processes and preserves Chinese and other East Asian languages. At present the collection has 15,000 Chinese books and one thousand each in Japanese, Korean, Tibetan, Nepali and Thai languages.

Germanic Languages Collection

The Germanic Languages division was formed in the library in the year

1985. The division has books in German, Dutch, Norwegian and Swedish. But the largest number of books is in German. The division has book exchange agreements with seven Germanic language-speaking countries. Berliner Zeitung, a newspaper published from former East Germany is available in this collection.

Romance Languages Collection

Romance Languages division came into existence in 1985, along with other foreign languages divisions. Although the collection includes books and other materials in languages belonging to the Romance group, the largest number of books is in French, about 5000. About 2000 Romanian and a handful of books in Italian and Spanish are also available.

Slavonic Languages Collection

The collection has books in Slavonic languages, spoken in Russia, Poland, Bulgaria, the Czech Republic, Slovakia, former Yugoslavia and other countries and peoples of the region. It deals with reading materials in 28 languages. But the largest collection is in the Russian language. At present the division has 65,000 books.

West Asian and African Languages Collection

The Buhar Library may be considered the nucleus of West Asian and African languages collection. The division has a handful of books in other West Asian languages such as Hebrew and Amharic. The largest number of books is in Persian and Arabic, approximately 12,000 in Arabic and 12,000 in Persian. The collection includes the lexicons compiled and prepared by Indians authors of the past and edited by the 'native' scholars of the College of Fort William and European orientalists of the said college.

The division also holds a large numbers of historical works published under the Bibliotheca Indica series of the Asiatic Society of Bengal in the 19th century. A large number of Arabic and Persian books and manuscripts can also be found in Sir Abdur Rahim Collection, Hidayat Husain Collection, Zakaria Collection and Imambara Collection. Sir Jadunath Sarkar Collection also has 200 Persian manuscripts. These manuscripts relate mainly to the later Mughal period and the early years of British rule.

Rare Books

The National Library has an impressive number of rare books and other reading materials. In 1973, a separate Rare Books division was established. At present the books published prior to 1860 are considered rare books, along with limited and first editions, books distinguished by their design, illustration or history, and a few other criteria. Along with rare books, manuscripts and microfilms of the library are also stacked in this division. The division also provides reading facilities to the users who wish to consult these items. At present the division has 4700 monographs, 3000 manuscripts and 1500 microfilms

Manuscripts

National Library has about 3600 rare and historically important manuscripts in different languages. These manuscripts are preserved separately along with other important and rare books in the Rare Books division.

Science and Technology Collection

Following the recommendations of the Reviewing Committee, the Science and Technology division was set up in 1972. The basic function of this division is to collect and disseminate the core material in science and technology. At present the division holds about 17,000 books and monographs and 800 current print periodicals. The division provides reading facilities and has an open access stack system.

Indian Official Documents

All the publications of Government of India, State Governments, Union Territories, Government Undertakings, Autonomous Bodies are collected, processed and preserved separately. A separate division for this purpose was established in 1972. The library owns a rich collection of Indian official documents from the days of the East India Company to the present.

The collection also includes the documents published by the Government of Great Britain relating to India. A good collection of Myanmarese documents and few documents of Aden, Sri Lanka, Persian Gulf Political Residency are also part of this collection. At present, the division holds around 4,90,000 documents.

Foreign Official Documents

The National Library is one of the repository libraries for United Nations Organisation and its agencies. Thus all the publications of UNO and its agencies are received by the library free of cost. These documents are processed and stacked separately.

The library also receives publications of the governments of the United States of America, Great Britain, Canada, the Commonwealth nations, and the publications of the European Economic Committee.

Almost all the volumes of the sessional sets of British Parliamentary papers since the beginning of the 19th century are available. Apart from the depositary copies, the library acquires selected foreign publications through purchase. At present the library has around 400,000 foreign official documents.

Newspapers and Periodicals

All the newspapers and periodicals in Indian languages are received and processed in their respective language divisions. But English newspapers and periodicals, both the Indian and foreign, are acquired and processed separately. A separate Serials division is responsible for acquiring and processing of English newspapers and periodicals.

The library has a rich collection of late 19th and early 20th century newspapers and periodicals, but almost all of them are incomplete sets. There are catalogues for periodicals, newspapers and gazettes available in the library up to 1953.

Maps and Prints

The library has an extensive collection of maps from the 17th century onwards. Indian topographical sheets of earlier days and maps of natural resources, population, transport and communication systems, agricultural production, soil, vegetation and the geology of India form the major part of the collection. At present the library has 85,000 printed maps, 54 cartographic manuscripts, and 280 atlases

Microforms

The library has around 500 rolls of Microfilms and 1000 Microfiches. These are preserved in the Rare Books division. The Census of India is one of the most important and rare document available in the form of Microfiches...

CONSERVATION ACTIVITIES

One of the basic functions of the National Library is to conserve the printed heritage for future generations.

For this purpose the library has separate divisions for physical, chemical, reprographic and digital conservation:

- *Physical Conservation*: Books damaged by human error or by natural causes are mended, repaired and bound in the Binding division. Journals are bound by volume.
- *Chemical Conservation*: The Laboratory division of the library, established in 1968, is taking care of the chemical treatment of books. Advanced procedures of chemical treatment are adopted to restore brittle and damaged books. The library is in the process of developing non-chemical treatment system for the preservation of printed materials. An indigenously developed fumigation chamber is being used to destroy the eggs and larvae of insects and termites. Encapsulation is another method of preservation that has been developed by the library.
- *Reprographic Preservation*: Most of the 19th century newspapers, Arabic, Persian and Sanskrit manuscripts have already been microfilmed. 5000 rolls of microfilms are already produced so far by the Reprography division.
- *Digitisation*: The scanning and archiving of rare and brittle books and other documents on compact disc has started. English books and documents published before 1900 and Indian publications preceding 1920 are considered for digitisation. 9140 selected books in

Indian and English languages have already been scanned and stored—a total of over 3.2 million pages.

ACADEMIC LIBRARY

An academic library is a library that is attached to academic institutions above the secondary level, serving the teaching and research needs of students and staff. These libraries serve two complementary purposes: to support the school's curriculum, and to support the research of the university faculty and students.

The support of teaching requires material for class readings and for student papers. In the past, the material for class readings, intended to supplement lectures as prescribed by the instructor, has been called reserves.

In the period before electronic resources became available, the reserves were supplied as actual books or as photocopies of appropriate journal articles. Traditionally, one copy of a book was made available for each 10 students—this is practical for large classes only if paperback copies are available, and the books reused from term to term.

Academic libraries must decide what focus they take in collecting materials since no single library can supply everything. When there are particular areas of specialization in academic libraries these are often referred to as niche collections. These collections are often the basis of a special collection department and may include original papers, artwork, and artifacts written or created by a single author or about a specific subject.

ACADEMIC LIBRARIES IN INDIA: A PRESENT-DAY SCENARIO

Education aims to impart knowledge and makes good citizens. Libraries are the repositories of knowledge and form an integral part of education. Libraries have a long history, starting with the chained and closed-access libraries of earlier times to the present-day hybrid, digital, and virtual libraries that use the latest technology for provision of information through various services.

Librarians have also changed from storekeepers who were concerned with protection of books against theft, mutilation, and pilferage, to that of information officers, navigators, and cybrarians who find themselves in the vast ocean of reading material and are busy in satisfying their clients who want anytime and anywhere information.

With the advent of computers, the nature of libraries has changed dramatically. Computers are being used in libraries to process, store, retrieve and disseminate information. As a result, the traditional concept of library is being redefined from a place to access books to one which houses the most advanced media including CD-ROM, Internet, and remote access to a wide range of resources.

Libraries have now metamorphosed into digital institutions. Gone are the days when a library was judged by its quantitative resources. Today, libraries are surrounded by networked data that is connected to a vast ocean of Internet-based services. Moreover, electronic resources relevant to the professions are developing at an unprecedented pace.

Academic libraries are considered to be the nerve centres of academic institutions, and must support teaching, research, and other academic programmes. The situation in academic libraries of India is the same as that of academic libraries the world over; however, Indian libraries must provide maximum information with limited resources.

The Educational System of India

India has a large higher education system. The growth rate of educational institutions in India was very slow before independence in 1947. Today there are a total of 237 universities, including 116 general universities, 12 science and technology universities, 7 open universities, 33 agricultural universities, 5 women's universities, 1 language universities and 11 medical universities along with 12,600 colleges that provide education in all disciplines. The number of teachers is 3.1 million, and 7.8 million students are enrolled in higher education.

University Grants Commission (UGC)

UGC, established by an act of parliament in 1956, coordinates and monitors the higher education system in India and provides grants to the universities and colleges. Two hundred ninety four universities/institutions in the country are directly under the purview of UGC.

It also advises the union and state governments on measures to university education. It frames rules and regulations for overall teaching and research at higher education. As a result, it also looks after the academic libraries, *i.e.*, sets various standards for library education, library staff, library services, etc. A number of committees have been set up by the UGC for the support of higher education in general and the library services in academic libraries in particular.

UGC has also set up three information centres covering different disciplines—the *National Centre for Science Information* (NCSI) at Indian Institute of Science Bangalore, SNDT Women's University Mumbai, and National Social Science Information Centre at M.S. University at Baroda, to provide the document delivery services to students, teachers, and researchers.

Information and Library Network

The University Grants Commission has set up an autonomous Inter-University Centre in 1991 called INFLIBNET. It is involved in modernizing university libraries in India and connects them through a nation-wide high-speed data network. It promotes automation of libraries, develops standards, creates union catalogues of serials, theses, books, monographs and non-book materials; provides access to bibliographic information sources; creates database of projects, institutions, specialists; provides training, etc.

Almost all academic libraries, especially university libraries, are members of INFLIBNET. It has also developed library automation software called SOUL (*Software for University Libraries*) and has distributed the same free of cost to its member libraries.

Other Networks

Besides INFLIBNET, a number of other national networks and various library networks have also been developed including:

- NICNET (National Informatic Center's network),
- INDONET,
- ERNET,
- CALIBNET,
- DELNET:
  - ADINET is associated with INFLIBNET,
  - DELNET with NIC and
  - MALIBNET with CFTRI.

A number of educational institutions are members of such networks. These networks, especially DELNET are engaged in compiling union catalogs, creating various databases of experts, providing training to library staff, ILL, online facilities, reference service, assistance in retrospective conversion, etc.

Library Consortia

Due to a financial crunch and the rising costs of journals, many Indian university and college libraries cannot subscribe to all the required journals and databases. To overcome this problem, libraries are forming consortia.

Some special libraries and organizations like the Indian Institute of Astrophysics Library, Inter-university Centre for Astronomy and Astrophysics Library, *National Centre for Radio Astrophysics* (NCRA) Library, Physical Research Laboratory (PRL) Library, Raman Research Institute (RRI) Library, Tata Institute of Fundamental Research (TIFR) Library, Council of Scientific and Industrial Research, Department of Atomic Energy, etc., have established consortia to share electronic access to journal literature.

NISCAIR (formed by the merger of INSDOC and NISCOM) is developing a consortium for CSIR labs for accessing e-journals. Consortia in India are still a new concept that requires proper guidelines and methodologies. In a survey by UGC in 2001, it was noted that although 142 university libraries had computer and Internet facilities and were interlinked to INFLIBNET, they were subscribing to printed journals only.

In order to solve this problem, UGC launched a major initiative called UGC-INFONET that provides high speed Internet connections so as to have electronic access to professional literature including research journals, abstracts, review publications, and databases from all areas in science and technology, as well as in social sciences and humanities.

Today, a number of professional journals are available over UGC-INFONET to all universities. The e-subscription initiative under UGC-Infonet is an important portal for sharing print as well as electronic resources amongst university libraries. INFLIBNET functions as a resource center with an aim to cater to the needs of its members for resources not accessible to them in electronic media or are available in print media.

INDEST Consortium

The Ministry of Human Resource Development (MHRD) has set up the "Indian National Digital Library in Science and Technology Consortium". The ministry provides funds required for the subscription to electronic resources for 38 academic institutions, including the Indian Institute of Sciences, Indian Institute of Technology, Regional Engineering Colleges, Indian Institute of Managements, and about 60 centrally-funded/aided government institutions through the consortium.

The INDEST consortium is the most ambitious initiative so far in the area of engineering and technology disciplines. The primary objective of libraries is to organize and provide access to information, and it remains the same although the format and methods have changed drastically.

Under the present scenario of declining budgets and higher subscription costs of journals in India, it is becoming very difficult to meet the demands of library/information users. The only solution to the problem is the pooling and sharing of resources—print as well as electronic—by way of consortia.

New technology has provided great opportunities for delivery of services within consortia. More and more libraries must unite, which of course requires a change in the attitudes, practices, and policies to get the maximum benefit.

SCHOOL LIBRARY

A school library is a library within a school where students, staff, and often, parents of a public or private school have access to a variety of resources. The goal of the school library media center is to ensure that all members of the school community have equitable access "to books and reading, to information, and to information technology."

A school library media center "uses all types of media... is automated, and utilizes the Internet for information gathering." School libraries are distinct from public libraries because they serve as "learner-oriented laboratories which support, extend, and individualize the school's curriculum... A school library serves as the center and coordinating agency for all material used in the school."

Researchers have demonstrated that school libraries have a positive impact on student achievement. More than 60 studies have been conducted in 19 U.S. states and one Canadian province. The major finding of these studies is that students with access to a well-supported school library media programme with a qualified school library media specialist, scored higher on reading assessments regardless of their socio-economic statuses.

In addition, a study conducted in Ohio revealed that 99.4% of students surveyed believed that their school librarians and school library media programmes helped them succeed in school. A report that reported similar conclusions was compiled by Michele Lonsdale in Australia in 2003.

HISTORY OF SCHOOL LIBRARIES

The later part of the 19th century marked the beginning of the modern American library movement with the creation of the American Library Association (ALA) in 1876 by a group of librarians led by Melvil Dewey. At these beginning stages of development, the school libraries were primarily made up of small collections with the school librarian playing primarily a clerical role.

1920 marked the first effort by the library and education communities to evaluate school libraries with the publication of the *Certain Report*, which provided the first yardstick for evaluating school libraries.

School libraries experienced another major push following the launch of Sputnik in 1957, which forced the United States to re-evaluate its priorities for math and science education. As a result, the 1960s were one of the greatest periods of growth and development for school libraries due to an increased flow of money and support from the private sector and public funding for education. Most notable during this time was the *Knapp School Libraries Project* which established model school library media centers across the country.

Hundreds of new school libraries were expanded and renovated during this time. Most recently, school libraries have been defined by three major guidelines documents: *Information Power* and *Information Power II*. Globally important mission statement is the Unesco School library Manifesto.

THE PURPOSE OF THE SCHOOL LIBRARY

The school library exists to provide a range of learning opportunities for both large and small groups as well as individuals with a focus on intellectual content, information literacy, and the learner.

In addition to classroom visits with collaborating teachers, the school library also serves as a place for students to do independent work, use computers, equipment and research materials; to host special events such as author visits and book clubs; and for tutoring and testing.

The school library media center programme is a collaborative venture in which school library media specialists, teachers, and administrators work together to provide opportunities for the social, cultural, and educational growth of students. Activities that are part of the school library media programme can take place in the school library media center, the laboratory classroom, through the school, and via the school library's online resources.

THE SCHOOL LIBRARY COLLECTION

School libraries are similar to public libraries in that they contain books, films, recorded sound, periodicals, realia, and digital media. These items are not only for the education, enjoyment, and entertainment of the all members of the school community, but also to enhance and expand the school's curriculum.

STAFFING OF THE SCHOOL LIBRARY

In many schools, school libraries are staffed by librarians, teacher-librarians, or school library media specialists who hold a specific library science degree. In some jurisdictions, school librarians are required to have specific certification and/or a teaching certificate.

The school librarian performs four leadership main roles: teacher, instructional partner, information specialist, and programme administrator. In the teacher role, the school librarian develops and implements curricula relating to information literacy and enquiry. School librarians may read to children, assist them in selecting books, and assist with schoolwork.

Some school librarians see classes on a "flexible schedule". A flexible schedule means that rather than having students come to the library for instruction at a fixed time every week, the classroom teacher schedules library time when library skills or materials are needed as part of the classroom learning experience.

In the instructional partner role, school librarians collaborate with classroom teachers to create independent learners by fostering students' research, information literacy, technology, and critical thinking skills.

As information specialists, school librarians develop a resource base for the school by using the curriculum and student interests to identify and obtain library materials, organize and maintain the library collection in order to promote independent reading and lifelong learning. Materials in the library collection can be located using an *Online Public Access Catalog* (OPAC).

This role also encompasses many activities relating to technology including the integration of resources in a variety of formats: periodical databases; Web sites; digital video segments; podcasts; blog and wiki content; digital images; virtual classrooms, etc. School librarians are often responsible for audio-visual equipment and are sometimes in charge of school computers and computer networks. Many school librarians also perform clerical duties. They handle the circulating and cataloging of materials, facilitate interlibrary loans, shelve materials, perform inventory, etc.

RESEARCH LIBRARIES

A research library contains an in-depth collection of material on one or more subjects. A research library supports scholarly research and will generally include primary as well as secondary sources; it will maintain permanent collections and attempt to provide access to all necessary material.

A research library is most often an academic or national library, but a large special library may have a research library within its special field and a very few of the largest public libraries also serve as research libraries. A large university library may be considered a research library; and in North America they may belong to the Association of Research Libraries.

A research library can be either a reference library, which does not lend its holdings, or a lending library, which does lend all or some of its holdings. Some extremely large or traditional research libraries are entirely reference in this sense, lending none of their material; most academic research libraries, at least in the U.S., now lend books, but not periodicals or other material.

REFERENCE LIBRARIES

A reference library does not lend books and other items; instead, they must be read at the library itself. Typically such libraries are used for research purposes, for example at a university. Some items at reference libraries may be historical and even unique. Examples of reference libraries include the British Library in London and the Bodleian Library at Oxford University.

Many libraries contain a "reference section", which holds books, such as dictionaries, which are common reference books, and are therefore not lent out. Such references sections may be referred to as "reading rooms", which may also include newspapers and periodicals.

SPECIAL LIBRARIES

All other libraries fall into the "special library" category. Many private businesses and public organizations, including hospitals, museums, research laboratories, law firms, and many government departments and agencies, maintain their own libraries for the use of their employees in doing specialized research related to their work.

Special libraries may or may not be accessible to some identified part of the general public. Branches of a large academic or research libraries dealing with particular subjects are also usually called "special libraries": they are generally associated with one or more academic departments. Special libraries are distinguished from special collections, which are branches or parts of a library intended for rare books, manuscripts, and other special materials.

ARCHIVE, MUSEUM AND RECORDS MANAGEMENT

ARCHIVE

An archive is a collection of historical records, or the physical place they are located. Archives contain primary source documents that have accumulated over the course of an individual or organization's lifetime, and are kept to show the function of an organization.

In general, archives consist of records that have been selected for permanent or long-term preservation on grounds of their enduring cultural, historical, or evidentiary value. Archival records are normally unpublished and almost always unique, unlike books or magazines for which many identical copies exist. This means that archives are quite distinct from libraries with regard to their functions and organization, although archival collections can often be found within library buildings.

A person who works in archives is called an archivist. The study and practice of organizing, preserving, and providing access to information and materials in archives is called archival science.

When referring to historical records or the places they are kept, the plural form *archives* is chiefly used. Archivists tend to prefer the term "archives" as the correct terminology to serve as both the singular and plural, since "archive," as a noun or a verb, has acquired meanings related to computer science.

The use of keeping official documents is very old. Archeologists have discovered archives of hundreds of clay tablets going back to the IIIrd and IInd millennia BC in sites like Ebla, Mari, Amarna, Hattusas, Ugarit, Pylos. And these discoveries have been fundamental to know ancient alphabets, languages, literatures and politics.

Archives were well developed by the ancient Chinese, the ancient Greeks, and ancient Romans. However, they have been lost, since documents were written on organic materials like papyrus and paper.

On the contrary, many archives founded since Middle Age by churches, kingdoms and cities survive and often have kept their official status uninterruptedly till now. They are the basic tool for historical research on these ages.

Modern archival thinking has many roots in the French Revolution. The French National Archives, who possess perhaps the largest archival collection in the world, with records going as far back as A.D. 625, were created in 1790 during the French Revolution from various government, religious, and private archives seized by the revolutionaries.

Users and Institutions

Historians, genealogists, lawyers, demographers, film-makers, and others conduct research at archives. The research process at each archive is unique, and depends upon the institution in which the archive is housed. While there are many different kinds of archives, the most recent census of archivists in the United States identified five major types: academic, business, government, non-profit, and other.

There are also four main areas of enquiry involved with archives:

- Material technologies,
- Organizing principles,
- Geographic locations, and
- Tangled embodiments of humans and non-humans.

These areas help to further categorize what kind of archive is being created.

Academic

Archives in colleges, universities, and other educational facilities are typically housed within a library, and duties may be carried out by an archivist. professors may also run a smaller archive. Academic archives exist to preserve and celebrate the history of their school and academic community.

An academic archive may contain items such as the administrative records of the institution, papers of former professors and presidents, memorabilia related to school organizations and activities, and items the academic library wishes to remain in a closed-stack setting, such as rare books or thesis copies.

Access to the collections in these archives is usually by prior appointment only; some have posted hours for making enquiries. Users of academic archives can be undergraduates, graduate students, faculty and staff, scholarly researchers, and the general public.

Many academic archives work closely with alumni relations departments or other campus institutions to help raise funds for their library or school. Because of their library setting, a degree certified by the American Library Association is preferred for employment in an academic archive in the United States.

Business

Archives located in for-profit institutions are usually those owned by a private business. Examples of prominent business archives in the United States include Coca-Cola, Procter and Gamble, Motorola Heritage Services and Archives, and Levi Strauss and Co. These corporate archives maintain historic documents and items related to the history and administration of their companies.

Business archives serve the purpose of helping their corporations maintain control over their brand by retaining memories of the company's past. Especially in business archives, records management is separate from the historic aspect of archives.

Workers in these types of archives may have any combination of training and degrees, from either a history or library background. These archives are typically not open to the public and only used by workers of the owner company, although some will allow approved visitors by appointment. Business archives are concerned with maintaining the integrity of their company, and are therefore selective of how their materials may be used.

Government

Government archives include those maintained by local and state government as well as those maintained by the national government. Anyone may use a government archive, and frequent users include reporters, genealogists, writers, historians, students, and people seeking information on the history of their home or region. Many government archives are open to the public and no appointment is required to visit.

In the United States, *National Archives and Records Administration* (NARA) maintains central archival facilities in the District of Columbia and College Park, Maryland, with regional facilities distributed throughout the United States.

Some city or local governments may have repositories, but their organization and accessibility varies widely. State or province archives typically require at least a bachelor's degree in history for employment, although some ask for certification by test as well.

In the UK the National Archives, formerly known as the Public Record Office, is the government archive for England and Wales. The National Monuments Record is the public archive of English Heritage. The National Archives of Scotland, located in Edinburgh, serve that country while the Public Record Office of Northern Ireland in Belfast is the government archive for Northern Ireland.

A network of local authority-run record offices and archives exists throughout England, Wales and Scotland and holds many important collections, including local government, landed estates, church and business records. Many archives have contributed catalogues to the national Access 2 Archives programme and online searching across collections is possible.

In France, the French Archives Administration in the Ministry of Culture manages the National Archives which possess 406 km. of archives as of 2010 with original records going as far back as A.D. 625, as well as the departmental archives, located in the *préfectures* of each of the 100 *départements* of France, which possess 2,297 km. of archives, and also the local city archives, about 600 in total, which possess 456 km. of archives.

Put together, the total volume of archives under the supervision of the French Archives Administration is the largest in the world:

- In India the National Archives are located in New Delhi.
- In Taiwan the National Archives Administration are located in Taipei.

Most intergovernmental organisations keep their own historical archives. However, a number of European organi-sations, including the European Commission, choose to deposit their archives with the European University Institute in Florence.

MUSEUM

A museum is an institution that cares for a collection of artifacts and other objects of scientific, artistic, cultural, or historical importance and makes them available for public viewing through exhibits that may be permanent or temporary.

Most large museums are located in major cities throughout the world and more local ones exist in smaller cities, towns and even the countryside. The continuing acceleration in the digitization of information, combined with the increasing capacity of digital information storage, is causing the traditional model of museums to expand to include virtual exhibits and high-resolution images of their collections for perusal, study, and exploration from any place with Internet connectivity.

Purpose

Museum purposes change from institution to institution. Some favour education over conservation, or *vice-versa*. For example, in the 1970s, the Canada Science and Technology Museum favoured education over preservation of their objects. They displayed objects as well as their functions.

One exhibit featured a historic printing press that a staff member used for visitors to create museum memorabilia. Some seek to reach a wide audience, such as a national or state museum, while some museums have specific audiences, like the LDS Church History Museum or local history organizations.

Generally speaking, museums collect objects of significance that comply with their mission statement for conservation and display. Although most museums do not allow physical contact with the associated artifacts, there are some that are interactive and encourage a more hands-on approach.

In 2009, Hampton Court Palace, palace of Henry VIII, opened the council room to the general public to create an interactive environment for visitors. Rather than allowing visitors to handle 500 year old objects, the museum created replicas, as well as replica costumes. The daily activities, historic clothing, and even temperature changes immerse the visitor in a slice of what Tudor life may have been

Management

The roles associated with the management a museum largely depends on the size of the institution, but every museum has a hierarchy of governance with a Board of Trustees serving at the top. The Director is next in command and works with the Board to establish and fulfill the museum's mission statement and to ensure that the museum is accountable to the public.

Together, the Board and the Director establish a good system of governance that is guided by various other documents such as an institutional or strategic plan, institutional code of ethics, bylaws, and collections policy.

The *American Association of Museums* (AAM) has also formulated a series of standards and best practices that help guide the management of museums. Unfortunately, many small, local museums lack this guidance since accreditation with AAM requires a museum to operate on an annual budget of at least $25,000.

A change in leadership may ultimately effect changes at the museum, as new directors commonly have new ideas for the institution they work for. For instance, the Los Angeles County Museum of Art's Director and CEO,

Michael Govan, has made great strides for the museum since he started in 2006.

Undertaking elaborate building projects, acquiring large collections of objects, and creating new relationships with contemporary artists are just some of his accomplishments. While change and growth is often good for a museum, they should not reach outside the original mission statement of the institution.

Museum professionals Hugh H. Genoways and Lynne M. Ireland, "Administration of the organization requires skill in conflict management, interpersonal relations, budget manage-ment and monitoring, and staff supervision and evaluation. Managers must also set legal and ethical standards and maintain involvement in the museum profession."

Various positions within the museum carry out the policies established by the Board and the Director. These positions include but are not limited to curators, collections managers/registrars, public programmers/educators, exhibition designers, and building operators.

These positions and all other employees should work together towards the museum's institutional goal:

- *Curator:* Research the collection and most often write the text labels for exhibitions. In larger institutions, there may be a curator assigned to each collection of objects the museum holds. Ex: Curator of Modern Art, Curator of Natural History, Curator of History, etc.
- *Collections Management/Registrar*: Responsible for the care and maintenance of all objects in the museum's collection, tracks movement of objects in and out of the museum on loan or on exhibition, records information about objects in databases-such as an object's provenance. Registrars oversee the accessi-oning process, which formally accepts objects into the museum's collection with an accession number and detailed record. Collections Managers and Registrars uphold the Collections Policy, which guides what is and is not accepted into the museum collection.
- *Public Programmer/Educator:* Creates programmes for the public and designs interactives for exhibitions. This position also oversees volunteers and docents at the museum. Depending on the institution, educators may also research the collections and write text for exhibitions. Educators work with the Board, Director, and Curator to ensure that the needs of the public are met as laid out in the institution's mission statement.
- *Exhibition Designer*: Designs and installs the exhibition under the supervision of the curator and collections manager. They have the vital role of creating exhibition space that is navigable by the visitor.
- *Building Operators:* Oversee security and maintenance of the museum. In larger museums, building operators will work with

Collections Managers to maintain appropriate levels of temperature and humidity which can affect the stability of the objects.

RECORDS MANAGEMENT

Records management, or RM, is the practice of maintaining the records of an organization from the time they are created up to their eventual disposal. This may include classifying, storing, securing, and destruction of records.

A record can be either a tangible object or digital information: for example, birth certificates, medical x-rays, office documents, databases, application data, and e-mail. Records management is primarily concerned with the evidence of an organization's activities, and is usually applied according to the value of the records rather than their physical format.

In the past, 'records management' was sometimes used to refer only to the management of records which were no longer in everyday use but still needed to be kept-'semi-current' or 'inactive' records, often stored in basements or offsite. More modern usage tends to refer to the entire 'lifecycle' of records-from the point of creation right through until their eventual disposal.

- *The ISO 15489-1:* 2001 standard defines records management as " field of management responsible for the efficient and systematic control of the creation, receipt, maintenance, use and disposition of records, including the processes for capturing and maintaining evidence of and information about business activities and transactions in the form of records".
- *The ISO 15489-1:* 2001 defines records as "information created, received, and maintained as evidence and information by an organization or person, in pursuance of legal obligations or in the transaction of business". While there are many purposes of and benefits to records management, as both this definition highlights, a key feature of records is their ability to serve as evidence of an event. Proper records manage-ment can help preserve this feature of records.

It should be noted that the format and media of records is generally irrelevant for the purposes of records management. The ISO considers management of both physical and electronic records. Also, section DL1.105 of the United States Department of Defence standard DoD 5015.02-STD defines Records Management as "[t]he planning, controlling, directing, organizing, training, promoting, and other managerial activities involving the life cycle of information, including creation, maintenance, and disposal, regardless of media."

Practicing Records Management

A Records Manager is someone who is responsible for records management in an organization.

Section 4 of the ISO 15489-1:2001 states that records management includes:

- Setting policies and standards;
- Assigning responsibilities and authorities;
- Establishing and promulgating procedures and guide-lines;
- Providing a range of services relating to the manage-ment and use of records;
- Designing, implementing and administering specia-lized systems for managing records; and
- Integrating records management into business systems and processes.

Thus, the practice of records management may involve:

- Planning the information needs of an organization
- Identifying information requiring capture
- Creating, approving, and enforcing policies and practices regarding records, including their organi-zation and disposal
- Developing a records storage plan, which includes the short and long-term housing of physical records and digital information
- Identifying, classifying, and storing records
- Coordinating access to records internally and outside of the organization, balancing the requirements of business confidentiality, data privacy, and public access.
- Executing a retention policy on the disposal of records which are no longer required for operational reasons; according to organizational policies, statutory requirements, and other regulations this may involve either their destruction or permanent preservation in an archive.

Records management principles and automated records management systems aid in the capture, classification, and ongoing management of records throughout their lifecycle. Such a system may be paper based or may be a computer system, such as an electronic records management application.

Managing Physical Records

Managing physical records involves different disciplines and may draw on a variety of forms of expertise. Records must be identified and authenticated.

This is usually a matter of filing and retrieval; in some circumstances, more careful handling is required.

- *Identifying Records*: If an item is presented as a legal record, it needs to be authenticated. Forensic experts may need to examine a document or artifact to determine that it is not a forgery, and that any damage, alteration, or missing content is documented. In extreme cases, items may be subjected to a microscope, x-ray, radiocarbon dating or chemical analysis. This level of authentication is rare, but requires that special care be taken in the creation and retention of the records of an organization.

- *Storing Records:* Records must be stored in such a way that they are accessible and safeguarded against environmental damage. A typical paper document may be stored in a filing cabinet in an office. However, some organisations employ file rooms with specialized environmental controls including temperature and humidity. Vital records may need to be stored in a disaster-resistant safe or vault to protect against fire, flood, earthquakes and conflict. In extreme cases, the item may require both disaster-proofing and public access, such as the original, signed US Constitution. Civil engineers may need to be consulted to determine that the file room can effectively withstand the weight of shelves and file cabinets filled with paper; historically, some military vessels were designed to take into account the weight of their operating procedures on paper as part of their ballast equation. In addition to on-site storage of records, many organizations operate their own off-site records centers or contract with commercial records centres.
- *Circulating Records:* Tracking the record while it is away from the normal storage area is referred to as circulation. Often this is handled by simple written recording procedures. However, many modern records environments use a computerized system involving bar code scanners, or *radio-frequency identification technology* (RFID) to track movement of the records. These can also be used for periodic auditing to identify unauthorized movement of the record.
- *Disposal of Records:* Disposal of records does not always mean destruction. It can also include transfer to a historical archive, museum, or private individual. Destruction of records ought to be authorized by law, statute, regulation, or operating procedure, and the records should be disposed of with care to avoid inadvertent disclosure of information. The process needs to be well-documented, starting with a records retention schedule and policies and procedures that have been approved at the highest level. An inventory of the records disposed of should be maintained, including certification that they have been destroyed. Records should never simply be discarded as refuse. Most organizations use processes including pulveri-zation, paper shredding or incineration.

Commercially available products can manage records through all processes active, inactive, archival, retention scheduling and disposal. Some also utilizes RFID technology for the tracking of the physical file.

Managing Electronic Records

The general principles of records management apply to records in any format. Digital records, however, raise specific issues. It is more difficult to ensure that the content, context and structure of records is preserved and protected when the records do not have a physical existence. This has important implications for the authenticity, reliability, and trust-worthiness of records.

Much research is being conducted on the management of electronic records. The International Research on Permanent Authentic Records in Electronic Systems Project is one example of such an initiative. Based at the School of Library, Archival and Information Studies at the University of British Columbia, in Vancouver, British Columbia, Canada, the InterPARES Project is a collaborative project between researchers all across the world committed to developing theories and methodologies to ensure the reliability, accuracy, and authenticity of electronic records.

Functional requirements for computer systems to manage electronic records have been produced by the US Department of Defence, the National Archives of England and Wales and the European Commission, whose MoReq (Model Requirements for the Management of Electronic Records) specification has been translated into at least twelve languages and is used beyond the borders of Europe.

Development of MoReq was initiated by the DLM Forum, funded by the European Commission. Particular concerns exist about the ability to access and read electronic records over time, since the rapid pace of change in technology can make the software used to create the records obsolete, leaving the records unreadable.

A considerable amount of research is being undertaken to address this, under the heading of digital preservation. The Public Record Office Victoria (PROV) located in Melbourne, Australia published the Victorian Electronic Records Strategy (VERS) which includes a standard for the preservation, long-term storage and access to permanent electronic records.

The VERS standard has been adopted by all Victorian Government departments. A digital archive has been established by PROV to enable the general public to access permanent records. Archives New Zealand is also setting up a digital archive.

Electronic Tax Records

Electronic Tax Records are computer-based/non-paper versions of records required by tax agencies like the Internal Revenue Service. There is substantial confusion about what constitutes acceptable digital records for the IRS, as the concept is relatively new. The subject is discussed in Publication 583 and Bulletin 1997-13, but not in specific detail.

Businesses and individuals wishing to convert their paper records into scanned copies may be at risk if they do so. For example, it is unclear if an IRS auditor would accept a JPEG, PNG, or PDF format scanned copy of a purchase receipt for a deducted expense item.

Current Issues in Records Management

As of 2005, records management has increased interest among corporations due to new compliance regulations and statutes. While government, legal, and health care entities have a strong historical records management discipline, general record-keeping of corporate records has been poorly standar-dized and implemented.

In addition, scandals such as the Enron/Andersen scandal, and more recently records-related mishaps at Morgan Stanley, have renewed interest in corporate records compliance, retention period requirements, litigation preparedness, and related issues.

Statutes such as the US Sarbanes-Oxley Act have created new concerns among corporate "compliance officers" that result in more standardization of records management practices within an organization. Most of the 1990s has seen discussions between records managers and IT managers, and the emphasis has expanded to include the legal aspects, as it is now focused on compliance and risk.

Privacy, data protection, and identity theft have become issues of interest for records managers. The role of the records manager to aid in the protection of an organization's records has often grown to include attention to these concerns. The need to ensure that certain information about individuals is not retained has brought greater focus to records retention schedules and records destruction.

The most significant issue is implementing the required changes to individual and corporate culture to derive the benefits to internal and external stakeholders. Records manage-ment is often seen as an unnecessary or low priority administrative task that can be performed at the lowest levels within an organization.

Publicised events have demonstrated that records management is in fact the responsibility of all individuals within an organi-zation and the corporate entity. An issue that has been very controversial among records managers has been the uncritical adoption of Electronic Document and Records Management Systems.

One well known RM thinker, Steve Bailey, has stated:

- "As far as the average user is concerned, the EDRMS is something they didn't want, don't like and can't use. As such, its no wonder that so few users accept them–as one person once said to me "making me use an EDRMS is like asking a plasterer to use a hammer!
- "And now, finally, it is time to turn our eyes to the records management profession itself. In my opinion, we have come within a whisker of allowing our blind obsession with EDRMS to turn us into an intellec-tually-sterile, vendor-led profession. For the best part of a decade we have allowed others to do the thinking for us and have come to rely on EDRMS as our intellectual-crutch. But make no mistake about it, the blame for this rests squarely with us. Like children following the Pied Piper, we allowed ourselves to be so enchanted by the tune being played that we were led, without question or debate, wherever the tech-nology took us."

Another issue of great interest to records managers is the impact of social media, such as wikis, Facebook and Twitter, on traditional records management practice, principles, and concepts.

PUBLIC LIBRARY: BACKDROP AND GROWTH

A public library is a library that is accessible by the public and is generally funded from public sources and operated by civil servants. There are five fundamental characteristics shared by public libraries. The first is that they are supported by taxes; they are governed by a board to serve the public interest; they are open to all and every community member can access the collection; they are entirely voluntary in that no one is ever forced to use the services provided; and public libraries provide basic services without charge. Public libraries exist in many countries across the world and are often considered an essential part of having an educated and literate population.

Public libraries are distinct from research libraries, school libraries, and other special libraries in that their mandate is to serve the general public's information needs. Public libraries also provide free services such as preschool story times to encourage early literacy, quiet study and work areas for students and professionals, or book clubs to encourage appreciation of literature in adults. Public libraries typically allow users to take books and other materials off the premises temporarily; they also have non-circulating reference collections and provide computer and Internet access to patrons.

HISTORY

A public library is a library funded by public money, such as taxpayer money. The purpose of a public library is to provide books, Internet access and many other resources to the public for free. Even DVDs and movies are available for free rentals. Public libraries are not new, in fact the first organization that was considered to be a public library was created in the late 1500s.

- The first public library was created in England. At that time, the only people who were able to use libraries were individuals who joined a cathedral or were enrolled in college. This public library was called Francis Trigge Chained Library. This public library actually still exists and is famous for its long standing history of giving the people free access to all library resources. Although this library was the first, it stood nearly alone in its existence until the mid 1800s. That was the time period in which public libraries began to become popular.
- In England, Parliament decided to make a committee dedicated to considering the creation of multiple public libraries. The committee was supposed to decide if a public library was something that would benefit the public. The committee reported back that public libraries would be beneficial, since so many people were poor. The

recommendation was to open multiple public libraries throughout the country. This decision led to the Public Libraries Act of 1850. The act allowed all cities to collect taxes for public library support, providing that the population of the city had at least 10,000 people.

- This was quickly followed by the Public School Law, created in 1870. The point of this law was to raise the literacy rate of the public, since it was very low at the time. The only people who really knew how to read were rich people and scholars. Obviously, this literacy need increased the need for public libraries. By the 1870s, over 50 cities had created public libraries of their own. Only 30 years later, the number of public libraries hit 300. This was the time when public libraries began opening everywhere, and the United States began funding them as well. A public library was funded by public money, but it was also common for the people to help out these public libraries grow and flourish. Womens' clubs and the wealthy donated books to these public libraries to improve their selections.

Today, there are hundreds of thousands of public libraries in the world. The larger the city, the more public libraries will be found there. Unfortunately, despite the great need and desire for public libraries, funding for them are cut consistently by the state legislature. Large amounts of money to fund public libraries are made by private donors who have the wealth and desire to see a public library being used.

17th Century

In the early years of the 17th century, many famous collegiate and town libraries were founded throughout the country. Francis Trigge Chained Library of St. Wulfram's Church, Grantham, Lincolnshire was founded in 1598 by the rector of nearby Welbourne. Norwich City Library was established in 1608, and Chetham's Library in Manchester, which claims to be the oldest public library in the English-speaking world, opened in 1653.

Other early town libraries of the UK include those of:

- Ipswich (1612),
- Bristol (founded in 1613 and opened in 1615), and
- Leicester (1632).

Shrewsbury School also opened its library to townsfolk. In Bristol, an early library that allowed access to the public was that of the Kalendars or Kalendaries, a brotherhood of clergy and laity who were attached to the Church of All-Hallowen or All Saints. Records show that in 1464, provision was made for a library to be erected in the house of the Kalendars, and reference is made to a deed of that date by which it was "appointed that all who wish to enter for the sake of instruction shall have 'free access and recess' at certain times".

Early 18th Century

At the turn of the 18th century, libraries were becoming increasingly public and were more frequently lending libraries. The 18th century saw the switch from closed parochial libraries to lending libraries. Before this time, public libraries were parochial in nature and libraries frequently chained their books to desks. Libraries also were not uniformly open to the public. In 1790, The Public Library Act would not be passed for another sixty-seven years. Even though the British Museum existed at this time and contained over 50,000 books, the national library was not open to the public, or even to a majority of the population.

Access to the Museum depended on passes, of which there was sometimes a waiting period of three to four weeks. Moreover, the library was not open to browsing. Once a pass to the library had been issued, the reader was taken on a tour of the library. Many readers complained that the tour was much too short. At the turn of the century, there were virtually no public libraries in the sense in which we now understand the term *i.e.,* libraries provided from public funds and freely accessible to all. Only one important library in Great Britain, namely Chetham's Library in Manchester, was fully and freely accessible to the public.

However, there had come into being a whole network of library provision on a private or institutional basis. Subscription libraries, both private and commercial, provided the middle and middle to upper class with a variety of books for moderate fees. The increase in secular literature at this time encouraged the spread of lending libraries, especially the commercial subscription libraries. Commercial subscription libraries began when booksellers began renting out extra copies of books in the mid-18th century. Steven Fischer estimates that in 1790, there were 'about six hundred rental and lending libraries, with a clientele of some fifty thousand.

The mid to late 18th century saw a virtual epidemic of feminine reading as novels became more and more popular. Novels, while frowned upon in society, were extremely popular. In England there were many who lamented at the 'villanous profane and obscene books' and the opposition to the circulating library, on moral grounds, persisted well into the 19th century. Still, many establishments must have circulated many times the number of novels as of any other genre. In 1797, Thomas Wilson wrote in The Use of Circulating Libraries: "Consider, that for a successful circulating library, the collection must contain 70% fiction". However, the overall percentage of novels mainly depended on the proprietor of the circulating library. While some circulating libraries were almost completely novels, others had less than 10% of their overall collection in the form of novels.

The national average at the turn of the century hovered around novels comprising about 20% of the total collection. Novels varied from other types of books in many ways. They were read primarily for enjoyment instead of for study. They did not provide academic knowledge or spiritual guidance; thus they were read quickly and far fewer times than other books. These were the perfect books for commercial subscription libraries to lend. Since books were read for pure enjoyment rather than for scholarly work, books needed to become both cheaper and smaller. Small duodecimo editions of books were preferred to the large folio editions. Folio editions were read at a desk, while the small duodecimo editions could be easily read like the paperbacks of today. Much like paperbacks of today, many of the novels in circulating libraries were unbound.

At this period of time, many people chose to bind their books in leather. Many circulating libraries skipped this process. Circulating libraries were not in the business of preserving books; their owners wanted to lend books as many times as they possibly could. Circulating libraries had ushered in a completely new way of reading. Reading was no longer simply an academic pursuit or an attempt to gain spiritual guidance. Reading became a social activity. Many circulating libraries were attached to the shops of milliners or drapers. They served as much for social gossip and the meeting of friends as coffee shops do today. Another factor in the growth of subscription libraries was the increasing cost of books.

In the last two decades of the century, especially, prices were practically doubled, so that a quarto work cost a guinea, an octavo 10 shillings or 12 shillings, and a duodecimo cost 4 shillings per volume. Price apart, moreover, books were difficult to procure outside London, since local booksellers could not afford to carry large stocks. Commercial libraries, since they were usually associated with booksellers, and also since they had a greater number of patrons, were able to accumulate greater numbers of books. The United Public Library was said to have a collection of some 52,000 volumes—twice as many as any private subscription library in the country at that period. These libraries, since they functioned as a business, also lent books to non-subscribers on a per-book system.

Private Subscription Libraries

Private subscription libraries functioned in much the same manner as commercial subscription libraries, though they varied in many important ways. One of the most popular versions of the private subscription library was a gentleman's only library. The gentlemen's subscription libraries, sometimes known as proprietary libraries, were nearly all organized on a common pattern. Membership was restricted to the proprietors or shareholders, and ranged from a dozen or two to between four and five hundred.

The entrance fee, *i.e.,* the purchase price of a share, was in early days usually a guinea, but rose sharply as the century advanced, often reaching four or five guineas during the French wars; the annual subscription, during the same period, rose from about six shillings to ten shillings or more. The book-stock was, by modern standards, small and was accommodated, at the outset, in makeshift premises—very often over a bookshop, with the bookseller acting as librarian and receiving an honourarium for his pains. The Liverpool Subscription library was a gentlemen only library. In 1798, it was renamed the Athenaeum when it was rebuilt with a newsroom and coffeehouse.

It had an entrance fee of one guinea and annual subscription of five shillings. While no records survive of the commercial library lendings, we have the Bristol Library's continuous record of borrowings from 1773 to 1857. An analysis of the registers for the first twelve years provides some fascinating glimpses of middle-class reading habits in a mercantile community at this period. The largest and most popular sections of the library were History, Antiquities, and Geography, with 283 titles and 6,121 borrowings, and Belles Lettres, with 238 titles and 3,313 borrowings. Far below came Theology and Ecclesiastical History, Natural History and Chemistry, Philosophy, Jurisprudence, Miscellanies, Mathematics, etc., and Medicine and Anatomy, all with fewer than 100 titles.

The most popular single work was John Hawkesworth's Account of Voyages in the Southern Hemisphere which was borrowed on 201 occasions. The records also show that in 1796, membership had risen by 1/3 to 198 subscribers and the titles increased five-fold to 4987. This mirrors the increase in reading interests. A patron list from the Bath Municipal Library shows that from 1793 to 1799, the library held a stable 30% of their patrons as female. It was also uncommon for these libraries to have buildings designated solely as the library building during the 1790s, though in the 19th century, many libraries would begin building elaborate permanent residences. Bristol, Birmingham, and Liverpool were the few libraries with their own building.

The accommodations varied from the shelf for a few dozen volumes in the country stationer's or draper's shop, to the expansion to a back room, to the spacious elegant areas of Hookham's or those at the resorts like Scarborough, and four in a row at Margate. Private subscription libraries held a greater amount of control over both membership and the types of books in the library. There was almost a complete elimination of cheap fiction in the private societies. Subscription libraries prided themselves on respectability.

The highest percentage of subscribers were often landed proprietors, gentry, and old professions. Towards the end of the 18th century and in the first decades of the nineteenth the need for books and general education made itself felt among social classes created by the beginnings of the Industrial Revolution. The late 18th century saw a rise in subscription libraries intended for the use of tradesmen. In 1797, there was established at Kendal what was known as the Economical Library, "designed principally for the use and instruction of the working classes".

There was also the Artizans' library established at Birmingham in 1799. The entrance fee was 3 shillings. The subscription was 1 shilling 6 pence per quarter. This was a library of general literature. Novels, at first excluded, were afterwards admitted on condition that they did not account for more than one-tenth of the annual income.

Rate-supported Libraries

Although by the mid-19th century, England could claim 274 subscription libraries and Scotland, 266, the foundation of the modern public library system in the U.K. is the Public Libraries Act 1850. Prior to this, the municipalities of Warrington and Salford established libraries in their museums, under the terms of the Museums Act of 1845. Warrington Municipal Library opened in 1848. Salford Museum and Art Gallery first opened in November 1850 as "The Royal Museum and Public Library", as the first unconditionally free public library in England. The library in Campfield, Manchester was the first library to operate a free lending library without subscription in 1852.

Norwich lays claims to being the first municipality to adopt the Public Libraries Act 1850 but theirs was the eleventh library to open, in 1857, being the eleventh in the country after:

- Winchester,
- Manchester,
- Liverpool,
- Boltcn,
- Kidderminster,
- Cambridge,
- Birkenhead and
- Sheffield.

The Scottish-American philanthropist and businessman, Andrew Carnegie, helped to increase the number of public libraries from the late 19th century. County libraries are a later development which were made possible by the establishment of County Councils in 1888. They normally have a large central library in a major town with smaller branch libraries in other towns and a mobile library service covering rural areas.

NORTH AMERICA

Canada

In 1779 Frederick Haldimand, the Governor of Québec City, founded the first subscription library in Canada. Until then, Canada's libraries were mostly religious institutions, and the general public was not admitted. However, even though "Haldimand's library, like other subscription libraries, appealed primarily to an urban elite", it was the nation's first step towards the public library as it is known today. Haldimand's library later merged with the Literary and Historical Society of Quebec, which displays the original Québec Library collection within its library. This and similar association/social libraries were examples of early prototypes of public libraries.

They were public in that membership was allowed regardless of class or religion, and many in Canada eventually evolved into free public libraries. Subsequently legislative collections were established in 1791 in Upper and in 1792 in Lower Canada; and in 1796 the first public library was founded in Montreal. In 1800, libraries were established in King's College, Nova Scotia, and at Niagara, where the first public library in Upper Canada operated for twenty years, in spite of losses during the War of 1812. In Saint John, New Brunswick in 1883, following the efforts of Colonel James Domville in procuring a collection of materials to replace the many private collections lost in the Great Fire of Saint John, New Brunswick the first free, tax-supported public library was established. Guelph, Ontario and Toronto, Ontario opened public libraries that same year as well. Due to Canada's size and diversity, the development of the modern Canadian public library was more of a slow evolution than a quick transition as each of the provinces' specific conditions had first to be addressed.

The public library therefore took on many forms in Canada's earlier years; the three most prevalent of these forms were school-district libraries, Mechanics Institutes, and association/social libraries. In 1850, school-district libraries were initiated in Canada. Public servant Joseph Howe started one in Nova Scotia, and politician Egerton Ryerson started one in Ontario. New Brunswick and Prince Edward Island followed suit in 1858 and 1877, respectively. The hope was that both children and adults could benefit from the local school authorities, where financial assistance was provided from colonial legislatures, but the departments of education proved to be too centralizing for locals and this practiced was phased out. Mechanics Institutes also contained libraries that the working class could access inexpensively. The first Canadian library of its kind was established in 1828 in Montréal, Québec. Other communities took up this idea as well – notably those in Halifax, Nova Scotia, Hamilton, Ontario, Toronto, Ontario and Victoria, British Columbia. Like the school-district libraries, these institutes eventually ceased or were replaced by public libraries.

The public library that opened in Toronto, Ontario, was mostly due to a campaign by city alderman John Hallam. James Bain became the first chief librarian, and built a comprehensive collection of Canadian literature and history. The Toronto Public Library was one of the first libraries to choose free status, and it was the largest of them all. Its development flourished after 1900 when Carnegie grants began to aid in building construction and the expansion of collections and services. During this time, open access and children's departments were introduced, and standard cataloguing and classification systems were adopted. Many of the original branches, funded by a Carnegie grant, still stand and continue to be operated by the Toronto Public Library. Other provinces were affected by Carnegie as well and followed Ontario's lead in legislating tax support for library services. British Columbia acted in 1891, Manitoba in 1899, Saskatchewan in 1906, and in Alberta, the first legislation officially passed by the legislative assembly was the Library Act.

The act was passed March 15, 1907. The next provinces to follow were New Brunswick in 1929, Newfoundland in 1935, Prince Edward Island in 1936, Nova Scotia in 1937, Québec in1959, and then the Northwest Territories in 1966. As they stand today, public libraries in Canada are "governed by provincial statues and are primarily financed by municipal tax revenues and other local income, with provincial grants supplementing local funding. [They are also] the responsibility of a local or regional library board with authority to appoint or dismiss employees, control library property, establish policies, and budget for library operations."

Though the services offered vary from local branch to local branch, public libraries in Canada are not only places to read and borrow books; they are also hubs of community services, such as early reading programmes, computer access, and tutoring and literacy help for children and adults. Throughout the years, Canadian libraries have been subject to the political and economic influence of the nation. During World War II, public libraries experienced development setbacks, but expansion resumed in 1945. Then, in the 1960s, Canadian public libraries felt the benefits of the era's emphasis on education – service expanded, buildings were remodeled or constructed from scratch, and Centennial Grants were provided in order to improve the system.

This period of growth ended in due to the inflationary period in the 1970s and the two recessions during the 1980s. However, in the late 1990s this trend reversed and the National Core Library Statistics Programme reported in 1999 that public libraries served 28.5 million municipal residents – a total of 93% of the Canadian population. Nevertheless, in 2011 the tides turned for public libraries in Canada once again, specifically in Toronto. The city is now undergoing a heated debate regarding Mayor Rob Ford's proposed budget cuts for the Toronto Public Library, which is currently one of the most efficient public library systems in all of North America.

Mexico

In 1646, Don Juan de Palafox y Mendoza, bishop of Puebla and Viceroy of New Spain, expelled the Jesuits from New Spain, and with the confiscated books founded the Biblioteca Palafoxiana—the first public library in New Spain. It was in Puebla and open to all readers. The Biblioteca Palafoxiana exists today and is listed on the UNESCO Memory of the World Programme.

United States

As the United States developed from the 18th century to today, growing more populous and wealthier, factors such as a push for education and desire to share knowledge led to broad public support for free libraries. In addition, money donations by private philanthropists provided the seed capital to get many libraries started. In some instances, collectors donated vast book collections. William James Sidis in *The Tribes and the States* claimed the public library, as such, was an American invention. But exactly what constitutes a "free public library" is subject to dispute, and the term "invention" doesn't seem applicable to the many facets of an institution such as a library.

Throughout history, knowledge in different forms has been shared in different ways. Writing was recorded on papyrus and stored in scrolls and kept in vast libraries such as the Library of Alexandria in Egypt. In ancient Greece, knowledge was passed by one person reading aloud to a group of scribes from a text; this resulted in sometimes different and error-prone versions of the same text. Monks in the Middle Ages copied manuscripts by hand. After the invention of the printing press by Johann Gutenberg, books became prevalent, and different institutions such as universities and governments and churches found ways to keep and share them. There are disputes about which was the first public library in the nation. Early American cities such as Boston and Philadelphia and New York had the first organized collections of books, but which library was truly "public" is subject to dispute. Sidis claims the first public library was Boston's in 1636, although the official Boston Public Library was organized later in 1852.

In 1698, Charleston's St. Philip's Church Parsonage had a parish library. In 1731, Benjamin Franklin and his friends, sometimes called "the Junto", operated the Library Company of Philadelphia partly as a means to settle arguments and partly as a means to advance themselves through sharing information. Franklin's subscription library allowed members to buy "shares" and combined funds were used to buy more books; in return, members could borrow books and use the library. Today, the Library Company continues to exist as a nonprofit, independent research library.

A town in Massachusetts wanted to name itself Franklin in honour of the famous Pennsylvanian, and in return, Benjamin Franklin donated books for use by local residents; while Franklin had been asked to donate a church bell instead, he declined on the basis that "sense" was preferable to "sound". One source considers the Franklin library in Massachusetts to be the first public library in the United States. Another source claims the library in Darby, Pennsylvania which opened in 1743 is the "oldest continuously operating free public library" in the United States. But other libraries claim to be the first public library, including the Scoville library in Salisbury, Connecticut, which was established in 1803. The library in the New Hampshire town of Peterborough claims to be the first publicly-funded library; it opened in 1833. And a library in Massachusetts in the town of Arlington claims to have had the first free children's library; it opened in 1835.

Finances

In the trend from private to public libraries, big city libraries had the largest book collections and the most funding. The forerunner of the New York Public Library in Manhattan was a library established by the Earl of Ballamont around 1700. A newspaper described the call for the "first public librarian" demanding that "he must not be too young, for this would render him liable to be despised by the youth" and "he must be of an even temper" with "great diligence" and "sufficient learning" and "have a genius peculiarly adapted to the calling." In 1849, the library was officially established, and consolidated in 1901.

Today, it is considered to be one of the most important public libraries in the nation. New York governor and book lover Samuel J. Tilden bequeathed millions to build the New York Public Library. He believed Americans should have access to books and a free education if desired. In 2005, the library offered the "NYPL Digital Gallery" which made a collection of 275,000 images viewable over the web; while most of the contents are in the public domain, some images are still subject to copyright rules.

In 1902, one account suggested "the village library is growing more and more an indispensable adjunct to American village life." Around the turn from the 19th to the 20th century, Scottish-American businessman Andrew Carnegie donated over $60 million, which was a vast fortune in 20th century dollars, to build over 2,811 free public library buildings in the United States. They were often known as Carnegie libraries. Carnegie envisioned that libraries would "bring books and information to all people." Libraries have been started with wills from other benefactors; for example, the Bacon Free Library in South Natick, Massachusetts was founded in 1881 after a benefactor left $15,000 in a will; it has operated as a public library since then. Once the idea of the public library as an agency worthy of taxation was broadly established during the nineteenth and early twentieth centuries, librarians through actions of the American Library Association and its division devoted to public libraries, the Public Library Association, sought ways to identify standards and guidelines to ensure quality service.

In 2009, with the economic downturn, many public libraries have budget shortfalls. The library in Darby, Pennsylvania found expenses were greater than revenues from local property taxes, state funds, and investment income; it was on the risk of closing, according to a newspaper report. Many public libraries face budgetary problems; the report noted that "tax dollars that support them are dwindling as property tax revenue declines along with home values and sales taxes fall as consumers spend less. As local funding drops, libraries are turning to their endowments and draining the investments." Many libraries have foundations behind them to support them financially, and rely on the help of well-heeled donors as well as local corporations for funds.

Services

Most public libraries today are supported by tax monies from local and state governments, and some have foundations to support them with additional capital. Libraries lend books and materials freely, but charge fines if materials are returned late or damaged. Libraries often keep many historical documents relevant to their particular town, and serve as a resource for historians in some instances; for example, the Queens Public Library kept letters written by unrecognized Tiffany lamp designer Clara Driscoll, and the letters remained in the library until a curator discovered them. In 2009, big city libraries have multiple branches and offer numerous services. For example, the Boston Public Library has 26 neighbourhood branches and offers free Internet service; it has two restaurants and an online store which features reproductions of photographs and artwork; and it promotes itself with a web site. It answers more than one million reference questions annually.

The library uses wireless technology software networks to offer more services and keep costs under control. The Boston library offers digitized content, video, a wider range of formats and, as a result, "research documents now have broader accessibility within the community and around the world," and help communities by offering public access computers, mobile Wi-fi access, and free job search tools. Libraries promote cultural awareness; in Newark, New Jersey, the public library celebrated black history with exhibits and programmes. Libraries also partner with schools and community organizations to promote literacy and learning. One account suggested libraries were essential to "economic compet-itiveness" as well as "neighbourhood vitality" and help some people find jobs. Some library buildings are notable for their particular architectural styles; in the town of Beaver Dam, Wisconsin, architects designed the Williams Free Library in the style of Richardsonian Romanesque.

EUROPE

France

The National Library of France is one of the oldest libraries in the world still in service today as it traces its origin to the royal library founded at the Louvre by King Charles V in 1368, but at the time it was conceived as the private library of the French kings and it opened to the public only in 1692, during the reign of Louis XIV. Claude Sallier, the philologist and churchman, had an idea that was advanced for its era—to make culture accessible to all. From 1737 to 1750 he made books available to the town of Saulieu, forming France's first public library. The pioneer of modern public libraries in France was Eugène Morel, a writer and one of the librarians at the Bibliothèque nationale. He put forward his ideas in the 1910 book La Librairie publique.

Italy

The Malatestiana Library also known as the Malatesta Novello Library, is a public library dating from 1452 in Cesena, Emilia-Romagna. It was the first European civic library, *i.e.,* belonging to the Commune and open to everybody. It was commissioned by the Lord of Cesena, Malatesta Novello. The works were directed by Matteo Nuti of Fano and lasted from 1447 to 1452.

Poland

The Zaluski Library was built in Warsaw 1747– 1795 by Józef Andrzej Zaluski and his brother, Andrzej Stanis³aw Zaluski, both Roman Catholic bishops. The library was open to the public and indeed was the first Polish public library, the biggest in Poland and one of the earliest public libraries in Europe. In 1794, the library was looted on orders from Catherine II of Russia. Much of the material was returned in the period of 1842-1920, but once again the library was decimated during World War II during the period following the Warsaw Uprising. The Zaluski Library was succeeded by the creation of the National Library of Poland in 1928.

Australia

Library services in Australia developed along different paths in the different States. In 1809 the Reverend Samuel Marsden advertised in England for donations to help found a 'Lending Library for the general benefit of the inhabitants of New South Wales'.

The library would cover 'Divinity and Morals, History, Voyages and Travels, Agriculture in all its branches, Mineralogy and Practical Mechanics'. No Public Library came to fruition from this although some of the books brought to the colony after this call survive in the library of Moore Theological College.

The place of Public Libraries was filled by Mechanics' Institutes, schools of arts, athenaeums and literary institutes. Some of these provided free library services to visitors. However lending rights were available only to members who were required to pay a subscription. In 1856, the Victorian colonial government opened the Melbourne Public Library. This was however purely a reference library. In September 1869, the New South Wales (NSW) government opened as the Free Public Library, Sydney by purchasing a bankrupt subscription library. In 1896, the Brisbane Public Library was established. The Library's collection, purchased by the Queensland Government from the private collection of Mr. Justice Harding. In 1932, the Carnegie Corporation of New York, funded a survey into Australian libraries. It found 'wretched little institutes' which were 'cemeteries of old and forgotten books'.

There was also criticism of the limited public access, poor staff training, unsatisfactory collections, lack of non-fiction, absence of catalogues and poor levels of service for children. Lending libraries in Sydney and Prahran were praised as examples of services which were doing well, but these were seen as exceptions. In NSW, The Free Library Movement was established in response to the Munn-Pitt Report. This collection of concerned citizens, progress associations, returned servicemen and trade unions advocated a system of public libraries to serve the needs of all people. The birth of the movement took place at a public meeting in the Chatswood-Willoughby School of Arts, Sydney, in 1935. George Brain, President of the Middle Harbour Progress Association, ran the meeting.

George Brain initiated the resolution which brought the Free Library Movement into existence in NSW as well as the election of provisional office bearers, including himself as Honourary Secretary. This movement was stalled by the onset of World War II in 1939. In 1943, the Queensland Parliament passed the Libraries Act, establishing the Library Board of Queensland to manage the operations of the Public Library of Queensland, and coordinate and improve library facilities throughout the State of Queensland. In November 1943, at the official opening of the new Public Library of New South Wales building, William McKell, the New South Wales Premier, announced that the Library Act would be fully proclaimed from 1 January 1944. After the war, and with George Brain now in NSW parliament as a principle advocate for the Free Library Movement, the passing of Library Acts in NSW and the other states at the end of the war marked the beginning of modern public libraries in Australia.

Even after the war, the development of free lending libraries in Australia had been agonizingly slow: it was not until the 1960s that local governments began to establish public libraries in suburban areas. Currently there are 1402 Australian public libraries plus 78 mobile libraries. Australians generate more than 110 million library visits per year. There are more than 9.9 million library members more than 41.5 million items to use and borrow, plus more than 11,600 computers for public use. It costs $882.3 million to run Australian public libraries. They return at least $2.6 billion-worth of community benefits. All this costs Australians $830 million - just over 10c a day each with a benchmark for best practice funding being 20c per day.

The 2007 Americans for Libraries Council (ALC) report on library valuation stated, 'A benefit-to-cost ratio of 3:1 or better is common among the library valuation studies ALC reviewed. Because this type of economic analysis is commonly used across industries and businesses, it puts libraries into an evaluative framework that permits comparisons with other types of organizations. When this occurs, public libraries consistently outpace other sectors, such as transportation, health, and education, on the efficient use of tax dollars'.

FUNDING PROBLEMS

Most public libraries rely heavily on local government funding. Some proactive librarians have devised alliances with patron and civic groups to supplement their financial situations. Library "friends" groups, activist boards, and well organized book sales supplement government funding. With the cost of running local government increasing at a rate far above inflation, libraries are compelled to look beyond the tax base of the communities they serve. In the United States, among other countries, libraries in financially strapped communities compete financially with other public institutions, such as police, firefighters, and schools.

Many communities are closing down or reducing the capability of their library systems, at the same time balancing their budgets. Jackson County, Oregon, closed its entire 15-branch public library system for six months in 2007, reopening with a private-public 'partnership' and a reduced schedule. This example of a funding problem followed the failure to pass of a bond measure and cessation of federal funding for counties with dwindling timber revenue, in a state with no sales tax. In December 2004, Salinas, California almost became the first city in the United States to completely close down its entire library system. A tax increase passed by the voters in November 2005 allowed the libraries to open, but hours remain limited.

The American Library Association says media reports it has compiled in 2004 showed some $162 million in funding cuts to libraries nationwide. Survey data suggests the public values free public libraries. A Public Agenda survey in 2006 reported 84 per cent of the public said maintaining free library services should be a top priority for their local library. Public libraries received higher ratings for effectiveness than other local services such as parks and police. But the survey also found the public was mostly unaware of financial difficulties facing their libraries. Recently, many US cities, including Philadelphia, New York, Trenton and San Diego, have been facing the issue of making job cuts and service reductions in order to save money.

Most of these cities have decided to cut library funding by closing down several branches and cutting hours and staff members in the branches that will remain open. Philadelphia, however, has decided to keep their 54 branches open. In order to save money during this financial crisis, Mayor Michael Nutter has proposed to cut funding for recreational parks and decrease the budget for police and fire services. Nutter has announced that the Philadelphia public library branches will not be affected by the budget cuts at this time. In various cost-benefit studies libraries continue to provide an exceptional return on the dollar. A 2008 survey discusses comprehensively the prospects for increased funding in the United States, saying in conclusion "There is sufficient, but latent, support for increased library funding among the voting population." Public libraries, long supported by various government entities, have seen a decline in monetary support for several decades, due to various influences.

The American Library Association states that 41% of states saw a decline in state budgets for public library funding in 2009 Cases in point are the libraries in Salinas, California, Rochester, New York, and Buffalo, New York, but there are many other long-standing public libraries now having to find new sources of income to keep them operating.

- In California, the passage of Proposition 13 in 1978 removed the property tax as a source of funding for libraries, school programmes, and other public services. This action provided tax relief for homeowners on one hand, but forced severe budget cuts to the services they enjoyed.
- The cost of creating, maintaining, and upgrading electronic hardware, networks, and resources has put a strain on many library budgets.
- The cost of printed matter such as books and magazines has risen over time, while funding has remained static or declined.

DEVELOPMENT OF PUBLIC LIBRARIES IN INDIA

Public libraries arose worldwide along with growth in education, literacy, and publications. Every country has its own public library history with influential leaders. Monarchs, wealthy people, and philanthropists have all made a contribution to society in the form of public library development. India is no exception. Libraries were established in ancient India mainly by the patronage extended by emperors, major capitalists, and scholars. Indian emperors and kings were supported scholars and scholarship. There is evidence of well-developed libraries even in the sixth century A.D. The famous Nalanda University in Bihar had its own magnificent library with a massive collection of manuscripts covering the universe of knowledge. Admission to library was restricted to scholars.

Other ancient universities, such as Taxila and Vikramashila, also had valuable libraries. Muslim influence in India during the 13th century A.D. marked the dawn of another era of learning and scholarship. The Mughal period gave a further stimulus to the growth of libraries. Mughal rulers attached considerable importance to libraries and appointed scholars as librarians. The Mughal emperors were patrons of art and literature. In the period of Emperor Babur, Humayun, and Akbar many new libraries were established and existing ones further developed. Mughal libraries featured magnificent buildings, rare manuscripts, and scholar librarians.

The names of Maharaja Sawai Man Singh of Jaipur and Maharaja Ranjit Singh of Punjab will be remembered with appreciation in the history of library services in India. The Maharaja of Tanjuar started the famous Saraswati Mahal Library in 17th century A.D. It remains a unique institution in its nature of collection and services Libraries established by the kings and capitalists functioned like private institutions and the admission was limited. Service to the general public had to wait for the British. Unfortunately, the arrival of the British and resulting political disorder also brought chaos to the Indian way of life.

This was a severe blow to the cultural heritage of India, which had arisen from the Indus valley civilization. When libraries began developing in India during the early nineteenth century, they were a western product. In 1808, the Government of Bombay proposed to register libraries, which were to be given copies of books published from the "funds for the encouragement of literature". The "Sinha Committee", this was the beginning of the first phase of public library development in India. During the first half of the 19th century, the three presidency towns of Bombay, Calcutta, and Madras had public libraries. These libraries were mostly financed by Europeans residing in these towns. Of these, the establishment of the public library at Calcutta in 1835 was the most significant. This was the library which later developed into the National Library of India. Almost simultaneous, subscription libraries were started in many Indian cities.

These were, of course, not public libraries in the true sense of the term, and did not provide free books for all. Founded in imitation of their western counterparts, the use of these libraries was confined to small, affluent portion of society. The first three decades of the 20th century can be looked on as the golden age of the Indian library system. On January 31, 1902, the Imperial Library Act was passed and Lord Curzon transformed the Calcutta Public Library into the Imperial Library in 1906. Developments in Baroda were also notable.

The development of public libraries in Baroda was unique. Baroda developed a network of public libraries to serve the entire Princely State. Maharaja Sayaji Rao Gaekwad III of Baroda who traveled all over the world was deeply impressed by the role played by public libraries in the promotion of education in the United States and thought of extending such benefits to his own subjects. In 1910 he invited an American expert, William Alson Borden to organize the public library system for his state. The public library movement that flourished in Baroda was a glorious one. But that was not a general trend of that period because in no other part of India, a parallel development occurred.

Yet another development during the period was the organisation of a host of conferences such as:

- The first conference of library workers and persons interested in the library movement was held at Beswada, Andhra in 1914.
- The first All India Library Conference of Librarians was held in 1918 at Lahore.
- The first All India Library Conference was held at Calcutta in 1933.
- The first All India Public Library Conference was held at Madras in 1934.

With the existence of democratic governments in several provinces beginning in 1937, another phase of the library movement began. Between 1937 and 1942, a number of village libraries and travelling libraries sprang up in Assam, Bihar, Punjab, and Travancore. It was estimated that there were about 13,000 village libraries in India in 1942. Another remarkable development was the appointment of the 'Library Development Committee' by the Government of Bombay, with A.A.A. Fyzee as its chairman. The Committee ambitiously recommended a comprehensive library system to be implemented in three successive stages. Because of financial constraints, the government could only implement part of the recommendations.

After Independence

After independence, the growth of libraries in general has been remarkable, although not as remarkable as that of academic and special libraries. At the time of independence, India was facing a host of challenges. Those in the rural population, 88 per cent of the total, were nearly all illiterate. Transportation was poor and mass media merely nominal. Nevertheless, the public library scene in India improved considerably during the post independence period, though it is still lacking on several fronts.

Verma and Agrawal argue that to compare our public libraries with those of the developed nations on equal footing, we have to go a long way. The 1951 census, the first conducted after independence, found 2,843 local governments in the urban and rural areas in India, of which 320 were rural district boards.

Only about one third of local governments maintained public libraries, about 950. In addition, there were about 1,500 subscription libraries. So-called public libraries were primarily reading rooms with a few hundred books for reading on the premises. The Delhi public library deserves special mention. It was founded in 1951 as the first UNESCO Public Library Pilot Project under the joint auspices of UNESCO and Government of India.

The purpose of the library was to adapt "modern techniques to Indian conditions" and to serve as a model public library for Asia. The establishment of Delhi Public Library, the involvement of union government in the public library movement, and the enactment of public library legislation in some states are the main factors which contributed to the improvement of public libraries after independence. Although the government of India allotted funds for public library development in its five-year plans, this funding was not connected to effective planning.

Advisory Committee for Libraries

The Government of India appointed a committee in 1957 to report on the status of public library development in the country. It is also called the Sinha Committee, after its chair, the late Dr. A.P. Sinha, who was at that time Director of Public Instruction in Bihar.

The Sinha Committee's charge included:

- Determining present reading needs, how they are met, and what part existing library systems play in meeting the needs;
- Determining reading tastes, what agencies provide suitable literature, and how reading taste can be improved;
- Recommending future library structure in India;
- Recommending areas of cooperation between libraries and education systems;
- Considering the training of librarians and the conditions of their service;
- Recommending the administrative and financial measures necessary to support public libraries in India.

The committee submitted its report to Dr. K.L. Shrimali, who was Minister for Education, on the 12th of November, 1958. The Committee described the situation as dismal and called libraries in most cases, "a stagnant pool of books," because new books were not added regularly. The committee at the same time observed that wherever large collections did exist, they were not fully used because of rigid rules. Library users were not trusted and were required to deposit large sums of money as a kind of insurance, which lower income people could not afford.

As of March 1954 there were 32,000 libraries in India, with a little more than 7,100,000 books and a total circulation of about 37,700,000. The report observed that genuine public library service was rarity, and that public library service throughout the country was unsatisfactory. The committee recommended creating state library networks based on uniform library legislation.

The chief recommendations of the report were:

- Library service should be made free to every citizen of India;
- The hierarchy of public library service in the country should begin with National Library, and proceed to State Central Library, District Library, Block Library, and Panchayat Library;
- An independent Director of Social Education and Libraries should be set up in every state, with a fulltime senior class-1 officer of the rank of Deputy Director of Education to plan, organize, and administer library services;
- An All India Library Advisory Council should be constituted as a central agency to review and assess the work done at the state level;
- Library Associations should actively assist the development of libraries in the country;
- University libraries should cooperate with public library systems by allowing selected public readers to use their collection;
- State governments should accept responsibility for public library services in their states;
- Librarians and social education workers should cooperate to promote literacy;
- A library cess of six paisa for each rupee of property tax should be levied with the permission of local bodies.
- The Government of India should match the amount collected in the states. State governments should also give matching grants to local bodies over the succeeding 25 years, their contribution should be raised to three times the cess collected.
- State and national governments should enact comprehensive state library laws incorporating the right of every citizen to have free access to libraries. The Government of India should provide necessary financial assistance to the state governments for this purpose.

RAJA RAM MOHAN ROY LIBRARY FOUNDATION

Another positive step taken by the Central Government was the establishment of the Raja Ram Mohan Roy Library Foundation (RRRLF) at Calcutta on May 22, 1972, as a part of the bicentenary celebrations of the birth of Raja Ram Mohan Roy, a social reformer of the early 19th century.

Its objectives are library development in general and rural library development in particular. It provides financial assistance to public libraries in the form of matching grants. It assists State Central Libraries and District Central Libraries, which has helped many states and Union Territories develop rural public library services.

Main Objectives of RRRLF

The main objectives of RRRLF are:

- Promotion of the library movement in India;
- The adoption of a national library policy by the central and state governments;
- Development of a National Library System by integrating the services of National Libraries, State Central Libraries, District Libraries, and other types of libraries through an interlibrary lending system;
- Propagation and adoption of library legislation in the country;
- Provision of financial and technical assistance to libraries;
- Provision of financial assistance to voluntary organizations and library associations for the promotion of library development;
- Periodic publication of reports on library development;
- To act as a clearing house for ideas and information on library development in India and abroad;
- To advise the Government of India library development;
- Promotion of research in problems of library development

The primary objective of RRRLF is the promotion of the library movement. The rest are subsidiary objectives. RRRLF is the first government-sponsored body specifically created for this purpose.

The foundation also has a programme of assistance to libraries for workshops, conferences, and exhibits. The foundation has taken the major initiative for the formulation of a national policy on library and information systems by the Government of India.

The current programmes of assistance are:

- Collection building;
- Rural libraries and mobile library service for rural areas;
- Seminars, workshops, conferences, training courses, and exhibits;
- Facilities and equipment for storage and display of materials;
- Public library buildings;
- Television and VCR equipment for educational purposes;
- Assistance to voluntary organisations providing public library services;
- Assistance to children's libraries or children's sections of general public libraries

During the last three decades, the foundation has assisted more than 500 libraries, including many in rural areas

NATIONAL POLICY ON LIBRARY AND INFORMATION SYSTEM (NAPLIS)

In 1985, a committee was set up under the chairmanship of Prof. D.P. Chattopadhyay to formulate a National Policy on Library and Information System (NAPLIS). The Committee submitted its report in May 1986. Following that, another committee looked at implications of the report and created an action plan for its implementation. The Empowerment Committee submitted its report in April 1988 and an Implementation Cell was formed to implement its recommendations within a period of six months. Yet another Working Group, under the Joint Secretary to the Government of India in the Department of Culture, was constituted to examine its recommendations for implementation. The Working Group submitted its report in July 1993 and suggested implementing only 29 of 60 recommendations made by the NAPLIS.

The following are some of the recommendations of NAPLIS related to public libraries:

- Proposals for maintenance and development of public libraries should preferably come from State Legislative Enactment. The Central Government may revise the Model Public Library Bill. Funds for library development should come from each state, either from general revenue or from local taxation. Central Government agencies may provide funds under Plan Expenditure.
- Efforts should emphasize rural public libraries. A village or a cluster of villages with an adequate population should have a community library/rural community centre, which will also serve as an information centre. Resources from various agencies engaged in the public health, adult education, State and central government, etc., should be used to build up and maintain this centre.
- The central government increase its assistance to state governments in the development of public libraries. The RRRLF, as the national agency for coordinating and assisting the development of public libraries, should be suitably strengthened in order to do this.
- Standards and guidelines for library service should be created.
- There should be a system of national libraries consisting of National Library, Calcutta as the National Library of India, National Depository libraries in Delhi, Bombay, Madras, National Subject Libraries, and others. These national libraries should form part of one integrated system.
- A National Commission on Libraries and Information System or National Commission on Informatics and Documentation may be constituted by an Act of Parliament to serve under the Ministry of Human Resource Development. The Commission will have representation from appropriate central and state agencies and could

provide guidance and coordinate library development programmes in all sectors. This body will have the primary responsibility for the implementation of NAPLIS programmes.

- National Depository libraries; Connemara Public library, Chennai; Central Library, Bombay; and Delhi Public Library, Delhi should concentrate on development of collections and preservation of Indian culture produced in the languages of their regions, supplementing and complementing the efforts of the Indian National Library.
- The Indian National Bibliography should have a comprehensive coverage of the national output of documents and should be updated regularly. This responsibility should be vested in the National Library.
- Government should create a national awareness of the need to preserve the nation's cultural heritage. National libraries should be responsible, with preservation facilities created there. Links between libraries, archives, and museums should be established for the purpose of national preservation.
- The Ministry of Rural Development has a plan for one community centre in every Panchayat Centre. The Department of Culture and the Ministry of Rural Development have agreed to provide library services at each of these Rural Community Centres.
- An important link should be established between community centre library and primary schools. If the schools do not have libraries of their own, the community centre library should provide children with adequate services.
- A community centre library should have an important role in adult education programmes.
- A district library should provide facilities and recreation for the disabled and low-income people, *e.g.*, literature in Braille.
- Libraries should be built in areas of tribal concentration and in minority communities to help in developing and sustaining their distinctive cultures.
- Libraries should be equipped with relevant resources, such as publications covering Open University and vocational educational courses, for their role in support of distance education.
- All public libraries within a state should form a part of a network extending from village library through community centre library, district library, and state network, and should be linked to the national information grid.

1951-1956

- The first five-year plan for educational development included a proposal for "Improvement of Library Service." This proposal envisioned a network of libraries throughout the country, coordinated by National Central Library at New Delhi

- During the first five-year plan, nine state governments, *i.e.,* Assam, Madhya Pradesh, West Bengal, Punjab, PEPSU, Rajasthan, Savarashtra, Bhopal, and Vindhya Pradesh, decided to set up State Central Libraries.

1956-1961

- At this time, the government allocated funds to set up a national network of libraries in its 320 districts. As a result, most states established State Central Libraries and District Libraries as the main distributing centres

1961-1966

- During this period, the system of central government assistance to the states was changed, and funding for libraries was kept to a minimum. It was up to the individual states to take initiative and develop their public libraries. The programme to assist state governments in establishing state central libraries, district central libraries, and block development libraries was abandoned.
- The decision was a major setback to the development of public libraries. During this period four national libraries were established at Delhi, Calcutta, Bombay, and Madras. A Working Group on libraries was appointed by the Planning Commission in 1964 to take a stock of library development.

The working group submitted its report on 7th September 1965 with following recommendations:

- The central and state governments should share responsibility for providing adequate public library service. New government agencies in the central government under the Minister of Education, a directorate of libraries and a state library advisory council in each state should be set up to execute the programmes effectively.
- State central libraries should be established in four states: Madhya Pradesh, Mysore, Nagaland, and Orissa.
- States which do not possess adequate functional buildings for their state central libraries should be provided with library buildings.
- The state central library must have a children's section.
- There should be 335 District Libraries for the 327 districts in the country, *i.e.,* in large and populous districts, two district libraries may be provided.
- New buildings should be constructed for the existing 100 district libraries.
- Block libraries are the chief feeding centre for the rural reading public, and therefore, 2,500 new block libraries, covering 75% of blocks in the country should be constructed.

- A sum of 10 million rupees shall be provided for distribution of grant in aid to such libraries of urban and rural areas which depend on subscription and donations.
- Three public libraries on model of Delhi Public Library should be set up
- The Institute of Library Science established by the Ministry of Education at Delhi University in 1958-59, and then closed in 1962, should be reopened. Such institutes should be established at the state levels also to train graduate and undergraduate librarians to meet future requirements.
- A sum of ₹.10,000 shall be allocated as financial assistance to all national level and state level library associations to create library consciousness in the country by organizing seminars, conducting surveys, and producing library literature.
- A programme of book production should be undertaken.
- A draft of the Library Act should be produced

1969-1974

This plan proposed a substantial sum for the social education programme. A much lower sum was allocated. Of this, only a very small amount was available for the development of libraries in the country.

1974-1979

This plan included measures to strengthen the buildings, collections, and staff of the central and state libraries, as well as strengthening the district, block, and village libraries. During this period, attempts were made to develop a district-level library system, so that district library could act as a leader for the smaller libraries in the district. The adult education programme was the hallmark of this plan. The programme was to be supported by a network of libraries at the village and block levels and various community centres. Thus steps were taken to strengthen not only the village and block libraries, but also the central, state libraries and the district libraries

1980-85

This plan emphasized establishing a network of rural public libraries to sustain literacy and disseminate information to rural areas. It discussed the necessity of integrating school and college libraries with the system of public libraries. During this period, 26 states or union territories out of 31 had established state central libraries and 291 district libraries.

1985-90

During this period, the Commission's objective was to address the needs of 90 million people in the Adult Education Programme. The network of libraries was to play a role in the development of literature for neo-literates. Library systems were to be strengthened, with specific attention given to improvement of facilities at national level institutions. An important development was the 1986 adoption of National Literacy Mission, which emphasised the education of women and the establishment of rural libraries. In addition, the RRRLF set up an Integrated Research Cell-cum-Computer Unit for promoting research in librarianship and database of public libraries in the country There were two annual plans for the years 1990-91 and 1991-92.

1992-97

During this period it was proposed to reorganize the Central Reference Library into the National Bibliographical and Documentation Centre, which would also have a computer centre. The Delhi Public Library set up two new libraries in its service area. RRRLF created programmes to help state central libraries purchase reprographic equipment, to help libraries process rare books, and to give special assistance to networks of public libraries that were at least 100 years old.

1997-2002

During the 9th five year plan, the National Library, Kolkatta, undertook several major initiatives to upgrade and modernize its collection building programme, reader services, and conservation of library material. The major activities completed during the period were automation of the circulation system in the lending section, setting up of a local area network, improved reader services, and more efficient collection management. The conservation activities in the library got a major advance with the purchase of modern equipment to preserve rare books and other materials. The Central Reference Library, Kolkatta computerised various functions during the Ninth Plan.

As a result, the publication of the Indian National Bibliography is now up to date, with records available online. Funds were provided to the Delhi Public Library and Central Secretariat Library, Delhi, for acquisition of new material in different languages and media as well as for modernizing their infrastructure. The benefits of these efforts can be seen in improved reader services, networking, and resource sharing.

The Central Secretariat Library organized a number of computer training programmes for resource sharing, standardization of cataloguing formats, and co-operative acquisition. Funds for modernizing and computerization were also provided from central grants to the Connemara Library, Chennai, Thanjavur Maharaja Serovji Sarasvati Mahal Library, Thanjavur and the State Central Library, Mumbai. Besides these, the RRRLF provided assistance to public libraries across the country for collections and storage, construction, and seminars and workshops.

Tenth Five-year Plan (Action Plan)

The Planning Commission proposed further modernization of central and public libraries during the Tenth Plan. A national bibliographic database would be developed to encourage resource sharing, networking, and to improve reader services. The Commission resolved to strengthen public library infrastructure through the RRRLF. The Tenth Plan focused on upgrading existing libraries, including private collections, and widening the programme for bibliographic control and documentation. To make readers services more comprehensive and effective, the National Library is expected to act as the ultimate referral centre for various subjects. To keep pace with the latest developments in information technology in public libraries, the upgrading and networking of central and state libraries was also planned.

2

Assessing User Needs, Satisfaction, and Library

INTRODUCTION

The University of Washington Libraries has utilised a number of approaches during the past decade to assess the effectiveness of service programmes and library support of faculty and student research, teaching, and learning. Among the most valuable methods employed have been large-scale surveys of faculty and students conducted every three years beginning in 1992. Focus groups, usability and observational studies, targeted surveys, and interviews are also used to assess library programmes and services as well as user needs. Results from the triennial surveys have played a critical role in supporting the transition to a user-centred library and in creating a culture of assessment.

The large representative data sets generated by these surveys have also proven to be powerful information sources in the campus political environment. These surveys, though quite valuable, are expensive and time-consuming to design, administer, and analyse. Participation in the ARL-sponsored SERVQUAL pilot provided an opportunity to use a well- established survey tool with a different methodology, design, content, and delivery mechanism. It also afforded the chance for inter-institutional comparisons using a standardised survey instrument.

Another attractive feature was the ability to gain experience with a Web based survey that might reduce survey costs associated with printing, mailing, and data entry.

This chapter will compare the UW Libraries' surveys with LibQUAL+ results from the University of Washington in such areas as response and representativeness of survey population, similarities and differences in results, and whether the right questions are being asked.

USER SURVEYS

Library user surveys have become widespread in academic libraries during the past twenty years. Surveys have often been used as a tool to assess service quality and user satisfaction. The Association of Research Libraries issued four Systems and Procedures Exchange Centre (SPEC) kits on user surveys and studies between 1981 and 1994. A substantial body of litreature has been developed on surveys and service quality, led by studies and reviews from such library educators/professionals as Hernon and McClure; Van House, Weil and McClure; Hernon and Altman; Nitecki and Franklin; and Hernon and Whitman. Library applications of the SERVQUAL instrument have been covered by Nitecki, and Cook and Heath, among others. Rapid changes in library services and operations, demands for internal institutional accountability, and assessment expectations by external accrediting agencies have contributed to further development and application of user surveys within academic libraries during the past decade.

User surveys can be designed and administered in a number of ways. Self-administered surveys are often employed to reach a large number of potential respondents with a minimum of direct contact and cost. Individuals are given or sent surveys to complete and return and the responses turned into data that can be analysed. Surveys can range from broad and comprehensive to those narrowly focused on specific services or activities. When properly designed and administered, user surveys can provide both quantitative and qualitative data directly from the target population.

UNIVERSITY LIBRARIES' SURVEY OF WASHINGTON METHODOLOGY AND DESIGN

The University of Washington Libraries began an active programme of assessing user needs, satisfaction, and the impact of library services and resources in 1992. Prior to this time, user input to the UW Libraries was generally informal and unsolicited through such channels as suggestion boxes and anecdotal comments from service desks. Other opportunities for user comment came through the Faculty Senate Council on University Libraries, a biennial meeting between subject selectors and faculty liaisons on collections-related issues and some earlier in-library surveys that focussed on specific activities within the library unit.

The catalyst for the development of a broad-based survey of faculty and students came from the UW Libraries' first strategic plan in 1991 that called for a user-centered approach to services. Specifically, the strategic plan recommended that the libraries: "Develop and implement a study to identify user populations, their information needs and how well they are being met".

The Task Force on Library Services was appointed by the Director of Libraries in late 1991 to design and implement a user survey that would provide information on the following:

- Determine who users and potential users are;
- How and why the library is used;
- What sources are used for library-related information;
- What faculty and students' library-related needs are;

- How satisfied faculty and students are with the libraries.

The litreature on academic library user surveys available at the time of the early 1990s revealed a wide spectrum of applications and uses.

Some common characteristics of these surveys were:

- Distribution within the library to users was more prevalent than mailed surveys;
- Focus on physical use of the library;
- Concentration on specific services;
- Interest in user satisfaction.

The task force designed the initial survey in 1992 in consultation with library staff and the University's Office of Educational Assessment (OM). The decision was made early in the design process to survey all user groups, distribute the survey through the mail in order to reach potential non-users, and provide similar survey content for each group to enable comparisons.

The survey would be sent to all faculty and a random sample of graduate and undergraduate students. While distributing the survey to all faculty would increase costs, it would also facilitate survey promotion and publicity, obtain sufficient number of responses to do analysis by academic subject areas, and foster positive political outcomes. Survey questions were similar for faculty and graduate students, with about 75 per cent consistency between faculty and undergraduates. Adequate space was provided for survey respondents to write comments. Content evolved with each subsequent survey in 1995 and 1998, and some aspects of survey design changed. Rapid changes in library services and programmes during the 1990s and usefulness of the data provided by some questions were prime factors in survey revision.

However, there was a core group of questions in each survey that dealt with:

- Information sources needed for research, teaching, and learning;
- Reasons and frequency of library use;
- Campus computer network connectivity;
- Use of electronic resources;
- Instructional needs and effectiveness;
- Library unit use;
- Satisfaction;
- Services availability or satisfaction.

The initial survey in 1992 was pilot tested in March with a group of faculty and students, revised, and then mailed mid-way through the Spring quarter to 3,900 faculty and a random, non-stratified, sample of 1,000 graduate and 1,000 undergraduate students. An incentive was offered to students who returned completed survey forms. Two weeks after the initial surveys were mailed, students were sent a second survey form, while faculty were sent a reminder notice. Completed surveys were returned to the Office of Educational Assessment (OEA) who arranged for data entry. Data were made available in SPSS format and results were available in early September 1992. Subsequent surveys in 1995 and 1998 generally employed a similar methodology and design. Survey design work began in January of each year, pilot testing took place in March, and surveys were mailed in late April to early May.

The undergraduate sample was increased to 2,000 for 1995 and 1998, and the 1998 survey also included a specialised set of questions for faculty and graduate students in the biological and health sciences, and one for faculty and students in the fine arts. Focus groups were also held prior to the 1998 survey to provide input from users on their perception of issues and concerns.

The bookstore gift certificate drawing was extended to all groups beginning with the 1995 survey. Reminder notices were sent in 1995 but not a follow-up survey form. In 1998, a survey accompanied the reminder letter. Both the cover letter and survey form included the name, phone number, and e-mail address of a librarian as a contact person for questions or clarification.

The few questions received generally requested another survey be sent to replace a lost one. Sending this type of survey to nearly 7,000 faculty and students is not inexpensive. Direct survey costs in 1998 totaled $19,000, about $7 per returned survey. Survey costs in 1992 and 1995 were about $12,000.

The 1998 costs were distributed in the following manner:

- Printing 30 per cent
- Mailing 30 per cent.
- Data entry 30 per cent
- Other 10 per cent

Staff time for the 1998 survey was estimated at approximately 500 hours, including analysis and reporting.

LIBQUAL+

The UW Libraries was one of twelve libraries that participated in the ARL-sponsored LibQUAL+ pilot administered in Spring 2000. Survey design and methodology were handled primarily by a team from Texas A&M where a SERVQUAL based library survey had been used several times. In addition to the twenty-two basic SERVQUAL questions which covered the standard dimensions of accountability, assurance, reliability, responsiveness, and tangibles, nineteen additional questions were added to test two additional dimensions: access to collections and the library as place.

Thus, there were forty one questions that used the SERVQUAL three-column response format of minimum, perceived, and desired. Another fourteen behavioural questions, two on frequency of library use, and an overall service quality question were also added which used just one response column. The survey also collected demographic data. The survey team at Texas A&M determined that the survey be administered to a random sample of 600 faculty, 600 graduate students, and 900 undergraduates at each institution based on an anticipated return of 200 surveys from each group. The UW Office of

Educational Assessment extracted the sample from the faculty and student databases, and e-mail ad- dress lists created for each group were sent to the UW Libraries.

The UW Libraries systems office created separate mailing lists for each group. A cover letter from the director of the UW Libraries was sent by e-mail to each participant. The letter included information about the survey and the university's reasons for participation, and also provided a URL address where respondents could complete the survey. The initial message was sent May 2 and a reminder notice was sent on May 11.Almost immediately after the initial e-mail notification was sent, there was a steady stream of messages back to the director and the local survey coordinator.

LibQUAL+ implementation at the University of Washington ultimately generated more than fifty e-mail messages, most coming from faculty members. The messages fell into two basic groups: technical problems trying to complete the survey, and comments, usually negative, on survey design and content. Direct expenses were $2,000 for the UW Libraries paid as a participant in the ARL project. This worked out to be about $5 per completed survey. Library staff contributed about 150 hours to the project, including responding to e-mail messages, analysis, and report writing.

SURVEY RESPONSE AND REPRESENTATIVES

Survey return rates for the 1992, 1995, and 1998 UW Libraries' surveys and the 2000 LibQUAL+ survey are shown in table.

Table. Surveys Distributed and Returned

Survey		Faculty		Graduate Students			Undergraduates		
Year	Sent	Returned	Rate	Sent	Returned	Rate	Sent	Returned	Rate
2000	600	128	21.3 %	600	131	21.8 %	900	137	15.2 %
1998	3750	1503	40.1 %	1000	457	45.7 %	2000	787	39.4 %
1995	4400	1359	28.4 %	1000	409	40.9 %	2000	489	24.5 %
1992	3900	1108	28.4 %	1000	561	56.1 %	1000	422	42.2 %

A second survey mailing appeared effective in raising the response rate as seen in the 1992 return rates for students and for all groups in 1998. The number of faculty surveyed varied according to criteria used to define the faculty pool, but all surveys included tenure track and research faculty as well as full-time lecturers.

The overall response rate as shown is slightly understated as undeliverable surveys were not subtracted from the total sent out. Undeliverable survey rates ranged from approximately.5 per cent of faculty to 2 per cent of undergraduate students. Response rates to the LibQUALt survey were substantially lower.

The definition of faculty was the same as used in the UW Libraries' 1998 survey. LibQUALt response rates were calculated by matching the number of completed surveys against the number of e-mail addresses to which the survey message was sent. Approximately 1percent of these messages were undeliverable.

REPRESENTATIUENESS OF SURVEY RESPONDENTS

The large number of responses to the UW Libraries' surveys generated correspondingly large data sets, especially for the faculty survey.

Table. Faculty Population and Respondents by Academic Area, 1998 and 2000 In Percentage

Academic Area	2000 LibQUAL+ Respondents n=128	1998 Faculty Population n=3750	1998 Survey Respondents n=1503
Health Sciences	43.0	48.6	44.7
Sciences/Engineering	25.8	26.2	27.1
Humanities/Arts/ Social Sciences	31.2	21.0	24.4
Other (non- Health Sciences)		4.2	3.8

As table shows, the faculty survey respondent population in 1998 was reasonably representative of the population as a whole when grouped by broad subject areas. Faculty in the Health Sciences were slightly underrepresented, while those in the Humanities/Social Sciences/Fine Arts group were somewhat over-represented compared to the actual population. Response rates by academic schools ranged from 31 per cent in Business to 54 per cent in the Social Science departments within the College of Arts and Sciences. Graduate student responses were similar to the faculty with Health Sciences respondents again lower than their percentage of the actual population while those from Humanities/Arts/Social Sciences were slightly higher.

Response rates by academic schools ranged from 24 per cent in Dentistry and 28 per cent in Education to 62 per cent in Nursing and '72 per cent in Social Sciences. Health Sciences does have a larger proportion of faculty and graduate/ professional students located away from the main UW campus, and this may be a factor in the under representation of respondents from those areas.

Table. Graduate/Professional Student Population and Survey Respondents by Academic Area In Percentage

Academic Area	2000LibQUAL+ n=131	1998 Graduate Population n=8183•	1998 Survey Respondents n=457
Health Sciences	22.1	30.4	26.0
Sciences/Engineering	28.20	29.4	30.2
Humanities/Arts/ Social Sciences	45.0	40.3	43.8
Other (non- Health Sciences)	4.6		

Note:

*Law was not included in the 1998 survey, 1998 graduate population with Law is 8,785, Law is 69. per cent to total.

Determining how representative undergraduate respondents are is more complicated. Undergraduates in earlier UW Libraries' surveys appeared to identify with certain academic majors before they were actually accepted into those programmes, thus skewing responses by academic areas. Year in school appeared to be a more reliable measure. Table shows undergraduate population and respondent population by year in school. Again, the respondent population is reasonably similar to the entire population. Freshmen were somewhat underrepresented in the 1998 survey and sophomores underrepresented in the LibQUAL+ survey.

Table. Undergraduate Student Population and Survey Respondents by Year In Percentage

Class	2000LibQUAL+ n=137	1998 Undergraduate Population n=23413	1998 Undergraduate Respondents n=787
Freshman	22.6	19.0	14.4
Sophomore	13.9	18.3	17.0
Junior	27.7	26.3	26.9
Senior	35.8	32.9	33.9
Other (including 5th Year		3.4	7.8

Compared to the population as a whole, and UW survey respondents in 1998, the LibQUALt respondent pools, although significantly smaller than those generated by UW surveys, appear reasonably representative when grouped by broad academic areas for faculty and graduate students, and by class for undergraduates.

The under representation of Health Sciences and overrepresentation by those in the Social Sciences mirrors the respondent population achieved in the large-scale UW Libraries' surveys. This is probably reflective of the way faculty and students in these areas use libraries as well as the larger proportion of the Health Sciences population located away from the main Seattle campus.

SURVEY RESULTS

Results from the UW Libraries' surveys provide an effective record of changes in the way that students and faculty used library and information resources during the 1990s. These results also documented significant variations within groups and between groups in some areas. Information from these surveys has been used extensively by the University of Washington Libraries to revise existing programmes and services and promote new ones.

Survey results showed:

- High satisfaction levels;
- A shift towards remote use and increased importance of electronic re- sources;

- Continuing importance of libraries as place for students;
- Increased complexity of finding and using information for teaching, learning, and research.

Although the University of Washington Libraries' surveys and the LibQUAL+ survey differs substantially in design and content, it is interesting to compare results where questions were similar.

The large respondent pool for the 1998 UW Libraries survey can serve as a benchmark for viewing the LibQUALt results based on a much smaller sample. For example, UW Libraries' surveys results revealed that faculty generally viewed the libraries through a collections-related focus, while undergraduate students placed a high value on the library as a place.

Even though the questions and design in these surveys differ, would LibQUAL+ results also show similar responses? Results from the UW Libraries' survey in 1998 and the LibQUALt survey in 2000 will be compared in the areas of overall satisfaction, opening hours, collections importance, the library as a place, and remote use of library services and resources. These areas are often barometers of service quality.

OVERALL SATISFACTION

Responses to overall library satisfaction questions on the 1998 survey showed faculty had the highest satisfaction while undergraduate students the lowest.

Table. Overall Satisfaction: UW Libraries 1998 Survey and Libqual+ 2000 Survey by Group In Percentage

Level	Libqual+ Faculty	1998 Faculty	Libqual+ Grad Students	1998 Grad Students	Libqual+ Undergrads	1998 Undergrads
Very satisfied	78.0%	91.3%	80.9%	84.9%	72.9%	78.5%
Satisfied	21.2%	7.8%	18.3%	13.5%	24.0%	19.9%
Not satisfied	0.8%	0.9%	0.8%	1.6%	3.1%	1.6%
Mean Score	7.17	4.33	7.13	4.11	6.88	3.99

The LibQUAL+ survey phrased the questions as overall quality of services but still produced similar results although the difference in Likert scales can lead to a different type of response. For LibQUALt, the differences between undergraduate scores and graduate and faculty ones were significant at the.10 level using t-tests.

LIBRARY HOURS

The 1998 survey asked whether libraries were open when needed on evenings, weekends, summer, and interim periods. Graduate students had the lowest satisfaction with hours while faculty had the highest, as shown in figure. Undergraduate student satisfaction had slipped from 1995 when it was similar to faculty satisfaction.

When asked to choose from a list of priorities, more than 37 per cent of graduate students and 42 per cent of undergraduates chose increased library hours as a priority compared to 17 per cent of faculty. Graduate students also wrote more comments about hours than any other group. The LibQUAL+ question was concerned about expectations and perceived level of service related to whether the library had convenient business hours.

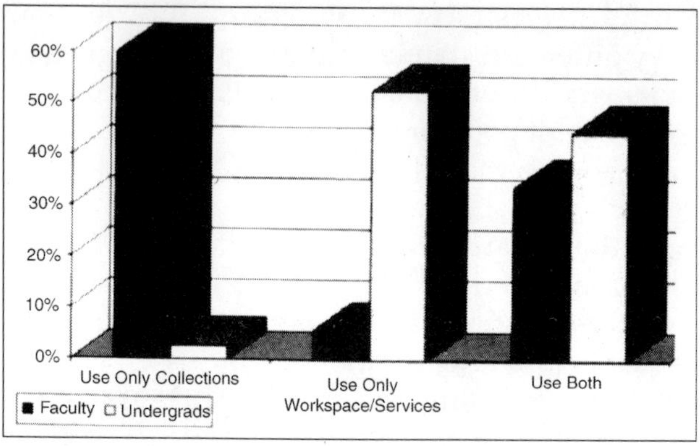

Table. LibQUAL+ Convenient Business Hours

	Faculty Minimum	Faculty Perceived	Grad Minimum	Grad Perceived	Undergrad Minimum	Undergrad Perceived
Convenient Business Hours	6.45	6.56 (.11)	6.68	6.63 (-.05)	6.50	7.13 (.63)

As table shows, graduate student minimum expectations for convenient business hours exceeded their perception of library performance. Faculty minimum expectations were lower, and the gap between expectations and performance, while small, was positive. Undergraduate students had both the highest perceived value and most positive gap. One likely reason for this positive response in LibQUAL+ was the Undergraduate Library's move to 24 hour opening in autumn 1998.

COLLECTIONS

A valuable part of each one of the UW Libraries' surveys is asking users to identify their library priorities from a list of ten to twelve choices. The list of potential priorities is compiled from comments provided on the pretests as well as areas the libraries are interested in. The first survey in 1992 showed that all three groups had the same priorities in their top three choices, while in 1998 the top three priorities for undergraduates were different than those for graduate students and faculty. Faculty, in particular, showed an almost exclusive focus on collections/information resources-related areas as shown in table.

Table. 1998 Survey: Library Priorities by Group In Percentage

	Faculty	Graduate Students	Under-graduates
Maintain quality of print collections	69.6%	52.3%	28.2%
Deliver full-text to your computer	60.4%	55.8%	34.4%
Deliver bib databases through the web	52.1%	40.0%	17.7%
Provide reserves electronically	18.8%	36.6%	50.8%

Add more computers in the library	8.6%	20.1%	54.5%
Provide training in use of web/ library resources	28.3%	27.4%	47.5%
Increase library hours	17.0%	37.5%	41.9%
Preserve library materials	40.0%	34.9%	24.7%
Add group study/seminar rooms			35.5%
Provide consulation on how to do library research		13.3%	39.8%

The LibQUAL+ survey reinforced the primacy of collections and information resources for faculty. This was the only area where faculty had negative gap scores. Faculty minimum expectations were generally higher as well. Graduate student results also showed high expectations for collections-related questions and negative gaps for full-text delivered electronically and complete journal runs. Undergraduate students had lower expectations and positive gaps in all collections related areas. Reviewing mean scores for six collections-related questions on LibQUAL+ showed higher mean scores for faculty and graduate students in minimum expectations.

Table. LibQUAL+ Collections Expectations/Perceptions

Question		Faculty Minimum	Faculty Perceived	Grad Minimum	Grad Perceived	Undergrad Minimum	Undergrad Perceived
10.	Resources added on request	4.23	6.10 (-.13)	6.04	6.27 (.23)	5.97	6.37 (.40)
17.	Timely document delivery/IIL,	6.41	6.82 (.41)	6.61	7.22 (.61)	6.31	6.88 (.57)
23.	Full text delivered electronically	6.32	5.84 (-.48)	6.20	6.16 (.04)	5.96	6.24 (.28)
27.	Comprehensive print collections	6.30	6.64 (.34)	6.65	6.65 (.02)	6.14	6.98 (.84)
36.	Interdisciplinary needs addressed	6.89	6.44 (.55)	6.24	6.55 (.31)	6.05	6.65 (.60)
37.	Complete journal	6.52	6.40 (-.12)	6.77	6.58 (-.19)	6.22	6.61 (.39)

However, the differences between undergrads and faculty were not significant at the.05 or.10 level according to t-tests. There were differences at the.05 level between grad students and undergraduates in complete runs of journal titles and comprehensive print collections, and at the.10 level for timely document delivery and interlibrary loan.

LIBRARY AS PLACE

A consistent theme revealed through each of the UW Libraries' surveys has been the different perspectives of faculty and students on the library as a place. Faculty use of the library is primarily collections driven, while students view the library as a place to do work, including finding and using information resources.

This difference shows up dramatically in responses to a 1998 survey question on reasons for visiting the library as well as other questions dealing with priorities and needed services. LibQUAL, clearly showed similar differences between faculty and students on the library as a place.

Table. LibQUAL+ Library as Place

Question		Faculty Minimum	Faculty Perceived	Grad Minimum	Grad Perceived	Undergrad Minimum	Undergrad Perceived
14.	Comfortable and inviting location	6.08	6.12 (1.04)	5.72	6.12 (.40)	5.98	6.73 (.75)
21.	Secure and safe place	6.77	7.51 (.74)	6.81	7.26 (.45)	6.80	7.23 (.43)
22.	Center for intellectual interaction	5.61	5.31 (1.15)	5.20	5.97 (.59)	5.75	6.24 (.49)
29.	Space for group/individual study	5.57	5.94 (1.34)	5.90	6.07 (.17)	6.20	6.78 (.58)
30.	Haven for quiet and solitude	4.74	6.02 (1.28)	6.12	6.08 (-.04)	6.53	6.46 (-.07)
40.	Space that facilitates quiet study	4.69	5.75 (1.06)	6.23	6.30 (.07)	6.52	6.62 (.10)

On seven questions related to the library as place, the differences in minimum expectations were significant at the 0.01 level except for 'safe and secure space.' With the exception of 'secure and safe space," faculty minimum expectations were generally below 5 and gaps between minimum and perceived were larger than 1.O. While graduate student expectations were higher than those of faculty, they were still lower than those of undergraduates. Both student groups were concerned about quiet study areas.

REMOTE USE

The 1995 UW Libraries' survey revealed for the first time that more were' going so remotely than physically visiting the library. This trend continued in 1998, and table shows degrees of remote use among all groups both in the 1998 survey and LibQUAL+.

Table. Type and Frequency of Library Use among Faculty and Students who Use Library at Least Weekly In Percentage

Type of Library Use	Visit in Person	Visit Remotely Using Computer
LibQUAL+ Faculty	54.5%	81.1%
1998 Faculty	47.3%	73.4%
LibQUAL+ 1998 Grad	77.0%	80.2%
1998 Grad	77.9%	66.1%
LibQUAL+ Undergrad	66.7%	48.8%
1998 Undergrad	70.3%	45.5%

Responses to other survey questions in 1998 revealed that more than 97 percent of faculty had access to the Web through a desktop computer. While remote use is not itself a measure of service quality, this information is critical for planning and delivering electronic services and resources. In general, LibQUAL+ results tended to correlate with results from the libraries' surveys which had a much larger number of respondents for each group, especially faculty. Differences between groups, especially faculty and undergraduates, that were evident in earlier UW Libraries' surveys, were also found in the LibQUAL+ results.

SUB-GROUP ANALYSIS

One of the benefits of a large respondent pool is the ability to do analysis on differences within the group. While there may be a set of similar characteristics that define a group, there may also be significant variation within that group. Academic user communities are not homogeneous in the way they use libraries nor in their needs for library resources and services. In addition to differences between faculty and students, there may also be significant differences between those in different academic areas or by gender or some other demographic component.

These have important implications for identifying user needs, concerns, and issues that may be missed in analysing aggregate results. The number of respondents to the UW Libraries' 1998 survey, especially for faculty, was sufficiently large to examine the degree of variation within the group and between subject areas. The sample size and response rates of the LibQUAL+ survey generally precluded analysis by academic area and made it difficult to find differences among demographic characteristics. Increasing the LibQUAL+ sample size and the response rate would provide larger data sets that could be used to examine variation within and between groups.

Factors related to the low response rate for LibQUALt include survey length, complexity, perceived redundancy, technical problems, behavioural issues associated with Web-based surveys, and how related survey content is to actual library use and issues of the respondent. While the LibQUAL+ sample appears representative of each group as a whole, it is not large enough to perform sub- group analysis. How important is it to have a respondent pool large enough to do analysis at the subgroup level? UW Libraries' surveys have consistently shown significant differences in how faculty from different academic areas use libraries and in their needs for library resources and services.

They also show surprising uniformity in areas such as connectivity arid remote use where differences might be expected based on traditional use patterns. Although graduate student response numbers are lower, they were similar to faculty in the same academic areas. Satisfaction responses, while showing some variation, generally do not differ significantly by academic area. Priorities, on the other hand, clearly do as shown in figure.

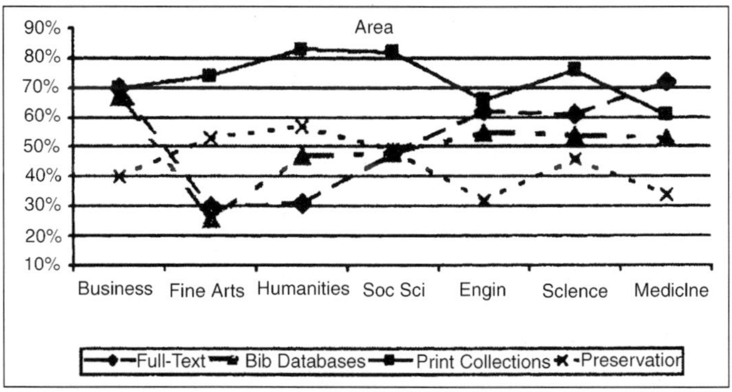

Fig. 1998 Survey. Faculty Top Priorities by Academic Area

The 1998 results showed significant variation among academic areas in the top four overall priorities, especially for de- livery of full text to the desktop and preservation. Variation within undergraduate responses to the UW Libraries' 1998 survey were more difficult to determine. There were some gender differences, especially in areas related to computer access and library instruction as well as differences by class year.

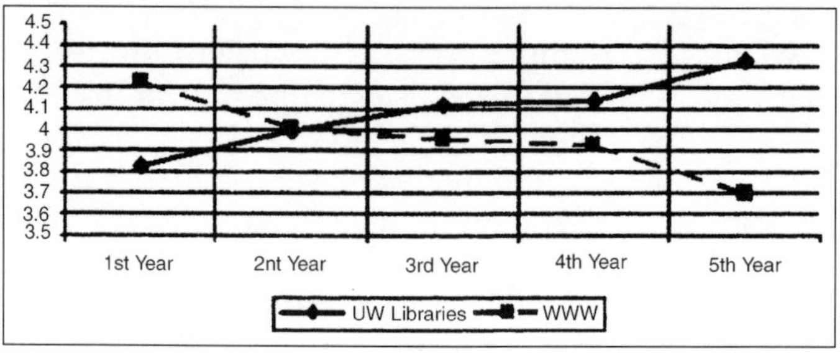

Fig. 1998 Survey. Importance of World Wide Web and UW Libraries by Undergraduate Class (Scale of 1 not important to very important)

Figure shows the importance of UW Libraries and the World Wide Web to the work of undergraduates by year in school. The differences between first year and upper division students were significant at the.05 level using a simple t-test. However, LibQUALt survey results did not show any statistical differences in responses either by gender or class year.

The importance of different resource types such as journals, books, bibliographic databases, and foreign language materials also showed significant variation between academic areas. When asked to rank these resource types on a scale of 1 to 5, faculty in all academic areas ranked journals as very important. A large number of responses also enables analysis within smaller sub- groups. For example, the 1998 faculty survey had 241 responses from those in science departments.

Table. 1998 Survey (Faculty). Importance of Resource Types

Department (Responses)	Books	Journals > 1980	Journals < 1980	Bibliographic Databases
Chemistry (36)•	4.28	4.83	3.92	4.39
Geology-Geophysics* (22)	4.54	4.91	4.27	4.18
Math-Stat (37)*•	4.89	4.89	4.57	3.51
Physics (39)•	4.21	4.56	4.08	3.69
Psychology (24)	4.13	5.00	3.75	4.42
Zoology (27)	4.11	5.00	4.30	4.63
All Science (241)	4.26	4.76	4.09	4.05

Table shows mean scores by department on responses to questions dealing with type and frequency of library use and importance of resource types. Only departments with at least twenty responses were included. While current journals are important to all groups, the importance of books, earlier journals, and bibliographic databases showed variation within each group. Understanding the importance of these resource types to different subject areas is useful in allocating the collection-development budget as well as making decisions on what materials to house on-site or in storage. There were also significant differences in the frequency of physical visits to the library by science faculty. Perhaps it is not surprising that distance from the library appeared to play an important role. Not only did the departments located closest to their primary library visit those libraries more often, the frequency of their physical visits exceeded the frequency of library use from an office computer.

A comparison between large-scale user surveys done by the UW Libraries and the LibQUALt survey administered to UW faculty and students shows good agreement in population representation and in broad result categories at the group level. However, the ability to do subgroup and intra group analysis can provide valuable results and efforts to increase the number of responses if the Web based LibQUAL+ survey should continue.

ASKING THE RIGHT QUESTIONS

Whether the survey results are statistically reliable, representative, valid, or significant, doesn't necessarily mean that they provide information that can be used to assess and improve library service quality. It is also important to examine whether these surveys are asking the right questions in the right way to the right group. Survey design is a complex and evolving process that requires substantial interaction between the surveying group and the surveyed population. At many large academic research institutions, user communities are diverse and differ in their needs for library resources and services.

It is essential to recognise that these differences exist when designing and administering surveys. Undergraduate students, based on their understanding or experience, may respond quite differently from faculty to some questions, making it difficult to do cross group comparisons. It is also important to remember that surveys are just one method of acquiring user input. While surveys offer the prospect of obtaining quantifiable data from large populations at reasonable costs, they need to be employed in the right situation. Surveys should be de- signed from the user perspective. Questions should be short, simple, and clear to the user. Complex issues may be better addressed using other techniques.

There should be sufficient motivation for faculty and students to take the time to complete a survey. The evolution of SERVQUAL to LibQUALt is a positive step. The ability to move away from the twenty-two question SEKVQUAL core pack- age to a design that provides a library focus, and perhaps a simpler format, is welcome. Grounding the survey based on user-provided information on library needs and use is critical to maintain currency and relevancy. Such qualitative data obtained at regular intervals enables the library to keep on top of user issues and concerns.

The library and information environment is changing rapidly. The continued growth in remote use of library services and resources and in user self-sufficiency calls for new ways to measure user needs and library performance that can be done quickly, inexpensively, and flexibly enough to catch environ- mental changes. The ARL New Measures Initiative plans to provide libraries with tested tools that can help provide information that will assist in meeting these challenges. The underlying concept of developing a standard instrument to mea- sure service quality across libraries is a powerful one and certainly one deserving institutional support.

However, it cannot supplant local efforts to work closely with faculty and students to assess user needs and library collections and services. There are local issues at each institution that probably cannot be effectively addressed in a standardised survey tool. The University of Washington Libraries expects to continue both its participation in LibQUALt as well as utilising a variety of ways to assess user needs and library performance, including the deployment of locally based large-scale user surveys.

3

Library Automation and its Impact on Strategic Planning

HRD ASPECTS OF LIBRARY AUTOMATION IN COLLEGE LIBRARIES OF GUWAHATI

Guwahati is the gateway of North East and capital city of Assam. It is an ancient city having mentioned in Mahabharata and Purans. Of course in those days it was known as Pragjyotishpur and Kamrup. It has been a glorious city since, old days.

It was famous for astrological studies besides the regular studies in education and philosophy. It is covered by 340 sq km in area with a population of about 11 lakks. With the passage of time, the city is also trying to develop its educational scenario by adopting the latest techniques in this field as far as possible. However, due to different factors, such as geographical isolation, political situation, insurgency problem there has not been much improvement as compared to other cities of India.

COLLEGE OF GUWAHATI CITY

At present the city of Guwahati has a total number of 20 colleges including deficit and non-deficit colleges. Besides there are a good number of junior colleges, law colleges, B.Ed. colleges, technical colleges, which has not been taken into consideration in this study. The colleges under study are shown below which are arranged according to their year of establishment. From the table, it is seen that some colleges are very old while some are newly established. Cotton College established in 1901 is the oldest while West Guwahati Commerce College was established in the year 1992. Out of 20 colleges, 6 college libraries are named on the great legendary of Assam.

Table. Name of College Library with Year of Establishment

S. No.	Name of College	Year of Estd.	Name of Library
1.	Cotton College Library	1901	Dr Surya Kumar Bhuyan

2.	Handique Girls' College Library	1938	Handique Girls' College
3.	B.Borooah College	1943	Hem Barua Library
4.	Pragjyotish College Library	1954	Pandit Tirthanath Sarma
5.	Arya Vidyapith College Library	1958	Arya Vidyapith College
6.	K K Handiqui Sanskrit College	1960	K K Handiqui Sanskrit College Library
7.	Gauhati Commerce College	1962	Dr Brinchi Kumar Baruah Library
8.	Pandu College	1962	Pandu College Library
9.	North Guwahati College Library	1962	North Guwahati College
10.	Gauhati College Library	1964	Surabala Bardoloi Memorial
11.	Lalit Chandra Bharali College	1971	Lalit Chandra Bharali College Library
12.	KRB Girls' College	1971	KRB Girls' College Library
13.	Kanya Mahavidyalaya Library	1977	Kanya Mahavidyalaya
14.	R G Baruah College	1978	R G Baruah College Library
15.	Dispur College	1978	Dispur College Library
16.	K C Das Commerce College	1983	K C Das Commerce College Library
17.	S B Deorah College	1986	S B Deorah College Library
18.	Karmashree Hiteswar Saikia College	1988	Dandeswar Gogoi Memorial Library
19.	Narengi Anchalik Mahavidyalaya	1991	Narengi Anchalik Mahavidyalaya Library
20.	West Guwahati Commerce College	1992	West Guwahati Commerce College Library

The colleges of Guwahati city are offering all the Stream of Gauhati University, *i.e.*, arts, science and commerce.

Collection of the Libraries

Collections of any type of library reflect the types of services offered by the library to its reader. A balance collection selected on a judicious basis is a must to offer the appropriate service by the library. The college libraries have to acquire a wide variety of learning materials both in printed and non-printed forms.

The table shows the collection of different college libraries of Guwahati. It reveals that the collection of Cotton College has highest collection and

Karmashree Hiteswar Saikia College has the least collection. The table further reveals that 5 colleges are having CD-ROMs, DVD-ROMs, VCD, etc.

Table. Collections

S. No.	Name of College	Collections		
		Printed	Non-Printed	Total
1.	Cotton College	119114	–	119114
2.	Handique Girls' College	38000	–	38000
3.	B.Borooah College	37000	20	37020
4.	Pragjyotish College	52100	–	52100
5.	Arya Vidyapith College	41065	45	41110
6.	K K Handiqui Sanskrit College	8680	–	8680
7.	Gauhati Commerce College	38499	–	38499
8.	Pandu College	35625	216	35841
9.	North Guwahati College	25897	–	25897
10.	Gauhati College	32000	–	32000
11.	L C B College	12800	–	12800
12.	KRB Girls' College	6935	–	6935
13.	Kanya Mahavidyalaya	16271	–	16271
14.	R G Baruah College	8684	–	8684
15.	Dispur College	10000	–	10000
16.	K C Das Commerce College	11500	120	11620
17.	S B Deorah College	6500	25	6525
18.	Karmashree Hiteswar Saikia College	2540	–	2540
19.	Narengi Anchalik Mahavidyalaya	4200	–	4200
20.	West Guwahati Commerce College	3820	–	3820

LIBRARY SERVICES

The colleges under the studies are having library facilities of different levels. The traditional services such as issue and return and reference service being common to most of the colleges a few of them are initiating the library automation to provide different modern information services to the users. The table reveals the different services being offered by the colleges of Guwahati.

LIBRARY AUTOMATION

Library Automation may be defined in simple sense as a process of mechanisation of library operations, which are of routine and repetitive in nature. This covers usually all the housekeeping operations, acquisition, serial control, cataloguing, circulation, reference, etc. Library Automation is a process that brought and will continue to bring profound changes to the library world, in terms of both technology and the involvement of people. Library automation refers to the processing of routine clerical function of the library with the assistance of computer or other mechanised or automation equipments. Actually it is nothing but the application of computer to the library operation.

Table. Services of College Libraries

1.	Arya Vidyapith College	Yes	Yes	Yes	–	–	–	–	Yes
2.	B. Borocah College	Yes	Yes	Yes	Yes	–	–	–	Yes
3.	Cotton College	Yes	Yes	Yes	Yes	Bibl	–	–	Yes
4.	Dispur College	Yes	Yes	Yes	–	–	–	–	Yes
5.	Guwahati College	–	Yes	Yes	Yes	–	–	–	Yes
6.	Guwahati Commece College	–	Yes	Yes	–	–	–	–	Yes
7.	Handique Girls' College	Yes	Yes	Yes	–	–	–	Yes	Yes
8.	K C Das Commerce College	Yes	Yes	Yes	Yes	Bibl, Ind, Abs, Book, Bk	–	–	–
9.	K K Handiqui Sanskrit College	Yes	Yes	Yes	–	–	–	–	Yes
10.	Kanya Mahavidyalaya	–	Yes	–	–	–	–	–	–
11.	Karmashree Hiteswar Saikia College	–	Yes	Yes	–	–	–	–	–
12.	KRB Girls' College	–	Yes	Yes	–	–	–	–	Yes
13.	Lalit Chandra Bharali College	–	Yes	Yes	–	–	–	–	Yes
14.	Narengi Anchalik Mahavidyalaya	–	Yes	Yes	–	–	–	–	–
15.	North Guwahati College	Yes	Yes	Yes	–	–	–	–	Yes
16.	Pandu College	Yes	Yes	Yes	Yes	Bibl	Yes	Yes	Yes
17.	Pragjyotish College	Yes	Yes	Yes	–	Book bk	–	–	Yes
18.	R G Baruah College	–	Yes	Yes	–	–	–	–	–
19.	S B Deorah College	Yes	Yes	Yes	Yes	–	Yes	Yes	Yes
20.	West Guwahati Commerce College	–	Yes	–	–	–	–	–	–

Table. Automation Status of Libraries

S. No.	Name of College	Fully Automated	Partiallty Automated	Not Automated	Year of Automation
1.	Arya Vidyapith College	–	Yes	–	2007
2.	B. Borooah College	Yes	–	–	2002
3.	Cotton College	–	Yes	–	2002
4.	Dispur College	–	Yes	–	–
5.	Guwahati College	–	–	Yes	–
6.	Guwahati Commerce College	–	Yes	–	2004
7.	Handique Girls' College	–	Yes	–	2004
8.	K C Das Commerce College	Yes	–	–	2004
9.	K K Handiqui Sanskrit College	–	–	Yes	–
10.	Kanya Mahavidyalaya	–	–	Yes	–
11.	Karmashree Hiteswar Saikia College	–	–	Yes	–
12.	KRB Girls' College	–	–	Yes	–
13.	Lalit Chandra Bharali College	–	Yes	–	2006
14.	Narengi Anchalik Mahavidyalaya	–	–	Yes	–
15.	North Guwahati College	–	–	Yes	–
16.	Pandu College	Yes	–	–	1999
17.	Pragjyotish College	–	Yes	–	2003
18.	R G Baruah College	–	–	Yes	–
19.	S B Deorah College	–	Yes	–	2003
20.	West Guwahati Commerce College	–	–	Yes	–

Automation of academic libraries in Assam is a recent phenomenon. Pandu College started the library automation in 1999, which was followed by B. Boarooah College in 2002. In the same year Cotton College also initiated library automation followed by Pragjyotish College in 2003. The table gives a clear picture of automation status of college libraries of Guwahati. From the table it is clear that only 3 colleges have fully automated, 8 colleges have partially automated while 9 colleges are yet to start automation services.

Library Software

Table. Library Software

Sl No.	Name of College	Library software used
1.	Arya Vidyapith College	SOUL
2.	B.Borooah College	SOUL
3.	Cotton College	SOUL
4.	Dispur College	Third Eye Library Management
5.	Gauhati College	SOUL
6.	Gauhati Commerce College	SOUL
7.	Handique Girls' College	SOUL
8.	K C Das Commerce College	SOUL
9.	K K Handiqui Sanskrit College	–
10.	Kanya Mahavidyalaya	–
11.	Karmashree Hiteswar Saikia College	–
12.	KRB Girls' College	–
13.	Lalit Chandra Bharali College	SOUL
14.	Narengi Anchalik Mahavidyalaya	–
15.	North Guwahati College	–
16.	Pandu College	SOUL
17.	Pragjyotish College	Third Eye Library Management
18.	R G Baruah College	SOUL
19.	S B Deorah College	SOUL
20.	West Guwahati Commerce College	–

Software packages are brain of the hardware system, which runs the system as well as helps in particular assignment. In the field of Library and Information Science, though there is a good number of library software only Libsys, SOUL and CDS/ISIS are popular among the library professionals in Guwahati city. The table shows the availability of library software in college libraries.

From the table it is seen that out of 20 colleges under this study 11 colleges used SOUL software for library automation while 2 colleges used Third Eye Library Management software. The remaining seven doesn't have any library software. The study further reveals that the colleges without library software are not taking part in library automation.

Prerequisites for Library Automation

Library automation demands the following prerequisites:

- Willingness of the library committee and librarian.
- Adequate finance.
- Proper planning.
- Hardware requirement, such as PC, UPS, Scanner, Printer, Storage media, etc.
- Software requirement, such as operating system, system software, application software, etc.
- Human ware, such as trained staff or manpower.

Areas of Automation

Ranganathan's five law of library science stipulates that documents of the library should have the maximum number of users. With the application of ICT in the area of libraries there has been tremendous improvement in the library services offered to the users by the libraries.

Following are the main areas of library automation:

- Library management.
- Library house keeping operation.
- Information Retrieval System.

MANPOWER FOR LIBRARY AUTOMATION

Fully trained professional staff is a must for any type of library. The college libraries under the study are having a staff trends from 1-3 on average, however fully trained librarians in those colleges are not sufficient in relation to their work load arising out of number of users. The table shows the existing position of different professionals and non-professionals in the colleges.

Table. Library Staffs

S. No.	Name of College	Professional	Semi Professional	Non Professional	Total
1.	Arya Vidyapith College	1	–	2	3
2.	B. Borooah College	2	2	2	6
3.	Cotton College	3	3	5	11
4.	Dispur College	1	1	2	4
5.	Guwahati College	1	1	2	4
6.	Guwahati Commerce College	1	–	4	5
7.	Handique Girls' College	1	–	5	6
8.	K C Das Commerce College	2	–	2	4
9.	K K Handiqui Sanskrit College	1	–	2	3
10.	Kanya Mahavidyalaya	–	–	2	2
11.	Karmashree Hiteswar Saikia College	1	–	1	2
12.	KRB Girls' College	1	–	1	2
13.	Lalit Chandra Bharali College	2	1	4	7
14.	Narengi Anchlik Mahavidyalaya	1	–	2	3
15.	North Guwahati College	1	–	1	2
16.	Pandu College	1	1	4	6
17.	Pragjyotish College	–	1	2	3
18.	R G Baruah College	1	–	2	3
19.	S B Deorah College	1	–	2	3
20.	West Guwahati Commerce College	1	–	–	1

The table further reveals Cotton College has the maximum staff followed by LCB College, B. Borooah College, Handique Girls' College, Pandu College, etc., while West Guwahati Commerce College has the least number of library staff, *i.e.*, only one. From the observation it is found that out of the 20 colleges in 15 colleges the librarians besides being professionally qualified have acquired special skilled in library automation by attending different short-term courses, orientation, refresher course, etc.

However from the observation of the college library, it is found that the training skilled acquired by the librarians is reflected only in 5 colleges. It may be observed that simply acquiring library skill is not sufficient for ensuring library Automated services to the readers. The mindset of the librarians has to be changed in a positive way to make the benefit of library automation passed on to the users. Again the cooperation of college authorities also factors for which many college librarians are not in a position to reflect their library automation expertise in an effective manner.

Use and Usefulness of E-journals A Case Study of Research Scholars

We present and collocate the findings of a recent investigation that have been conducted under the Research Starter Fund at University of Madras, a Project that seeks to bring e-journals use and utilisation of the research scholars of the University of Madras. The results of this study bring a comprehensive detailed picture of the use of e-journals by the research scholars. This investigation is probably one of the first of its kinds in the University after implementing the University Grants Commission's Infonet Programme. The main aim of this chapter is to present the outcome of the research project undertaken to examine the use and utilisation of the e-journals by the research scholars of the University of Madras. The increasing move from print collection to digital collections has generated much significant research on scholars' reading patterns and the take-up the use of e-journals.

This project examines about the kinds of people use e-journals and their information seeking behaviour of the sample population. To understand how e-journals forms and functions may evolve, study examines the current role that e-journals play in scholarly work. This may provide some insight as to how e-journals will establish their niche within a broader set of scholarly resources and how they will complement and challenge traditional paper journals. This investigation applied a standard survey method to analyse the use and utilisation of e-journals. This study restricted only to the research scholars and excluded the faculty members, post-graduate students and M.Phil degree students.

REVIEW OF RELATED STUDIES

Many studies tell us that using of e-journals articles has increased during the last decade and has been boosted by the application of Information and Communication Technologies (ICTs) in scholarly communication. More use of e-journals by the scientists than social scientists, however, enthusiasm for e-journals and patterns of use vary even among field of science. Chemists and physicists use them frequently, while earth scientists and mathematicians see few advantages in using ejournals. Tenopir and King also found these variations that physicists and astronomers to be among the most enthusiastic users of e-journals articles, because of the digital archives and e-journals available and designed specifically to facilitate their natural work patterns. Dillon and Hahn report the use of e-journals with study conducted at the University of Maryland. More faculty member used e-journals daily or weekly than they did print journals.

This corresponds to the decrease in physical visits to the library by graduate students and faculty, especially in health sciences, sciences and engineering. Business school faculty reported the highest use, while Palmer and Sandler found economics faculty to be the most enthusiastic users of e-journals. Speier and Hahn found that among business faculty, finance and management information systems faculty were more aware of e-journals than those in other fields.

Faculty members for history, education, and the arts have been slower to adopt e-journals. Among the corporate users, investment and banking companies or departments spend a higher percent of their budgets on electronic products than do other types of business such as pharmaceutical firms, legal services, food services, or telecommunications. Rudner, Miller-Whitehead and Gellamn found graduate students, particularly Ph.D. students are to be heavy users of e-journals, most likely in their role as researchers.

As found in the SuperJournal Project, graduate students may be 'binge' users consulting e-journals extensively for a short period when they are writing a thesis or dissertation. There are some exceptions—under graduates were the most frequent users in an experimental study conducted by American Chemical Society. Different workplaces or types of institutions have varying use patterns as well. Davis examined e-journals users logs in libraries of the Northeast Research Library Consortium and found that each institutions has a unique pattern of use - medical institutions users had higher use of a smaller number of journals, while users at large universities and smaller colleges downloaded articles from a greater variety of journals title. Differences in e-journals use may be attributed to age, status or rank. Speire and Hahn found that young ARL University Business faculty members reported that they use e-journals more often and were aware than were older faculty.

Another study reported that more than half of the faculty members under the age of 40 reported using e-journals as compared with only 14 per cent of those over 40, although more than 80 per cent of the total respondents indicated that would consider using e-journals in the future. Antoir found that older people preferred print articles; Monopoli found that user between age 21 and 34 used e-journals most frequently. Tenner and Yang found that assistant professors are most likely to have used e-journals (44.7 per cent), followed by professors (34.5 per cent) and followed by associate professors (34.2 per cent).

Researchers in other studies found no relationship between age and searching skills, although the researchers observed that younger users are more likely to browse on the computers, while older users prefer print journals for browsing. Tenopir and King also found no relationship between age and reading patterns among astronmers. Monopoli et al studied amongst the staff of the University of Patras, Greece, found that male staff has frequent use of electronic journals than female staff. Dilhon and Hahn found 70 per cent of the faculty wants core journals in both print and electronic form, but the some member wanted non-core journals only in electronic form. Worlock found that articles recommended by colleagues were more often in print than in electronic format.

Tenopir and King found contradictory results that e-mail and listerv make it easier to share recommended articles with colleagues. University faculty members opined that the ability to send articles to their colleagues instantly as being one of the major advantages of ejournals. Use of electronic books is also clearly course driven-books with the highest usage are those required in a class, and most users come to an electronic book collection to use a single title.

Most college students now are computer litreate and they use the web frequently. This does not necessarily correlate with effective use, however, an study found that professors performed newspapers and journal articles significantly better than graduates. The perceptions that e-journals are of lower quality than print is another problem that may be diminishing as a high percentage of peer-reviewed journals are digitised. Reported that they did not perceive e-journals to be of as high quality as paper counterparts.

While more than 70 per cent of the faculty members in a British University believe the quality of articles in electronic journals is the same as in print journals, this same group of respondents cited the top disadvantage of electronic journals as being the impression that electronic publication is not 'real' publication. Tenopir found that more undergraduate students used the web and web search engines frequently, students are mostly unaware of the distinction between materials on the web and peer reviewed journals.

A nationwide survey of students and academics in the Netherlands found that 60 per cent of respondents in the humanities, 78 per cent of respondents in the social sciences, and 82 per cent of respondents in the sciences used the Internet for study or work and nearly all believed they had Internet skills. Waldman found that 97 per cent of psychology students access the Internet at least weekly, about 44 per cent of the time for educational information.

Lack of awareness was one of the contributing factors for non-use of e-journals. Science, engineering and health sciences faculty at the University of Washington favoured cancelling print journals in favour of electronic only, while humanities and social sciences faculty opposed this idea and responded that maintaining the quality of the print collection is their higher priority.

MEANS AND METHODS

A whole range of different methods with different approaches and objectives have been employed to the use of e-journals. Questionnaire surveys and interviews are the common favourite methodologies amongst the researchers. Transactional log analysis studies are not so common, but they are more popular to study the e-journals as well as digital libraries. A survey method would be adopted to carry out this research project.

In the process of surveying, a predefined questionnaire has been used to collect the necessary data. The questionnaire having questions like personal information, computer education, computer use, Internet and World Wide Web aware and use, search engines, browser, skills search techniques, awareness of the e-journals, level of use, purpose of sue, problems of using e-journals, etc.

The University Departments are spread into four campuses and located in different places with group of Departments. Social sciences and humanities in Chepauk, languages in Marina, life sciences and physical and chemical sciences in Guindy and basic medical sciences in Taramani. Questionnaires have been distributed with equal proportion based on the number of departments available in that campus.

DATA ANALYSIS

The data collected through questionnaire have been analysed using statistical tool and presented. The total questionnaire admired this study is two hundred and distributed to the research scholars of all the campuses. Only 72 per cent of research scholars responded. Among the respondents, male representation was 69 per cent and female represent 31 per cent under this survey.

The respondents are grouped into two broad categories for sake of convenient into data analysis, *viz.*, arts and science. Science (53 per cent) arts (47 per cent) and disciplines research scholars having same proportion in the sample population. This indicated that questionnaire have been distributed with equal proportion based on the disciplines. Among the researchers, young researchers are more (45 per cent) than the second year (22 per cent), third year (11 per cent) and fourth year (17 per cent). Research scholars can be grouped into full-time and part-time students. Fulltime students are again divided into stipendiary and non-stipendiary candidates. Part-time candidates are also included in the sample. Full-time non-stipendiary candidates are higher (59 per cent) than the stipendiary candidates. Very small number of part-time candidates responded.

This may be due to the non-availability of researchers in the departments during the survey period. Almost all the respondents are below 35years old except 5 per cent of respondents are above 35 years old. This is because sample population belonging to only the research scholars. The basic qualification for pursuing Ph.D. degree also taken into consideration with view of, is there any factor affecting the pattern of use? Respondents with Post-graduation are higher (60 per cent) than with M. Phil as qualification for pursuing Ph.D. degree programme. While study the e-journals use, access to e-journals requires computer knowledge some extend. Whether the respondents had acquired any formal computer education or not have been asked to correlate with e-journal use.

The level of education was divided into four categories such as level of degree, postgraduate diploma, diploma and certificate course. Amongst certificate course level is more (36 per cent) followed by diploma holder (20 per cent), 7 and 9 percentages of respondents acquired degree and P.G. diploma levels respectively. The remaining 28 per cent of respondents are having any level of formal computer education. Almost all the research scholars are using computer for one or other purposes, very less number of respondents are not using computer. Nearly half of the respondents are viewed that the computer is being used for purpose of communicate with others.

More than half (55 per cent) of the respondents are using computer for their project work. Now-a-day, digital and electronic resources are playing vital role in satisfying the users' requirements. Researchers and students are depending mainly on electronic sources. But the survey shows that less than half of the respondents (45 per cent) opined that computer is using for preparing assignments. Twothird of the respondents (70 per cent) are using computer for their research purpose.

Apart from their academic and/or research purposes the respondents were asked whether computing is being for entertainment purposes, very less segment of the sample population (24 per cent) is using computer for entertainment. Among the respondents, only 36 per cent are having either personal computer or laptop. Surprisingly 2 per cent of the research scholars respond that they are not aware of Internet and World Wide Web (WWW). Remaining respondents are aware and using Internet with varied years of experience. As far as years of experiences is concerned, more than five years of Internet using experience is more (27 per cent) than the other categories.

This was followed by very young users, *i.e.*, less than two years (21 per cent) and between 2-5 years experiences spread equally in three groups. Almost all the respondents are active users of Internet, either they are using daily (33 per cent) alternate days (22 per cent) or once in a week (22 per cent). A small percent of the respondents are occasional users. The possible places of using Internet are University's Internet Centre (34 per cent), cyber cafes (26 per cent) and home (5 per cent). More than half (52 per cent) of the respondents learnt Internet through self-learning method.

The second position occupy by the through friends (23 per cent), sixteen percent of the respondents are taken formal training course for Internet access and only 3 per cent of the respondents are through media/newspapers. The respondents mainly preferred Internet Explorer for browsing web pages. More than 90 per sent of the respondents are preferred this browser and only 4 per sent of the respondents are using other than Internet Explorer.

Google search engine is most preferred search engine among the respondents. More than three fourth of the respondents are using the search engine either often or sometimes. Yahoo and MSN are not in a significant place among research scholars. Only negligible amount of respondents are preferred Alltheweb, Altavista, Askjeeves, Excite, Hotbot, Lycosand and Infoseek. Alltehweb advanced, Altavista advanced, Google advanced, Hotbot advanced are taken into consideration for identify the usage of advanced search engines. Nearly 70 per cent of respondents are using Google advanced search either often, rare or sometimes.

One fourth of the respondents are not using advanced search, no significant numbers using other search engines. The preferred type of resources among the respondents were been questioned, nearly 20 per cent respondents are using databases often. Full-text publications often search by 42 per cent of respondents. In relation to library web sites, half of the respondents are often or sometimes visits to the library web sites. More than half of the respondents are not having interest to see health related web sites, others are visits rarely (6 per cent), sometimes (19 per cent) or often (17 per cent). Similar range of respondents engaged with job searching and newspaper reading areas.

However, recreational web sites gets high position among the researchers (73 per cent). The possible difficulties in Internet access have been identified, *viz.*, language barriers, broken links, instability of network, slow expansion, finding relevant, and information overload. The respondents opined in this survey that language is low degree of problem in searching the Internet. At the same time 16 per cent of respondents are opined that the language barrier is in moderate level. Broken link is also available in moderate level while searching the web. Regarding instability of network, high degree of responses occurs on that. Slow expansion is another problem among the respondents of the Internet users. High percentage of respondents opined that it occurs in moderate level.

Among the respondents, 30 per cent respondents are strongly agreed that Internet resources are up-to-date information. Very negligible number of respondents disagrees or strongly disagrees this and majority of the respondents are opined that that Internet has lot of information. Good accessibility was scored high (60 per cent) from the opinion about the accessibility of the Internet resources. Similarly optioned on accuracy of the resources available in the Internet, but very limited number of the respondents said that sources are excellent.

The opinion about availability, consistency, flexibility and usefulness, respondents gave rated high to good scale in all the attributes. Below 10 per cent respondents are says these attributes are excellent on availability, similar results one could see for other attributes. Internet and Internet resources have positive impact on studying and teaching strongly agreed by the majority of the respondents. One third of the respondents felt that some have had positive impact. The search methods and level of satisfaction on 'content' and 'keyword' search have been asked to determine the search skills of the respondents. Among the respondents, majority of the respondents are not a habit of searching items with content/topic in which they required. But significant respondents (38 per cent) among them using content/topic search often. Majority of the respondents use keyword searching often.

Similarly, majority of the respondents are opined that they are using sometimes. In the topical search, the respondents are received moderate level of satisfaction. Only 20 per cent viewed that they have received high level of satisfaction. High level of satisfaction received from the respondents on keyword search. Various search techniques such as Boolean Operators (AND, OR, NOT), nesting, truncation, phrase searching, controls, case sensitive and wildcard have been asked to find out whether users are using these search techniques while search the web. Majority of the respondents (60 per cent) are never using Boolean operators; the remaining respondents are using Boolean operators rarely, sometimes, or often.

Nesting also never used by the two third of the respondents. Only one third of respondents are using the nesting techniques on the other levels. In the text retrieval system, truncation is one of the techniques used to improve the recall in the search. The result shows that the majority of the respondents (70 per cent) are not using truncation method. Similar results arrived for phrase searching also.

The researchers of the Madras University do not have practice of using 'controls' while search the Internet resources. The result of use of case sensitive methods in searching is shows that 67 per cent of them are not suing case sensitive. The use of wildcard method also asked among the respondents. Almost all the respondents are opined that they never use this while searching.

The utilisation of resources such as bibliographic databases, full-text databases, images, audio-video information, e-books and e-journals by the researchers of the University have been ascertained. Among the respondents, 66 per cent of the respondents opined that they never browse the bibliographic databases, others browsing sometimes, often or rarely. Similar set of results are arrived in the case of full-text database also. Images, audio-video type of information also in the list of very often used sources of information by the one fourth of the respondents. E-books are not in their mind among 40 per cent of respondents, others are using often, sometimes or rarely.

Unlike the e-books, 70 per cent respondents are often use e-journals. Now-a-days open sources are dominant in the web resources. It is considered as one of media for scholarly communication. The awareness of the open sources among the researchers is determined, sharply 50 per cent of the respondents are aware of open sources, the remaining are unaware.

More than half (60 per cent) of respondents are aware of virtual libraries, other respondents are not aware of virtual libraries. Similar result is arrived for the awareness of electronic libraries (64 per cent). Nearly 40 per cent of respondents are not aware of consortium functioning in India. Among the three major functional consortia in India, UGC's Infonet is one of the aware and using consortia than All India Council for Technical Education's INDEST and CSIR's Consortia.

The use and utilisation of e-journals have been assessed with following questions:

- Whether you are using e-journals?
- What mod you are using (consortia or open source)?
- Is e-journals are useful?
- Is e-journals are substitute to the printed form?

Among the respondents, nearly 50 per cent of the respondents are not using e-journals either from open sources or through consortia. One fourth of the respondents (26 per cent) are using e-journals through consortium, remaining respondents are using open sources. Majority of the respondents (82 per cent) felt that the e-journals are useful sources of information. Regarding the substitution of e-journals, two third of the respondents (61 per cent) felt that e-journals are considered as a substitute to the print journals.

The remaining of them opined reverse. The e-journals characteristics such as accessibility, authenticity, availability and usefulness are asked and the results are: half of the respondents (51 per cent) are 'agree' about the accessibility. Nearly 30 per cent of respondents 'somewhat agree' on accessibility of e-journals. At the same time very few of them opined 'strongly agree'. Only 2 per cent of the respondents have opinion of 'disagree' and 'strongly disagree'. While asking the authenticity of the e-journals, the result is reflecting the same as in the accessibility. Nearly half of the respondents (47 per cent) of the respondents 'agree' about the authenticity of the e-journals.

One-third of the respondents are 'somewhat agree'. Similar result one could see from the results on availability of the e-journals. Majority of them (75 per cent) either 'agree' or 'somewhat agree'. The opinion of the usefulness of the e-journals slightly differs from the other characteristics. Majority of the respondents (82 per cent) are 'strongly agree' and 'agree' and 13 per cent respondents 'somewhat agree'.

INFERENCES

The following inferences have been arrived and summarised as follows:

- *Sex*: Male respondents are more than female in the sample population.
- *Department*: More or less equal number of distributions of respondents in both Arts and Science disciplines.
- Fresh-hand researchers are more than senior researchers among the sample population.

- Full-time non-stipendiary candidates are more than stipendiary candidates; very less number of respondents belongs to part-time researchers.
- *Age*: Majority of respondents are youngster rather old persons.
- *Qualification*: Post-Graduation qualified research scholars are more than with M.Phil qualified respondents in the sample population.
- *Computer Education*: Two third of the respondents are having formal computer education.
- *Computer Use*: Almost all the researchers are using computer one or other purposes.
- *Purpose of using Computer*: The research scholars are using computer for preparing assignment, project, research and some extend to entertainment rather business purpose.
- One-third of researchers under survey are having own computer system. Others dependent outside resources.
- *Internet and World Wide Web*: Almost all the respondents are aware of Internet and World Wide Web and one third of them having good experiences in using Internet and World Wide Web.
- All the respondents are active users of Internet and World Wide Web. They spent reasonable time in browsing the net.
- The research scholars are not only depending upon the University's Internet Centre's but also Cyber cafes. Only minimum number are using in their home.
- *Internet use Learning*: The researchers are learnt Internet browsing by themselves and through friends. This indicates that the syllabus does not have any course on Internet study area.
- *E-mail*: E-mail communication exists as one of the communication channels among the research scholars of the University of Madras.
- *Internet Browser*: Internet Explorer is popular Internet browser among the respondents. Mozilla Firefax occupies the second position. No other became popular to the research scholars.
- *Search Engines*: Google, Yahoo, MSN are the most popular search engines among the research scholars. Other search engines are rarely using by the respondents. No much use of the advanced search engines, except some respondents are using Google's advanced search engine.
- *Type of sites using*: The researchers mostly preferred full-text publications, Education and Job sites. Recreational, Health, etc are visiting by the researchers sometimes. Newspapers/Magazine, Travel and Tourism related web sites are least preferred.
- Internet Access Difficulties:
  - *Language Barriers*: Language is not at all considered as barriers in Internet access.
  - *Broken Links*: Broken/dead link problem affect the researchers in the moderate level.

- *Instability of Network*: The instability of network also not affects the use of Internet.
- *Slow Expansion of site*: Researchers opined that it is in moderate level.
- *Relevant Information*: The research scholars are found relevant information while searching the Internet.
- *Information overload*: The same opinion of the above could find this case also.
- *Internet Resources*: The researchers are strongly felt that the Internet resources are up-to-date and enormous information is available. But somewhat agree on ideal way of communication.

- The University research scholars felt that the attributes such as accessibility, accuracy, availability, consistency, flexibility and usefulness are good rather excellent or poor.
- *Impact of Internet*: The Internet had positive impact on research and academic activities of the research scholars.
- *Search Skills*: Keyword search is preferred search methods adopted by the majority of the researchers rather content/topical search. The moderate level of satisfaction they acquired through keyword search.
- *Search techniques*: Boolean operators, phrase searching are some of search techniques rarely being used by the researchers. The other techniques such as nesting, truncation, controls, wildcard, etc never being used by the almost all the research scholars.
- Advanced search by restricting type of resources, file format and period never being used by the University of Madras research scholars.
- Type of Resources browsing:
  - *Bibliographic databases*: It is not a preferred resource for browsing by the research scholars.
  - *E-books*: Almost all the researchers are not having the habit of using e-books.
  - *Audio-Video*: Rarely it being used by the researchers.
  - *Full-text databases*: Full-texts databases are preferred areas of interest of most of the scholars.
  - *E-journals*: The majority of the research scholars often use e-journals.
- *Open Sources*: The researches are aware of 'open sources' in the Internet and World Wide Web.
- *Virtual and Electronic Libraries*: They have knowledge about 'virtual library' and 'electronic library'.
- Consortia:
  - University of Madras is one of the member institutions in the

UGC's InfoNet Programme. The researchers are aware of it. But the other major consortia such as AICTE's INDEST and CSIR's Consortia are not aware of by the researchers.
  - The researchers of the University do not often use UGC's InfoNet. Science discipline research scholars fully aware about the programme and using, whereas Arts discipline researchers are not aware and used.
- E-journals:
  - E-journals are using by the research scholars of the University. Among the researchers, Science discipline researchers are using open sources as well as consortia.
  - Generally the e-journals are useful sources of scholarly communication
  - Both the opinions are found that Ejournals are considered as substitution to the print journals and not.
- E-journals characteristics:
  - Accessibility of the e-journals is easy than printed journals.
  - Though authenticity is one of the criticisms when the 'open sources', e-journals are considered as one of the authentic sources of information. Lot of e-journals is available in an electronic form, which made available through open sources and consortium.
  - Digital information has an attribute of manifestation. e-journals are considered as useful resources.

OPEN ACCESS JOURNAL PUBLISHING IN INDIA A STUDY WITH OJS SOFTWARE

Open-access (OA) litreature is digital, online, free of charge, and free of most copyright and licensing restrictions. Providing open access to the research work will help the researchers, especially in the developing world, to have access to the research litreature from across the world. Also, studies have shown that the citations for the open access scholarly litreature is higher than the subscription based scholarly litreature.

Open Access to scholarly information can be achieved by two methods:

- Open Access Journals;
- Open Archives.

Open Access Journals publish articles like conventional journal but are accessible in full without any fee or subscription charges. Open Archives are publicly accessible online repositories where the authors or their representatives or other right holders upload their pre-print or post-print articles.

OPEN ACCESS PUBLISHING

Open access publishing is the publication of material in such a way that it is available to all potential users without financial or other barriers. An open access publisher is a publisher producing such material. Many types of material can be published in this manner scholarly journals, known specifically as open access journals. Open access journals are scholarly journals that are available to the reader "without financial or other barrier other than access to the Internet itself."

Some are subsidised, and some require payment on behalf of the author. Subsidised journals are financed by an academic institution or a government information centre; those requiring payment are typically financed by money made available to researchers for the purpose from a public or private funding agency, as part of a research grant.

In 2002, the Budapest Open Access Initiative (BOAI) was launched to encourage science to be freely available on the Internet. To support this nowadays a scientific community can use different open source electronic publishing systems for the e-journals.

Some of the popular ones are Digital Publishing System (DPubs), ePublishing toolkit (ePubTk), Open Journal System (OJS). With its features, functionalities such as easy to use, modest system requirements, extensive documentation, user manuals, support, customisation and biggest user community Open Journal System (OJS) has become popular journal management system.

OPEN JOURNAL SYSTEM (OJS)

Open Journal Systems (OJS) is a journal management and publishing system that has been developed by the Public Knowledge Project (PKP) through its federally funded efforts to expand and improve access to research.

WHY OJS

OJS is open source software made freely available to journals worldwide for the purpose of making open access publishing a viable option for more journals, as open access can increase a journal's readership as well as its contribution to the public good on a global scale. OJS has been designed to reduce the time and energy devoted to the clerical and managerial tasks associated with editing a journal, while improving the record keeping and efficiency of editorial processes.

It seeks to improve the scholarly and public quality of journal publishing through a number of innovations, from making journal policies more transparent to improving indexing. OJS was designed to facilitate the development of open access, peer-reviewed publishing, providing the technical infrastructure not only for the online presentation of journal articles, but also an entire editorial management workflow, including article submission, multiple rounds of peer-review, and indexing.

OJS relies upon individuals fulfilling different roles, such as the Journal manager, editor, reviewer, author, reader, etc. As of January 2009, OJS is being used by at least 2000 journals worldwide. A selected list of OJS journals is available on the PKP web site.

OJS FEATURES

- OJS is installed locally and locally controlled.
  - Easy to install with moderate system requirements.
- Editors configure requirements, sections, review process, etc.
- Online submission and management of all content.
  - OJS moves submissions to the journal through easy steps in the editorial process, which will be managed by one or more of the editors.
- Subscription module with delayed open access options.
- Comprehensive indexing of content part of global system.
- Reading Tools for content, based on field and editors' choice.
  - The Reading Tools are designed to assist experienced and novice readers by providing a rich context of related materials from a wide variety of largely open access sources.
- E-mail notification and commenting ability for readers.
- Complete context-sensitive online Help support.
  - Help document is contextually embedded within OJS, with the relevant pages coming up depending on where the user is when requesting Journal Help.

OJS WORKFLOW

OJS management systems are structured around the traditional journal workflow required to move a submission through reviewing, and if accepted, editing and publishing, with records maintained of who is doing what and when. It uses roles to organise activities and spaces within the journal's management and publishing web site.

Roles in the Publishing Workflow are:

- Journal manager, who sets up journal by filling in templates and checking options; manages users, assigns roles; manages reading tools, indexing, prepared e-mails templates.
- Editors can assign one or more editors or a section editors to submissions; oversee editorial process and decisions; assemble and publishe issues.
- Section editor: he manages peer review process and makes editorial decision for submissions, in consultation with Editor.
- Subscription manager, who sets up different types of subscriptions and manages subscription processes.

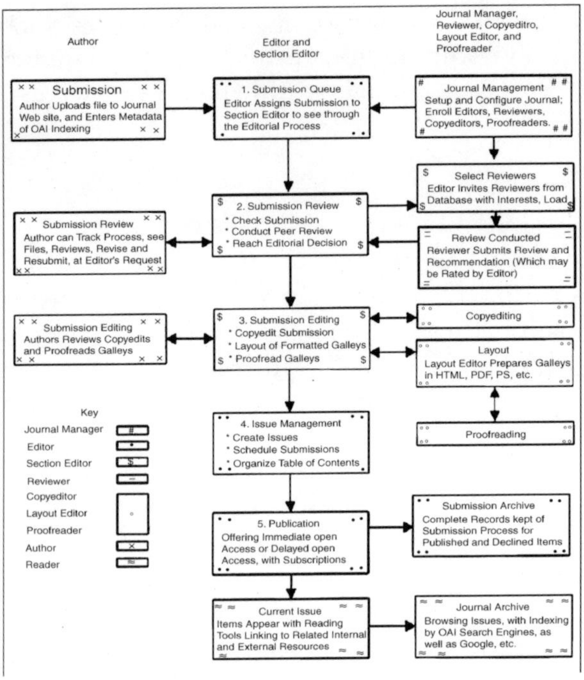

Fig. OJS Editorial and Publishing Process

OJS has a 'plugin' architecture, similar to other community-based projects such as WordPress, allowing new features to be easily integrated into the system without the need to change the entire core code base.

Some of the plugins contributed to OJS include tools to facilitate indexing in Google Scholar and PubMed Central, a feed plugin providing RSS/Atom web syndication feeds, a COUNTER plugin, allowing COUNTER-compliant statistics and reporting, and more. OJS is also LOCKSS-compliant, helping to ensure permanent archiving for ongoing access to the content of the journal. OJS has been translated into eight languages (English, French, German, Italian, Portuguese, Russian, Spanish, Turkish), with an additional languages (Arabic, Catalan, Chinese, Croatian, Persian, Hindi, Japanese, Norwegian, Thai, Vietnamese) in development. All translations are created and maintained by the OJS user community

OA IN INDIA

A small but the number of Indian journals moving towards open access is significantly increasing. There is a need to create a great deal of awareness of OA concepts and its impact on the visibility of scholarly information.

Present Scenario of Open Access in India

- 107 Journals found at DOAJ—Directory of Open Access Journals when searched with India.

- Browse India ROAR Registry of Open Access Repositories resulted in 39 repositories.

The Indian Academy of Sciences converted all its journals into OA. The Indian Medlars Centre at the National Informatics Centre brings out the OA version of 40 biomedical journals under its medIND programme. Four OA journals are from Indian National Science Academy. MedKnow brings out more than 70 OA journals on behalf of their publishers (although not all of them are Indian journals), Calicut Medical College brings out 3 OA medical journals.

It is also noted that inspite of their online presence the articles in some of these journals are less used because some of these journals do not comply with indexing standard of OA, *i.e.,* OAI-PMH (Open Access Initiative—Protocol for Metadata Harvesting) protocol. Hence, the articles in these journals are not easily 'discoverable' due to poor metadata and poor indexing.

As OJS is OAI-PMH compliant, it makes the content of the journal's metadata OAI–PMH compliant which will significantly increase the accessibility of content.

PRESENT ISSUES FACING SCHOLARLY PUBLISHING IN INDIA

- Fear that revenue loss from print subscriptions if journal becomes OA, even as it increases readership and circulation of knowledge.
- Lack of IT infrastructure or the funds to develop it for using far more efficient online means of managing and publishing journals.
- Other obstacles include uncertainty around copyright issues and a lack of management support and clerical support.

OJS INITIATIVES IN INDIA

SJPI

Project in partnership with PKP demonstrated electronic publishing through a prototype and disseminated the knowledge by conducting two workshops in which participants from different parts of India who are involved in publishing attended.

Open Knowledge Society (OKS)

OKS a non-profit organisation working for the dissemination of all forms of Open Access to the Knowledge. OKS as PKP partner in India supports publication of Open Access Journals through OJS and conversion of print journals into online versions. With the support of OKS Medicinal and Aromatic Plant Association of India the newly formed scientific society at National Research Centre for Medicinal and Aromatic Plants (NRCMAP) a constituent establishment of ICAR has launched an Open Access Journal on Medicinal and Aromatic Plants (OJAMP). Open Knowledge Society aims to facilitate all forms of Open Access to Knowledge.

It includes:

- Supporting publication of Open Access Journals;
- Supporting conversion of print journals into online versions;
- Supporting making online journals OAI-PMH complaint;
- Supporting creation of Institutional Repositories;
- Supporting automation of libraries;
- Supporting Digital Libraries;
- Other activities that promotes open access to knowledge.

Following are some of the test journals setup:

- Mysore Journal of Agricultural Sciences;
- Journal of Spices and Plantation crop;
- Journal of soil Science and management;
- Journal of Pest Management. etc...

SKILL ENHANCEMENT OF LIBRARY PROFESSIONALS AND USERS OF SHERUBTSE COLLEGE, KANGLUNG, BHUTAN

Bhutan is one of the Asia's smallest country located in the eastern Himalayas. The total population is 6.35 lakhs. Historically the education in Bhutan started with the early Monastic bodies. The monastic system of education has sustained the Bhutanese society in its spiritual fold for many centuries.

The monastic education system was practised through informal relationship between the master and the disciples. In total 4971 monks have registered with the Deratshang Lhentshog (Central Monastic Body). The development of a comprehensive modern education system in Bhutan was initiated in 1961.

In Bhutan two kinds of modern education system exits namely, Formal and Non-formal system. Education is free for all which is applicable to all types of educational system in Bhutan. Sherubtse College was first inaugurated in 1968 as a public school. It became a University College in 1983. It is the apex institution of higher education for Arts and Science of the country.

The total number of admission at the higher education level is 4373. Out of which, Sherubtse College alone occupies 1009 which is approximately one fourth of the total admission of the country for higher education. It is a residential college where 90 per cent of the students stay in hostels. The college library has over 30,000 volumes of books and hundreds of journals, magazines and ebooks. It also subscribes a good number of online journals. The annual budget for the library is over 10 lakhs per year and also receives some UNFPA fund. It is fully computerised.

The library has ten computers, two allotted for Online Public Access Catalogue (OPAC). The OPAC is also available on intranet. Recently a data security gate has been installed for security purpose. The Library is kept open from 7.30 a.m. to 10.30 p.m. on all days. The average visitors of the library per day will be around 350-400 patrons. There are two librarians and nine other staff members working in the library. Two simple types of questionnaire have been distributed, first one is for library staff and the second one is for the users.

The questionnaire for Library staff is distributed to all the ten library staff with their respective responses. The random selection method has been adopted to distribute the questionnaire to the users and 150 questionnaires have been distributed which is about 12.5 per cent of the total users (both Students and Staff).

ANALYSIS OF LIBRARY STAFF

Table. Library Staff Details

Design	Libn	SAL	AL-1	AL-2	LA-1	LA-2	LA-3	LA-4	LA-5	LA-6
Qin	PG	10	12	10	10	8	12	10	10	10
Yrs of Exp	1	19	10	10	2	7	14	3	2	1
Nature of Duty	Overall Mgt	Jrs Sec	Tbk Sec	Data Entry	Barcoding	Bk Process	Counter Service	Stacking	Stacking	Security

There is no Library Science programme in the country. Except the Librarians, all the Library staff are non-professionals. But they have good experience. As the library staff were sent to various countries to attend training programmes, they have good working knowledge in the library.

Except the temporary staff, almost all are familiar with the Dewey Decimal Classification System, processing of Library books and all other routines of the Library services. The library staff are user-friendly with computers and internet. They are independently working in their own sections of the library like journal section, internet section, reference section and so on. The following table will show the details of training programmes attended by the Sherubtse library staff:

Table. Training Programmes Attended by the Library Staff

Designation of Library Staff	No. of Progs.	Duration	Countries Visited	Funding Agency
Librarian (1)	1	Two years (PG)	UK	UNFPA - 1
Sr. Asst. Libn (1)	6	8 Months	Bhutan – 4 Philippines – 1 India - 1	SAARC – 1 UNFPA – 1 RUB - 4
Asst. Libns (2)	6	Each 4 Months	Bhutan – 3, India – 2, Thailand – 1	RUB – 2 UNFPA – 1 SAARC - 2
Library Assts (3)	8	2 Months – 1 4 Months – 2	Bhutan – 5, India – 2, Thailand – 1	RUB – 5 SAARC – 2 UNFPA - 1

To evaluate the feasibilities to work in the library and scope for the skill enhancement, the library staff were asked some relevant queries, and their responses are in the table. It says that library staff are getting good support from the management and there is good scope for self enhancement.

Table. Feasibilities to Work in the Library

	Best	Good	Normal	Poor	Worst
Work	2	6	2		
Eny					
Job Sat	1	7	1	1	
Rel lib	6	3	1		
Rel Users	1	5	3	1	
Self Dev	3	5	2		
Mgt Support	1	4	5		

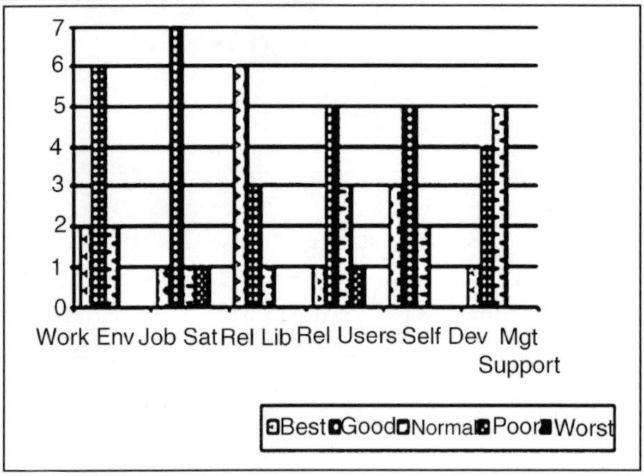

Fig. Feasibilities to Work in the Library

PERFORMANCE MANAGEMENT SYSTEM

The performance management system is being in practice to evaluate the performance skills of all civil servants.

This is to:

- Enable fairness in career advancement and promote competence, meritocracy, productivity and self-esteem.
- Enhance both organisational and individual development and effectiveness by introducing objective performance management mechanism.
- Enhance professionalism and accountability.

Every beginning of the academic year, each and every one of the staff will be asked to submit their goals to work for the year. At the middle of the year, the performance of individual staff against the goals will be checked and reviewed, and the same will be analysed thoroughly and the grades will be awarded.

Appraisal Cycle

All performance information, including the ratings shall be analysed and archived accordingly, and shall be computed through the use of appropriate software which shall be used to generate quantitative data as well as document of critical incidences. The Human Resource Officers shall be responsible for managing this information. Every Civil Service Organisation shall submit appraisal information when required by the Royal Civil Service Code (RCSC).

Performance Rating

The performance ratings of the immediate manager shall be final and binding. In case of the library, the Chief Librarian is the immediate manager. For the Chief Librarian, the Director is the immediate manager.

The average scores across both performance outputs and core competencies shall form the final rating of the employee as follows:

- *Average total scores of 3.5—4.00*: Outstanding.
- *Average total scores of 2.5—3.49*: Very Good.
- *Average total scores of 1.5—2.49*: Good.
- *Average total scores of 0—1.49*: Improvement Needed.

Use of the Performance Appraisal Results shall be used to:

- Identify and address development needs of employees.
- Determine appropriate performance increment.
- Recognise good performers and provide appropriate incentives and rewards.
- Promote an employee to a higher position available in Civil Service.
- Take other personnel actions like, transfer, confirmation of services for the probationers and assigning special tasks.
- Identifying non-performance.

Managing Non-performance

Analysis of Users

For this purpose 150 questionnaires have randomly been distributed to assess the skill enhancement of library users, out of which 30 were for staff and 120 were for students. Out 30 staff members, 9 are doctorates, 17 are PG and M.Phil degree holders of which 8 are research scholars, 4 are PG degree holders and in this group 3 are doing research.

To give an account of their experience, two staff has more than twenty years of experience, four are in between 16 and 20, six are in between 11 and 15, eleven in between 6 and 10, lastly 7 falls in the group of five and less than that. The staff members were to answer the queries regarding the articles they have published in the last five years. For this query, seven persons answered no as they have not published any such articles, nine members have mentioned 1-2 articles, 6 members have published 3-4 articles, 5 members have published 5-10 articles and 3 members have published more than ten articles in the last five years. Again the staff members were asked whether they have published any books in the last five years and if so how many.

Table. Time Spent in the Library

Time Spent in Library	No. of Respondents
Less than 1 hr a day	16
1-2 hrs a day	48
2-3 hrs a day	36
More than 3 hrs a day	28
1-2 hrs in a week	14
Occasionally	8

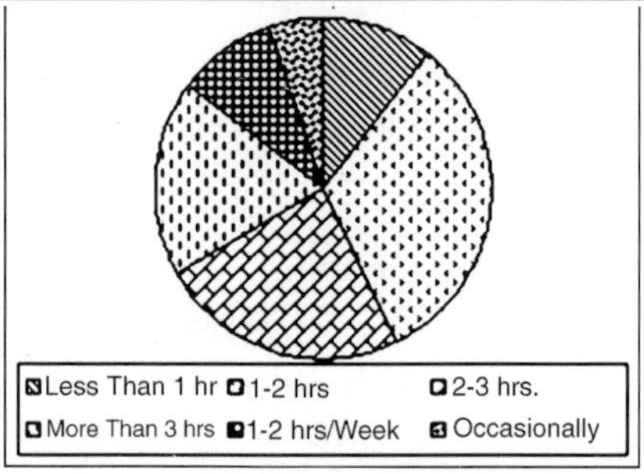

Fig. No. of Respondents

For this purpose, six members were told that they have published one or two books, two staff have responded for 3 to four books. In this survey of students group, 28 are first years, 45 are second years and 47 are final year students. All these basic information will notify the importance of Library for their skill enhancement.

In response to the query of time spending in the library, almost 75 per cent of the users responded that they are spending sufficient time for potential purposes. Out of 150 users only 8 have responded that they seldom visit the library.

PURPOSE OF VISITING THE LIBRARY

Staff

Table. Purpose of Visiting the Library

Purpose	R1	R2	R3	R4	R5	No. Res.
a.	17	4	4	3	2	
b.	7	9	9	4	1	
c.	6	14	8	1		1
d.		3	7	14	4	2
e.			2	8	8	12

Note:

a. To prepare lecture notes,

b. To get information for research work,

c. To enrich subject/GK,

d. To get current information,

e. For entertainment R—Rank, Res—Response

Regarding the purpose of visiting the library 17 staff have given top priority to prepare lecture notes, 14 members have given second priority to enrich their subject and general knowledge, 9 members have given second and third priority for research purpose and very few have responded for entertainment.

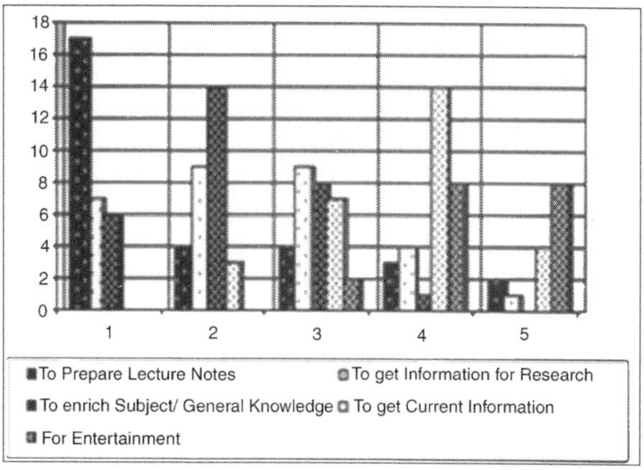

Fig. Purpose of Visiting the Library by Staff

Students

Since, Sherubtse College is running only undergraduate courses, there is no much scope for research at the student's level. In this group, the students mainly use the library to prepare for their class works, assignments, seminars, competitive examinations for further study and RCSC examinations. Only these criteria vary from the staff on the purpose of visiting the library.

Table. Purpose of Visiting the Library

Purpose	R1	R2	R3	R4	R5	No. Res
a.	48	36	27	9		
b.	35	41	28	13	3	
c.	18	26	39	31	6	
d.	15	14	22	40	21	8
e.	4	3	4	22	45	42

Note:

a. To prepare class notes and assignments

b. To develop subject/GK

c. To prepare for RCSC and other competitive exams

d. To get current information

e. For entertainment, R—Rank, Res—Response

In response to the purpose of visiting the library, 48 students have given top priority and 36 students have given second priority to prepare class notes and assignments. The other important criteria to enrich their subject and general knowledge, 35 and 41 students have given first and second priority. At the same time a large number of students responded with either last priority or no response to entertainments.

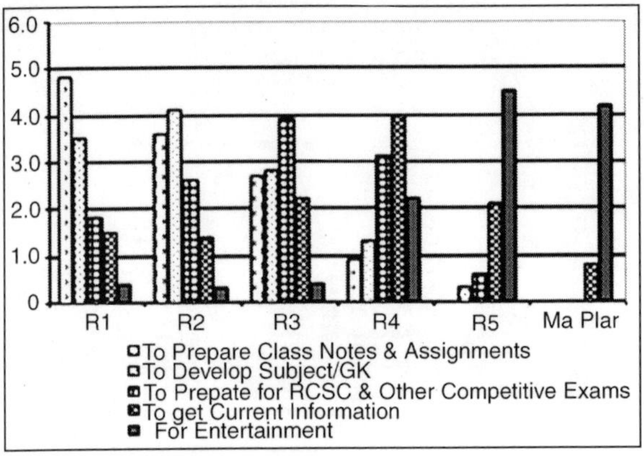

Fig. Purpose of Visit the Library by Students

EVALUATION OF LIBRARY FACILITIES AND SERVICES

To evaluate the services and facilities of the library, a few questions were framed for both students and staff. This includes the availability of reading materials such as textbooks, reference books, journals, e-books and online journals, also general facilities, library working hours, approach of the library staff, and overall services in the library. In response, about 63 per cent of users told that the library is above normal. However, few members have told that the facilities are very poor, which can't be neglected.

Table. Evaluation of Library by the Users

Lib Facilities and Services	Best	Good	Normal	Poor	Worst
Avail Tbk/Ref	14	71	44	17	4
Access of Jrs	20	75	43	10	5
E-bks and internet	12	53	54	23	8
Library working hrs	41	84	25		
Approach of Lib Staff	20	76	48	4	2
Lib infrastructure and Facilities	23	72	44	6	5
Overall Lib Services	15	84	42	8	1
Total	145	515	300	68	22

Note:
Lib: Library

Tbk/Ref: Text books and Reference Materials
Jrs: Jounals
hrs: Hours

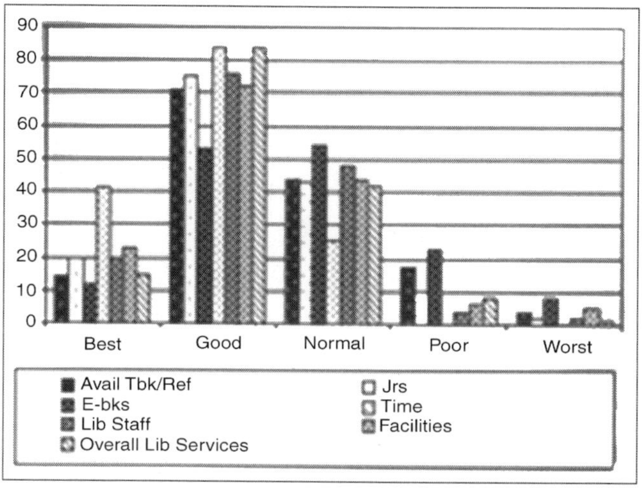

Fig. Evaluation of Library by the Users

It is easy to understand that the Sherubtse College Library is an ideal place for skill enhancement for both the library staff and the users. In addition, the Royal University of Bhutan Library Task Force Committee has recommended to start the Library and Information Science Course in the UG level at the earliest possible. This would be an effective solution for the skill enhancement of library professionals for the country in the near future.

CAMPUS NETWORK MANAGEMENT *BEST PRACTICE BY KUVEMPU UNIVERSITY*

UGC has launched an ambitious programme to bring about a qualitative change in higher education and research centres. In this direction UGC is extending help to modernise the ICT infrastructure in university campuses with state-of-the-art campus wide networks under UGC-Infonet programme. Under this programme, it is proposed to use Information and Communication Technology and Internet to transform learning environment from a monodimensional one to a multi-dimensional one. Campus wide network is the basic required infrastructure in the universities for the effective utilisation of UGCInfonet Digital library e-consortium as well as the internet e-resources.

Therefore, the structured campus network is a sine quanon for every university. The term 'campus' as used here refers to a main university location consisting of one or more buildings in close proximity to one another at the same locale. All buildings and floors on the campus are connected to shared resources and services in a data centre, the campus network may also be connected to remote location such as Off campus via a WAN. With the establishment of the well structured campus network most administrative, academic and research processes are carried out online, so any campus network down time or inefficiency has a negative impact on the university bottom line.

Secure, high performance, high available LAN services are crucial to ensure that each campus facility is always online, so that administrative, academic, research productivity as well as user satisfaction are maximized. This chapter focuses on the issues and challenges in establishing and maintaining the campus network at Kuvempu University for effective utilisation of the UGC-Infonet e-resource, internet services and for other administrative and academic applications through adopting proper planning and implementation. A campus network design that meets campus security, connectivity, and performance challenges while enabling key IT initiatives is needed. It also must scale, offer operational simplicity and flexibility, accommodate new computing trends without much alterations in the original structure and design.

OBJECTIVES

- To highlight the issues on how the Kuvempu University has planned and established campus network for effective utilisation of UGC-Infonet programme.
- To know the issues and challenges faced in establishing the campus Network.
- To know the issues related to changing campus needs.
- To know how best the UGC-Infonet and internet services reaches the end users of Kuvempu University.
- To know the use of campus network for different administrative and academic services.

UGC-INFONET DIGITAL LIBRARY E-CONSORTIA PROGRAMMES AT KUVEMPU UNIVERSITY

The Kuvempu University was established in year 1987. Till then it was functioning as a post-graduate centre of University of Mysore. The university has started to get the benefits and assistance provided by the UGC through Inflibnet Centre, Ahamadabad for automation of its library as early as 1995. In 1997, the university library has received financial assistance of ₹ 6.50 lakhs from Inflibnet for its automation activity.

The university library has taken a lot of initiatives in automating its library activities by making use of the grants and other assistance of the UGC. Again in 2004 the UGC has sanctioned ₹ 7.14 lakhs and considered the Kuvempu University as one among the 50 universities in the First phase of the UGC-Infonet programme. Under this programme the UGC has initially given 128 kbps BB VSAT for Internet purpose during 2004 and later it was upgraded to 256 kbps BB VSAT. In 2008 the bandwidth was upgraded to 2 MB leased line for better utilisation of UGC-infonet programme and other internet services for the benefit of the administrative, academic and research community.

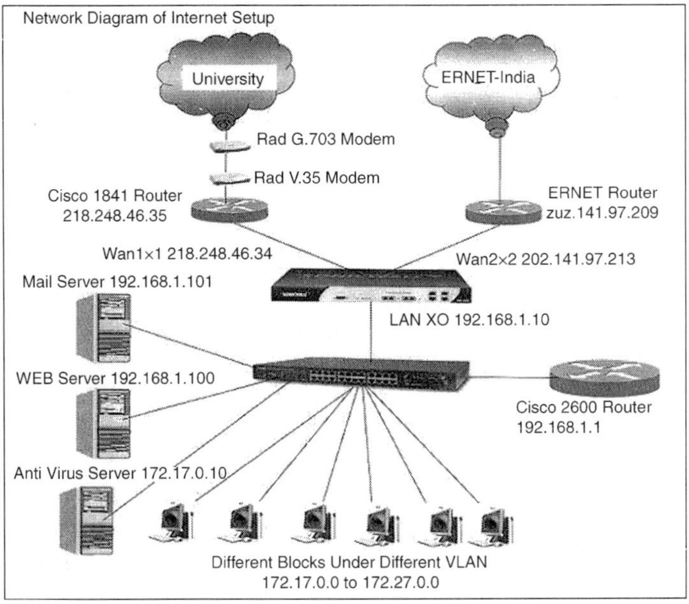

Fig. Integration of Two 2 MB Leased Line Connectivity

The university library was instrumental to initiate and implement the campus network, establishing Network Operation Centre in library building itself. Initially, the programme was confined to library by creating a LAN with 24 nodes for all its users. Then it was extended by establishing a campus network throughout campus to all the academic and administrative blocks in the campus by creating number of virtual LANs, by laying OFC backbone. Later through different stages the LAN network was extended to the other blocks in the campus including hostels, Guest House and Residence of the Statutory Officers. As for as the bandwidth of the internet is concerned the university on its own has subscribed additional 2 MB BSNL leased line connectivity and integrated the same with the 2 MB of UGCinfonet to meet the speed requirement.

The integrating techniques have been applied to integrate the Two 2 MB leased lines connectivities, by making use of Sonicwall Firewall and is as shown in the figure, for effective utilisation of the UGC-infonet programme and other internet based applications.

SERVICES UNDER CAMPUS NETWORK

Any campus network must provide the following high level services to optimise the administrative, academic and research activity in the university. In this direction the Kuvempu University has taken several measures under campus network.

They are:

- *LAN (Local Area Network) Connectivity*: The entire campus has been covered by extending secured wired and wireless LAN connectivity by creating independent virtual LANs.

- *WAN Connectivity*: The WAN connectivity has been created through reliable, and secured Network Operation Centre for maintaining servers for different application like Web server, Mail server, Proxy server, Antivirus server and Database server.
- *Remote Access Server*: Remote Access Server is also enabled for effective use of the e-resources, and other database service by the remote users.
- Antivirus, Anti-spy ware, Anti spam, Content Filter, and Intrusion Prevention Services: The Kuvempu University has taken much and top priority to protect the network and the data by applying antivirus solution by creating network based antivirus server with a powerfull antivirus as well as the antivirus control at the firewall level to avoid the virus from outside, along with Anti-spyware, Anti-spam, Content filtering and Instruction prevention facilities also taken at the firewall level.
- *Security*: Security is critical to all campus network services. Access to network and application must be open and pervasive, yet remain secure and controlled. Today's networks not only need to effectively handle unmanaged devices and guest users attempting network access, they also need to address support for unmanageable devices, post admission control, application access control, visibly and monitoring. A high end firewall with antivirus, anti-spyware, anti-spam, content filtering, and intrusion prevention, etc., installed at Network Operation Centre in the library takes care of the security.
- *High Performance*: The higher performance of the speed in the wired and wireless LAN must be provided at all time throughout the campus. Due to the creation of number of VLANs and strong OFC backbone the speed performance in both wired and wireless LANs is good. LANlike speed must also be maintained over the WAN when accessing any centralised applications or resources.
- *High Availability*: Downtime of the internet connectivity either by the services provider side or by the user side is not an option in today's campus network but it must offer at least 99 per cent of reliability with a goal of approaching the level of service. For this the university has taken several measures like opting high end core network devices, Softwares, and redundancy in the network structure, etc.
- *Centralised Management*: The centralised management is very much required to maintain the campus network activity. Kuvempu University has set up main Network Operation Centre at its central library and the library staff with the help of computer programmer is maintaining and controlling the entire campus network at all levels. From this

Network Operating Centre all network switches, firewalls, routers and other security devices and servers are installed and maintained. Centralised management solutions reduce the time and expense required to configure and manage network devices. In addition network traffic can be more easily analysed with such a system facilitating network performance optimisation.

PREREQUISITES FOR CAMPUS NETWORK LAN DESIGN

The following are the minimum basic prerequisites which we have considered under the functionality, scalability, adaptability and manageability issues while designing and establishing the campus network:

- The proposed network should be aimed at the goals of the organisation.
- Set up a technical expert committee chaired by the head of the institution comprising the technical experts from both inside/outside the institution.
- Campus Network must scale and accommodate emerging computing trends and additional network services without an entire redesign of the campus network.
- The adoption of unified communications including voice and data services is on the rise such deployments have a direct impact on the high performance and high availability requirements of a campus network.
- Requirements of suitable bandwidth from the service provider like BSNL in addition to the UGC allotted Bandwidth based on the load and requirement.
- Care should be taken for the network must be leveraged with high end service such as wireless coverage and remote access to maximize productivity by avoiding any LAN downtime or inefficiency that impacts the institution bottom line.
- Security issues to avoid any sort of internal and external attacks.
- *Wireless services*: One of the main drives of better business decisions is access to key information and resources at all times from all location in the campus. Administrators, Faculties, Students and researchers use their laptops, expect wireless access to all of their applications, data stores, resources and services. For this reason the wi-fi provision should be made available throughout the campus with suitable secure to access it. Such wireless services enable users to access whatever materials are needed to support their requirement.
- *Server centralisation or centralised operation*: Is highly opted to centralise and control the server and their operations from a single point. For this there is a need to establish Network Operation Centre to

operate, control, maintain the campus network to reduce costs, simplify operations and comply with regulatory guidelines.

- *Upgradation and expansion activity*: The network infrastructure in today's campus is no longer sufficient to satisfy the user requirements. Also due to the fast advancement in the computer and communication technology and in their services inevitably we have to invite and accept for upgrading the existing setup regularly.

Based on the increase in the number of users in the campus and new applications both in administrative and academic environment we have to expand the campus network for effective use of different resources:

- *Survey of the Campus*: Survey of the campus and all building blocks in the campus is very much needed before starting planning and establishing the campus network.
- *Manpower*: Skilled, technically qualified and sufficient number of staff required at different levels to operate and maintain campus network.
- *Budget*: Appropriate budget provision should be made for planning required campus network project.

KUVEMPU UNIVERSITY CAMPUS NETWORK ARCHITECTURE

Three layer approach of campus network at Kuvempu University consists of the following:

Core Layer Level

The Core Layer Level consists of all high end network accessories, Servers, and WAN Connectivity, established and installed in the centralised Network Operation Centre.

The Network Operation Centre of Kuvempu University consists of:

- 2 MB plus 2 MB leased line connectivity from ERNET-BSNL and KU-BSNL respectively.
- Both the connectivities have been integrated by using high end sonicwal Firewall device.
- High End CISCO Routers are used for Leased Line connectivity.
- CISCO-2600 series Router used for routing purpose.
- Sonic-wall Firewall device used as a Gateway and Firewall also used as a Anti-Virus, Anti-Spam, Anti-Spyware and Intrusion Prevention Control tool.
- Cisco L2 Catalyst Manageable Switch is used for maintaining different VLANs.
- Sufficient number of OFCs have been terminated by using appropriate OFC terminating network accessories.
- Proxy server with Linux OS platform is configured and using for campus net maintenance.

- WEB server is configured and hosted with university web site.
- E-mail services is also configured and implemented and maintained for university mail services.
- Importantly Antivirus server is also maintaining by installed 250 users Trend Micro network based antivirus software for taking care of antivirus problem in the campus network.
- Some D-link manageable switches are also used to maintain the Local LAN of the Library.

Aggregation Level Layer

The aggregation level layer sometimes referred to as the distribution layer aggregates connection and traffic flows from multiple access layer switches to provide high density connectivity to the LAN core. Due to their location in the network aggregation layer switches must provide scalability, high-density wirerate ports, and high availability hardware and software features that deliver carrier class, reliability and robustness. OFC-Optical Fibre cable with 4 Core and 6 core used and laid between the different blocks from the main network operation centre with redundancy between some important blocks/segments.

Access Level Layer

On a campus, the access level layer provides network connectivity to end users by connecting devices such as PC's Printers, IP Phones, etc., via wired and wireless LAN access points. In the access level layer the switches typically reside in the wiring closest of each floor in each campus facility. The access level layer provides connectivity Power over Ethernet (PoE), QoS, and Security with policy services and network access control.

Access Lavel Layer Design Consideration includes:

- Wired port connectivity
- Wireless LAN (WLAN) connectivity
- Power over Ethernet
- Virtual LAN (VLAN)

Campus network use VLANS to logically group sets of users, devices or data regardless of location into logical networks through software configuration instead of physically relocating devices on the LAN. The VLANs help to address issues such as scalability and network management. One such VLAN established in Bioscience block is illustrated.

OPTIMISATION IN UTILISING THE UGC-INFONET PROGRAMME

The university has taken up some of the following initiatives in creating awareness among the academic community as well as administrative staff for effective utilisation of internet based resources and services:

- Training and awareness programme to educate, operate and maintain the campus network for selected technical professionals
- Developing IT culture about the use and awareness of the existing available infrastructure
- Creating awareness about the worthiness of internet as an information source
- Accessibility to Internet Services
- Education and training programme
- Monitoring internet use for academics
- Ensuring the access speed of Internet
- Creation and compilation of web sites

ACTIVITIES UNDER KUVEMPU UNIVERSITY CAMPUS NETWORK

The University has established and utilising the campus network to meet its administrative, academic, research and other activities as mentioned below:

- Establishment of Network Operation Centre to control and maintain the campus network.
- Creation OFC Backbone structured segmentwise Campus LAN.
- Creation of Block-wise LANs and WLANs under different VLANs connecting more than 450 nodes.
- Functioning of Wireless LAN in Dynamic mode.
- Creation of Proxy Server for campus network maintenance on Linux Platform.
- Creation of Web server for hosting Kuvempu University web site and its application.
- Creation of Mail Server for Kuvempu University mail services.
- Creation of Antivirus server with 250 users to maintain the antivirus.
- Creation of database servers on different applications.
- Setup of Tele Medicine service facility at University Health Centre connecting with one of the popular and prestigious cardiology centre in Karnataka, *i.e.*, Narayana Hrudayalaya, Bangalore for the 24 hours online treatment of cardiac diseases for the benefit of the university staff.
- Conducting regular training/awareness programmes to make use of campus network as well as UGC-Infonet programme with the cooperation of Inflibnet Centre, Ahmedabad.
- Arrangement of online demonstration of products/services.

EXPANSION ACTIVITIES

The expansion of the campus network both physically and logically is a continuous process based on the requirements of the future programmes of the university and its Post-Graduate Centres. In this direction we have already planned and initiated the expansion task of campus network to the off campus at Post-Graduate Centre, Davanagere in the coming days. The execution of the task is in progress.

CHALLENGES

Any campus network task that should be in a position to accept the challenges at different levels and in different forms due to the continuous technological changes, environmental changes, financial constraints, human resources, user satisfaction, and for many other reasons as listed below:

- Maintenance of Campus Network by adopting new technologies as and when they available and discard the obsolete one.
- Constant upgradation of the existing setup along with upgradtion of bandwidth.
- Regular training to the technical staff and their retention.
- Recruitment of trained and skilled manpower to handle and maintain the campus network and its applications.
- Expansion activities.
- Effective utilisation of campus network for administrative, academic, research and many other purposes.
- Regular training/awareness programmes to the administrative staff, faculties, researchers and students.
- Provisions for making appropriate budget for maintenance, expansion activities.

FUTURE PLANS

Because of the technological revolution and globalised situation all most all the organisational functionaries are network based online applications. For this there is a need to make use of this campus network to the university's all online and network based applications in the coming days.

They are:

- Further strengthening of the digital library applications.
- Implementation of university e-governance application.
- Addition of different servers for different applications.
- Video-conferencing/Teleconferencing facility between the Main campus to its post-Graduate centres.
- Permanent setup of training/awareness training cell.
- IP based camera services for connecting important areas in the campus.
- On-line registration, examination services.
- Establishing e-learning centre.
- Online distance education mode.

ICT FACILITIES AND SERVICES AT M. K. TATA MEMORIAL LEARNING CENTRE FOR VISUALLY CHALLENGED

Disability can be defined as a physical or mental condition that prohibits an individual from the use of his or her body (either partially, completely and with ease) to perform daily tasks. It can also be defined as meaning that one cannot learn easily. It should be noted that in addition to the physical challenges, visually impaired and physically handicapped people face the ignorance barrier, a major prejudice and most harmful social discrimination.

These difficulties are not compensated for by emotional speeches. Public awareness and equal opportunities are necessary conditions to integrate them into society. It is already established that access to information is one of the most important human rights: it allows the individual to develop himself/herself, and participate actively within a democratic society, fully exercising his/her rights and duties. A badly informed community, or one that restricts information to an elite group, in the long term becomes a non-democratic society in which ignorance and inequality of opportunities will unfailingly lead to intolerance and discrimination among citisens.

All citizens should therefore have access to information that will enable them to be active and equal contributors and participants in society. The World Wide Web provides a great potential to the academic and research community as an instrumental tool that extends the content of the curriculum, enrich class room discourse, remote communication and enhance learning opportunity. It has become possible to connect with learning resources located in libraries and information centres across the globe, and TISS proposes to establish M K Tata Memorial Learning Centre for Visually Challenged students of TISS to access to such learning resources.

EARLY INITIATIVES AT SDTM LIBRARY

The present library, Sir Dorabji Tata Memorial Library, is one of the premier social science libraries in the world established with the support of Sir Dorabji Tata Trust and is used by people from all over the world. Presently the library is in the process of expansion of library facilities by having digital library, cyber library, document delivery system for the Asian library users. However, some of visually challenged students are at a disadvantage as they will not be able to make use of these facilities.

Since, the institute has admitted several visually challenged students in various programmes and library has only one Galileo Reading machine at present donated by Sir Dorabji Tata Trust in the year 1999 and inaugurated by Shri. Ratan Tata, Chairman, Tata Group. To ensure equality of access to ICT for Lifelong Learning, to Litreature, and for the Information needs for those with a disability, the library had submitted a proposal to M K Tata Trust in September, 2007 for the establishment of "M. K. Tata Memorial Learning Centre for Visually Challenged Students" at TISS Library. Development of M. K. Tata Memorial Learning Centre for Visually Challenged Students therefore bridges the gap between visually challenged and others and give an equal opportunity to access available information sources in the form of book, journal, online databases and electronic journals.

Objective

To establish a learning centre exclusively for the support of visually challenged students which will have computer assisted reading facilities.

Justification and Anticipated Impact

One of the major difficulties faced by visually challenged students is to access learning materials available in print and electronic version. Not all information is available in Braille version.

This learning centre will provide:

- Independent reading of books/journals and library services.
- Computer Training for Independent Access of Computers and other ICT equipments.
- Provision of curriculum in alternative format namely Braille, large print or soft copies on CDs.
- Congenial Classroom environment.

Funding and Sustainability

It is proposed that the M K Tata Trust be approached to support the establishment of the M K Tata Memorial Learning Centre for Visually Challenged. From the current academic year, TISS has started charging the students a small fee as 'Development Fund' to pay maintenance of these new facilities. The centre will cater to the Visually Impaired and Physically handicapped students. A computer reading facility for visually impaired will be provided which reads and stores all printed documents including letters, books, magazines and newspapers in floppy. Even stored information in the floppy can be read through this machine. The user can record it in tape and listen the information at home. This machine is used by the students as well as general public in and around TISS. Library will set up a separate unit for the Visually Impaired students where 10 dedicated computers with JAWS software loaded and Galileo Reading System have been installed.

SALIENT FEATURES OF M K TATA MEMORIAL LEARNING CENTRE

Provision of the following facilities is critical to the quality of teaching and learning experiences in Computer training centres for the visually impaired:

- Computer Training for Independent Access of Computers.
- Independent reading of text books/library services
- Provision of curriculum in alternative format namely Braille, large print or soft copies on floppies or CDs.
- Congenial Classroom environment.

- Barrier free access to the disabled.

Computer Training for Independent Access of Computers

Today the visually impaired, deaf, deaf blind and physically challenged can also learn computers. JAWS Software for the blind, which converts a normal PC into a talking PC, Magic Magnification Software for low vision persons and speech recognition software like the Qpointer Hands free, modified keyboards, switches, pointing devices for physically handicapped and Converser FM assistive listening devices for deaf make it possible to train the disabled in computers. Knowing computers would also help them in their education as they can acquire an ocean of knowledge and information from the Internet.

Independent Text Reading

The blind and low vision students today are dependent on voluntarily readers and are able to barely manage to study their textbooks but due to acute shortage of human readers these days, the problems have multiplied. However, with the use of Text Reading machines, like the K1000 OCR reading software, which using a PC and scanner convert any printed text into sound and magnify the text for low vision on a Standard TV/monitor, or even provide support for reading, writing and studying for dyslexic [learning disabled] they can simply borrow any book from the library and read the same independently and Prisma print magnifier connected to a 21 inch TV or monitor for low vision.

Provision of Curriculum in Alternative Format like Braille Computer Lessons

With the setting up of a high speed computerised mini Braille printer, they can get their lessons of their choice in Braille, even one copy, if so desired on demand as and when needed. They can also carry home notes or a few chapters of a textbook taken from the library duly converted into Braille for studying at their own pace at home. This facility can be extended not only to English language but one can also produce Braille text in Indian languages. Besides, one can also provide Braille print-outs not only in text but also charts, maps, diagrams, pictures incorporated along with the text.

M.K. TATA MEMORIAL LEARNING CENTRE: STATE OF- THE-ART ICT FACILITIES

M. K. Tata Memorial Learning Centre has been setup at Sir Dorabji Tata Memorial Library, TISS in 2008 to provide innovative teaching techniques and philosophy that continues to have far-reaching effects on the lives of visually challenged and taking them to new heights of independence. M. K. Tata Trust, Mumbai has funded the project. Ms. Piloo Tata, Chairperson, M. K. Tata Trust was inaugurated the centre on 7th May, 2008 during the Institute Convocation function. The Centre has acquired latest technologies to assist visually impaired readers. For the first time, partially sighted people can now read for long periods of time without tiredness. It is a unique computer reading facility for visually impaired with a congenial classroom environment. The Centre is aimed to provide barrier free access and independent reading of library materials. The Centre believes that with proper training and opportunity, visually challenged people can compete on terms of equality with their sighted peers. Provision of the following latest assistive technologies is critical to the quality of teaching and learning experiences in computer training centres for the visually impaired.

JAWS Pro Talking Software

For conversion of a normal PC into a Talking PC to enable the blind to operate computers independently including Internet Access and also to train blind persons on using the computer.

Kurzweil 1000 OCR Reading Software

An excellent support for blind students to read any printed books from the library to have independent access to not only their text-books but also other general reading. It is used with a combination of a scanner and a PC.

Magic Magnification Software Pro

Useful for enlarging the screen from 2x to 16x enabling Low vision students to view the monitor screen as well as use the add-on support tools for enhancing visibility.

Talking Typing Teacher Pro

Talking Typing tutorials specially designed for the blind with complete guidance and practice lessons for learning keyboarding skills and developing typing speed in a systematic manner. Since, the programme also has a complete display of all lessons, even the low vision students can read and learn to type.

Braille Scanning Software—OBR (Optical Braille Recognition)

Optical Braille Recognition (OBR) is a Windows software programme that allows you to 'read' single and double sided Braille documents on a standard A4 scanner. It scans the Braille document, analyses the dot pattern, and translates it into normal text that it presents on the computer screen.

Prisma Magnification Device for Low Vision

Prisma is a full colour video magnifier with a stylish, adjustable camera stand and integral table that allows a tremendous range of magnification in a convenient size. The simple controls allow you to view in full colour or enhanced reading modes. Magnification is achieved by raising or lowering the camera and re-focussing with the large focus control located on the top. Prisma uses a standard TV for its display, so you can take it just anywhere.

The clearance under the camera allows you to write easily and even perform hand tasks such as needlework or carving.

Zoom—Ex Instant Tex]t Reader

Zoom—Ex is a small portable device that uses the new generation Motion Sensor technology in combination with its proprietary Zoom Office software to make scanning and instant reading of text fast and easy. Place a book under the highly sensitive camera and start reading or listening instantly and that too with an Indian Accent Voice! and with every turn of a page, the camera takes a snapshot of the page automatically. It then converts these photographic images to readable text. A book of 200 pages is ready in 8 minutes! Now read it at your own pace for long hours.

Index Basic D Braille Embosser

Index Basic D low cost, High Speed, Double sided Tractor Feed continuous sheet, new generation technology Braille embosser.

Important features are:

- It produces 2 pages, *i.e.*, front and back at the same time; uses Tractor Feed paper which can be spiral bound using plastic wire making it very economical; does not require any special binding equipment; supplied with an acoustic cabinet. The acoustic cabinet is very important for reduction of noise level during printing as well as protection of the printer from heat and dust. It also enables collection of the paper in an orderly manner.

Freedom Scientific's SARA

Freedom Scientific's SARA™ (Scanning and Reading Appliance) is an affordable and easy-to-use solution for reading a wide variety of printed material including books, mail, newspapers, magazines, and so much more. SARA uses the latest in advanced optical character recognition technology to scan text and then read it aloud in crisp, clear speech. SARA automatically stores and remembers the contents of hundreds of thousands of scanned pages.

DSpace Digital Archive

A separate digital archive has been maintained in the DSpace Digital Library portal where all the essential reading materials required by visually challenged students are digitised and maintained in the archive.

Infrastructure Facilities

- *Desktop Computers*: 20 Hp Pentium computers under LAN environment.

- *LAN Connection*: For inter connecting the computers for better management and control by the computer trainer.
- *HP Scanners*: For use with K1000 for reading by blind students.
- *Headphones*: To avoid disturbance and confusion when listening to JAWS by many persons at the same time.
- *UPS units*: For providing stabilised and uninterrupted power supply for at least 10 minutes to prevent loss of data and damage to the equipment caused by frequent power breakdowns.
- *Air-conditioner*: Required to protect the equipment from heat and dust and also to maintain a cool temperature which is important in areas with high temperatures during summers.

4

Basic Preservation for Library and Archive Collections

COSTS AND BENEFITS OF COLLECTION PRESERVATION

Addressing collection preservation as part of library building design helps to protect the collection against catastrophic loss and to reduce library expenses by extending the collection's service life. The purpose of collection preservation is to manage risk to an acceptable level, while acknowledging that avoiding risk altogether is impossible. The collection is the library's single largest asset; designing the building that houses it to maximize protection against major losses, including earthquake, fire, water damage, and theft, is responsible management of public resources. Designing an indoor environment (including temperature, humidity, air quality, and light levels) conducive to preservation extends the collection's service life by slowing down its rate of physical deterioration.

Books and documents intended to be kept in the collection permanently will not need to be replaced as often, saving the library money. Preservation costs money to save money; it requires an initial investment in building features and systems to increase protection and reduce deterioration. The library's return on its investment comes as cost avoidance in the years that follow: fewer losses and longer service life. To minimize up front costs, actions to protect the collection and actions to optimise the collection environment should be addressed separately. All library collections represent a large investment of library funds. Consequently, all library building projects should optimise their design to protect the collections against earthquake, fire, water, and theft. Some collections have to last forever; many libraries have "special" and "local history" collections they want to last centuries, if possible. These collections largely are irreplaceable and therefore need additional features from the building design to maximize their service lives. However, most collection materials in most publicly funded libraries are not added to the collection with the expectation that they will continue to be part of the collection indefinitely.

These "general" collection materials are expected to be serviceable enough to meet current and anticipated future needs; they will be discarded when they no longer are needed or have been succeeded by more current works. Opportunities to minimize preservation-related construction and operating costs accrue from distinguishing between the needs of general and special collections. If the two types of collections can be segregated for storage and use, the higher cost solutions needed for special collections can be addressed without incurring the cost of applying the same solutions to the general collections. For example, irreplaceable special collection materials might be stored in a very secure part of the building where there are no emergency exits from the building decreasing the risk of theft, and without water lines or other utilities, decreasing the risk of water damage.

Special collection materials could be used in reading areas where sight lines from service desks are unobstructed, providing a sense of vigilance and security for the collection. The relatively challenging environmental conditions needed for storage of special collections might be met more readily and less expensively by locating special collections away from exterior walls and windows where environmental control is more difficult and more costly.

COLLECTION PROTECTION

The recommendations for collection protection below apply equally to general and special collections, are the top priority among preservation measures, and should be implemented for all new library construction or major renovations.

FIRE PROTECTION

Library fires are a very common and very serious risk to collections. In the United States alone, an average of 198 library fires has been suffered each year since, 1980— one library fire every 1.8 days. From the point of view of survival of collections, popular belief for some decades was that more books and documents were lost to malfunctions and unwanted discharge of water-based fire suppression systems than to fire. This led to deployment of non-aqueous systems, aqueous systems based on keeping sprinkler pipes filled with air rather than water until a fire triggered the system to fill with water, and even installation of fire detection systems instead of fire suppression systems.

With modern freeze-drying technology, this perspective has changed; wet materials can be salvaged, but burned materials cannot. Further, National Fire Protection Association (NFPA) fire tests have discounted the mistaken notion that library materials don't burn readily; studies have proven that library materials constitute a high concentration of combustible material that makes library stack fires, once underway, very difficult to extinguish.

Best Practices

Current best practices are to:

- Minimize exposure to arson which are accountable for nearly a third of all library fires;
- Use compartmentation to limit the spread of fire; and
- Employ fire detection AND water-based fire suppression systems for collection protection.

Minimize exposure to arson. Exterior doors in library buildings (public, staff, and emergency egress doors) need to be well attended and controlled, and they usually are. Windows, however, too often are left unattended during library open hours, and left unlocked or open when the library is closed, providing an arsonist with an opportunity to start a fire by tossing into the building burning rags, wadded up paper, or even (on record) Molotov cocktails.

Windows that do not open eliminate this risk, or the risk can be reduced by the use of screening to cover windows that can be opened. A second major exposure to arson comes from book returns that penetrate the exterior wall into library space. A book return built into the wall of a library gives an arsonist easy access to the interior, and often is provided with a convenient fuel source in the form of other books that previously have been deposited in the book return. Much damage has been done by book return fires, including damage from smoke that spreads throughout the building. Best practice is to use stand alone book return bins located outside and away from the perimeter of the building. Use compartmentation to limit the spread of fire.

In any book stack, the risk of major damage to or loss of the entire collection is reduced by introducing "compartmentation," *i.e.*, subdividing the book stack by constructing fire-resistant walls, ceilings, and floors to limit the spread of fire, smoke, and to some extent, water. Compartmentation is a highly successful method of reducing risk if barriers are designed and installed properly. Fire ratings must be appropriate for book stacks, and there can be no breaks or interruptions to the barriers.

Points often overlooked in the use of compartmentation are continuation of the walls above drop ceilings to the floor above, installation of automatic dampers in air handling systems, sealing of gaps around utility tunnels, and use of automatic fire doors; all are measures designed to help isolate compartments from one another to prevent the spread of fire, smoke, and water. Vertical openings between floors for services, stairwells, and elevators need to be sealed if each floor is to become a separate compartment and barrier to the spread of fire.

Special collection storage areas often are especially suitable for compartmentation; the collection usually is housed in closed stacks (not accessible directly by library patrons) and often has additional security and environmental requirements that dovetail well with the use of compartmentation for fire protection. Employ fire detection AND water-based fire suppression systems. Fire detection systems include those based on heat sensors, smoke sensors, and products of combustion sensors. Fire detection systems can detect fires prior to triggering the suppression system and, consequently, can buy an extremely valuable few minutes for fire department response. Among fire detection equipment options, products of combustion sensors can detect fires sooner than heat or smoke detectors, so have been recommended when water damage from the suppression system is to be avoided if at all possible.

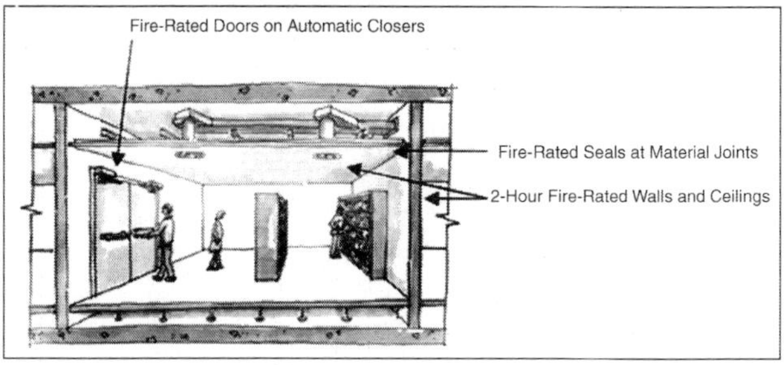

Fig. Special Collection Area Separated through Compartmentation.

Fire Suppression Systems

Most fire suppression systems in libraries are water-based sprinkler systems, but non-aqueous gas, expansion foam, and chemical powder suppression systems also are available. Non-aqueous fire suppression systems based on the use of carbon dioxide are not used in libraries because people can be suffocated by the system when it discharges. Non-aqueous systems based on use of fluorocarbons have been outlawed due to the damage the fluorocarbon discharge can do to the environment. Water-based fire suppression systems utilise a range of delivery technologies from "wet pipe" to "dry pipe" to high pressure "water mist" systems. Wet pipe systems keep the sprinkler pipes filled with water at all times and use temperature-triggered sprinkler heads that open the sprinkler valves at a predetermined temperature.

The wet pipe system has proven to be very reliable in many library installations for three reasons: it works when needed, it is unlikely to discharge when not needed (short of someone accidentally breaking off a sprinkler head), and it requires the least maintenance of all types of fire suppression systems. Part of the success of the wet pipe system is due to its simple technology and relatively low maintenance requirements; staff knowledge of suppression systems often is limited, and maintenance schedules are notorious for being deferred to higher priority needs.

"On/off" sprinkler heads, once a popular technology designed to limit the amount of water discharged by automatically turning on and off the flow of water, no longer are available from domestic manufacturers following failures and recalls of some designs in the late 1990s. "Water mist" systems are similar to wet pipe systems in design except that they deliver water under high pressure to specially designed nozzles, creating a fog of fine water droplets that quickly lowers the temperature below that needed to support combustion. The water mist system is designed to use the least water and cause the least water damage, but has not yet been widely deployed for the protection of library collections, so little is known about its long-term performance.

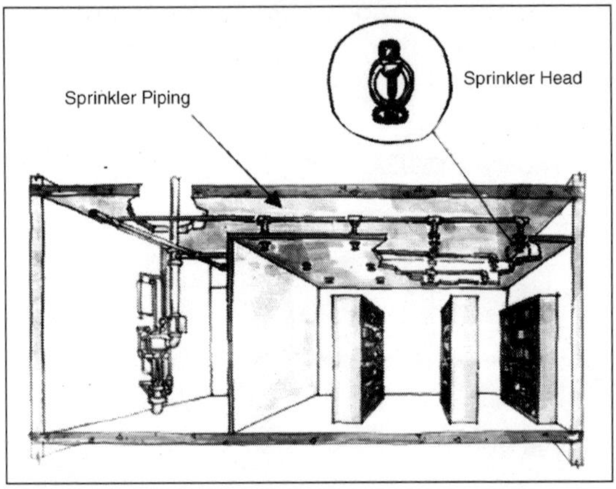

Fig. Typical Water-based Fire Suppression System.

However, the monetary and historical value of some special collections may justify investigation of the latest developments in this fire suppression technology. "Dry pipe" systems are filled with air rather than water until the fire detection system senses a fire, at which point the pipes fill with water. Alternately, a sprinkler head is tripped and opened, which releases the air from the pipes. The pipes fill with water, and water is discharged from the sprinkler head(s) that opened. Dry pipe systems suffer some disadvantages from the preservation perspective: they are slower to respond to a need for suppression than wet pipe systems, and they require more attention to maintenance. In the absence of the required maintenance, they are more likely to fail.

Fire Protection and Cellulose Nitrate Film

Cellulose nitrate film decomposes over time, becoming less stable and more combustible, a process exacerbated by elevated temperatures and storage in concentration. Early motion picture films were made of cellulose nitrate and most commonly have been stored in rolls in film cans. Over time, these films have become a sufficient fire hazard such that the National Fire Protection Association produced *NFPA 40: Standard for the Storage and Handling of Cellulose Nitrate Motion Picture Film*, to address their special needs. Many special collections have significant holdings of early cellulose nitrate sheet film (as distinct from motion picture film), much of it in protective paper sleeves or interfiled with related paper documents and in quite serviceable condition. The most recent edition of *NFPA 40: Standard for the Storage and Handling of Cellulose Nitrate Film, 2001 Edition,* was renamed and extended to the storage of cellulose nitrate still or sheet film, calling for segregation of cellulose nitrate still film from the rest of the collection with storage practices to match those for motion picture film.

The inclusion of sheet film in *NFPA 40* without recognition of its apparently greater stability than motion picture film has led to controversy within the photographic conservation field. As of this writing, the necessity for segregation of cellulose nitrate *sheet* film from the rest of the collection for increased fire safety is very unclear, while the costs of constructing separate storage facilities without justification discourage implementation of this NFPA Standard.

WATER PROTECTION

With the exception of the use of water to extinguish fire, water damage to collections is a consequence of a failure of a building system to work as intended. The roof, the windows, the plumbing, the heating, ventilating, and air-conditioning (HVAC) system, and rarely, the fire sprinkler system, cause water damage because they have failed. In addition to using well designed and constructed systems, there are two building-related approaches to optimise water protection for the collections: system avoidance and vigilance.

System Avoidance

System avoidance entails eliminating any systems from collection storage areas unneeded to meet the operational requirements for collection storage. While the primary concern usually is water damage, systems that could create a fire also should be reviewed for elimination. Unnecessary windows, restrooms, utility sinks and other utility plumbing, and roof drains that pass through the building should be eliminated from areas designed primarily to store collections. If areas are multi-use, including collection storage, compromises will need to be made to accommodate the multiple functions, but at increased risk to the collections.

Vigilance

Vigilance in the form of routine inspection and maintenance is an effective form of water protection. Routine inspection of gutters for clogging leaves, roofs for cracks, the support structure below for telltale water stains, joints on plumbing for evidence of corrosion and slow leaks, and interior drains for sluggish performance are among the often deferred facility services.

An alternative solution to some routine inspection is installation of automatic monitoring systems that detect water; equipment is available to monitor for roof leaks, water buildup on floors, and wet walls, with options for either local alarms or automated notification to 24/7 monitoring services. A search on the World Wide Web for "water detection" will yield a range of equipment designed for this purpose.

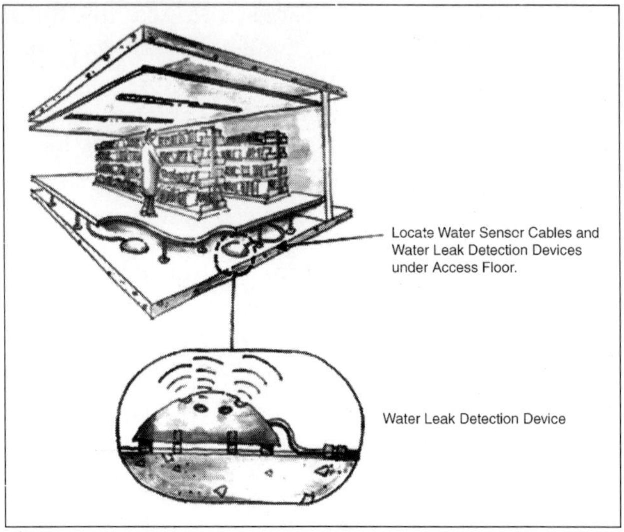

Fig. Water Leak Detection Under Access Floors.

Siting HVAC Equipment

Placing the HVAC equipment on the roof over the collection area is undesirable for two reasons. Vibration from the equipment can cause fractures to the roof's surface, leading to leakage, and the equipment itself can provide water an entry point through the roof to the interior below. Further, the discharge of water from the system has been known to back up until it overflowed into the building. For both reasons, siting the HVAC equipment alongside the building is better than any roof location, and failing that option for aesthetic or space reasons, siting it away from collection areas is recommended.

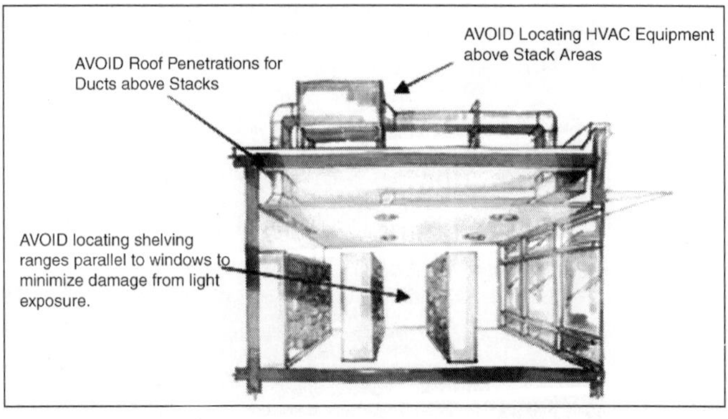

Fig. Illustration of Poor HVAC Equipment Siting.

THEFT AND VANDALISM PROTECTION

Managing access to and egress from the storage and reading areas is essential for provision of good service and protection of collections. Unobstructed sight lines for staff observation of user behaviour are a good deterrent to theft and vandalism, as well as beneficial for staff and patron safety. The design and layout of service desks need to consider points of entry and exit from the library. Key or card access to special collections areas needs to be different from that to the general collections areas to ensure that only authorised staff have access to the facilities and collections.

DISASTER RESPONSE AND COLLECTION SALVAGE

Good building design and good preparedness practices reduce, but do not eliminate, risk of disaster. When disaster strikes, the collection is best served by effective and efficient emergency response and salvage. A written disaster response and collection salvage plan, a trained staff collection salvage team, a cache of salvage supplies, and a list of priorities for collection salvage are essential elements of collection protection.

There are several reasons for maintaining a written plan rather than relying on a general shared agreement and understanding:

- To ensure that staff responsible for action have all the necessary information;
- To ensure that all response and salvage staff are using the same information;
- To help staff think clearly and work systematically in high stress emergency situations; and
- To better inform staff whose responsibilities are peripheral to the main emergency response and collection salvage effort.

A generic (fill-in-the-blanks) plan for disaster response and collection salvage is located at the California Preservation Clearinghouse, along with a wealth of information on disaster preparedness activities, resources for supplies and technical help, and "table top" exercises to test out the viability of an institutional disaster response and collection salvage plan in response to a particular disaster scenario.

Every disaster response and collection salvage plan needs to include several major components:

- Emergency notification procedures (*e.g.*, fire department, police, facilities management, library administration, library supervisors of affected staff);
- Outline of the collection salvage operation, including authority and responsibility for the several roles;
- Step-by-step procedures for identifying and packing wet materials;
- List and location of onsite salvage supplies, and resources for additional supplies;

- List of priorities for salvage in the event that time and staffing are too limited to salvage everything before parts of the collection become unsalvageable;
- Floor plans of the collection storage areas with the location of high priority materials for salvage marked on the plan.

The staff collection salvage team and a cache of salvage supplies are keys to quick action following a health and safety approval to re-enter earthquake-, fire-, or waterdamaged buildings. Time is limited for water-damaged materials; as few as 36-48 hours may elapse before irreparable damage (especially from growth of mold) begins. The success rate for collection salvage can be very high when salvage actions are taken quickly; recovery rates of 95+ per cent are possible when the library is prepared. At the other extreme, libraries without disaster response and collection salvage plans have been known to suffer near total losses of water-damaged collections.

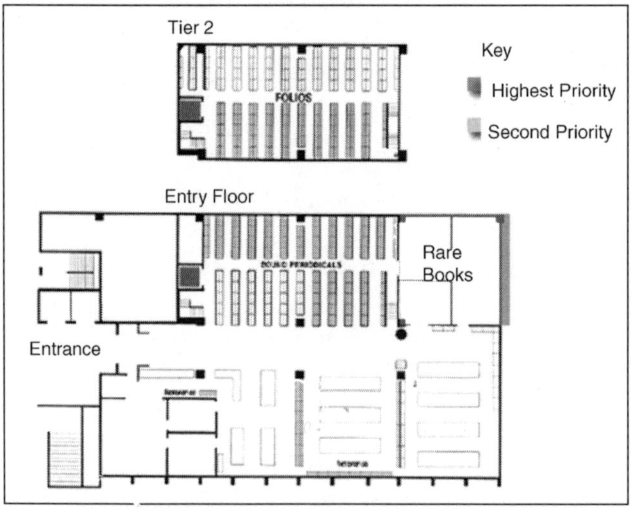

Fig. Sample Salvage Floor Plan Showing Areas of Highest Priority.

A secure space should be dedicated to storage of emergency supplies: mops, pails, wet vacuums, folded cartons and freezer paper (for salvaging wet books), plastic tarps, and paper toweling. The space should be located near an exit, if possible, to reduce the risk that impassable areas within a damaged building block access to the supplies. Equipping the library with a written disaster response and collection salvage plan demonstrates the library's commitment to responsible management and protection of institutional assets, and reduces the risk of accusations of administrative negligence. Engaging a representative of the library's insurance carrier in the preparation of the disaster response and salvage plan can lower premiums for collection insurance coverage. Further, reviewing insurance coverage with the insurance carrier *before* a disaster enables staff to know what steps can be taken immediately in response to the disaster without jeopardising coverage.

ENVIRONMENTAL CONTROL

After collection protection, environmental control is the most cost-effective investment in building design to extend the service life of the collection. The benefits of extended service life and reduced collection maintenance costs, in addition to considerations of human comfort, often can justify environmental control throughout the library.

However, if the project budget can support only part of the library to be environmentally controlled, the benefits to irreplaceable collections argue for controlling their environment above other collections in the library. Special and local history collections are California's documentary heritage. More than a financial investment and asset of the community, these collections often contain the only known copies of old local newspapers, books by local authors, publications about the area, and photos of the town and landscape as they were.

Additionally, some local history rooms serve as archives with collections of unpublished papers and scrapbooks of members of the community. These materials often are unique, almost always are irreplaceable, and need to last forever or as close to that as possible.

Categorising collection materials by environmental needs enables HVAC systems to be designed to achieve preservation goals, energy conservation goals, and to minimize HVAC system construction costs. General collections can be sub-divided usefully into "current collections" and "permanent collections" for HVAC design planning. If a library's general collection consists mostly of current materials, then the cost of achieving appropriate environmental conditions is less than for general collections that consist largely of materials of permanent value. *Current collections* are housed in combined stack and user areas, consist predominantly of high use circulating materials, and have a service life limited more by wear from use, and obsolescence from more current editions, than by chemically caused deterioration. Environmental requirements for these materials are minimal: control relative humidity to avoid desiccation from too dry air (which makes bookbindings more subject to cracking and magnetic media subject to static electricity), avoid mold growth from too damp air, and set the temperature to meet human comfort needs consistent with energy conservation goals.

Permanent collections usually are housed in combined stack and user areas, often have low use relative to "current" collections, but have continuing value even as they age. Protecting the investment the library has made in these materials can be enhanced by creating environmental conditions that extend the service life of the collection. In addition to avoiding desiccation and mold growth, the service life of the permanent collection can be extended by reducing temperature to the lowest level of comfort able to be tolerated by users and staff, and by stabilising relative humidity to help maintain the physical condition of the collection.

Special ("local history") collections usually are housed in stacks separated from users for security, thus providing an opportunity to create desirable environments for each. For these largely irreplaceable materials, preservation goals include both protection of investment and taking all prudent steps to ensure the materials' survival for future generations of library users. Desirable environmental conditions include setting the temperature as low as possible to minimize temperature-induced deterioration and controlling relative humidity to avoid collection damage.

The minimum set point for temperature is determined by the limit of the HVAC equipment to achieve the desired relative humidity, and by the difference between the stack conditions and reading room conditions: too great a difference could lead to condensation of moisture on cold materials when they are transferred from the cooler stack to the warmer reading room.

Collection **Category**	Temp.°F **(Incl. Fluctuation)**	RH % **(Incl. Fluctuation)**
Current	User comfort	35-65
Permanent	68-72	35-45
Special	60-65	35-45

RELATIVE HUMIDITY (RH) SPECIFICATIONS

Library materials absorb and release moisture when the surrounding air becomes damp or dry in an effort to achieve equilibrium with it. With each gain or release of moisture, the materials change in dimensions, not enough for the casual observer to see, but enough to cause damage when two different materials are bonded together and try to expand or contract different amounts. Paper text leaves glued to cloth covers, microfilm emulsions on plastic film bases, and the multiple layers of a CD or DVD all expand and contract at different rates, creating tensions between layers that split them apart. Practical consequences of not stabilising relative humidity are a shorter collection service life and more costly collection maintenance.

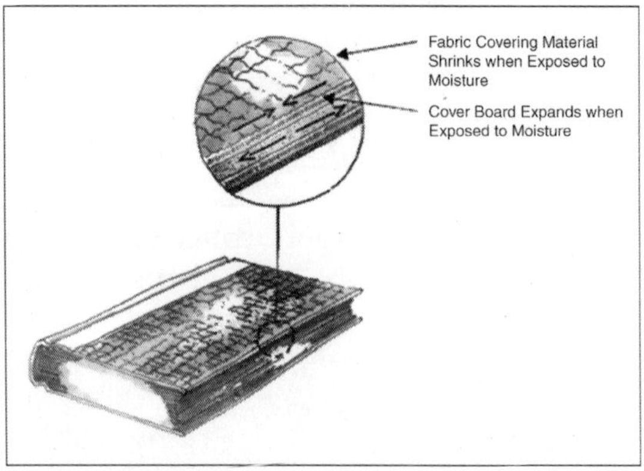

Fig. Different Rates of Expansion between Adhered Materials Produce Damage when Exposed to Moisture.

At one extreme, materials that are too dry (less than 30 per cent RH) desiccate and become brittle; at the other, materials that are too damp (greater than 70 per cent RH) encourage mold growth; consequently 35-65 per cent RH is recommended as the maximum acceptable range for any library collection. However, to minimize damage from expanding and shrinking layers, library materials need to be kept as close as possible to constant relative humidity. For collections of mixed media, a design specification of 40 per cent RH and a maximum of 5 per cent fluctuation (*i.e.*, 35-45 per cent RH including fluctuation) around the clock is an acceptable compromise among different ideal conditions for different media. This specification applies to both permanent and special mixed media collections, in storage areas and in reading environments, where maximizing collection service life is a major goal.

TEMPERATURE SPECIFICATIONS

Heat degrades all organic materials, including paper, photographic film and prints, and analog and digital media. More heat speeds up the chemical reactions responsible for degradation of materials, shortening their service lives. So colder is better, down to reasonable tolerance limits for staff and patrons who need to work in the stacks.

For permanent collections, where book stacks and user spaces often are combined, the low end of the human comfort zone (68-72°F, including fluctuation) is recommended as the range. Special and local history collections should be separated from staff work and reading areas, enabling the temperature in the collection storage area to be reduced to as close to 60ºF as possible to maximize the service life of the collections.

A range of 60- 65°F (including fluctuation) is recommended for closed stacks for three reasons:

1. Most HVAC systems use "chiller" technology because it is relatively easy to service, but cannot maintain 40 per cent RH at temperatures much below 65°F;
2. Moisture condensation on the surface of books is avoided when they are removed from the colder storage area to the warmer reading environment; and
3. 60°F appears to approach the limit of staff tolerance of differences in temperature between the book stack and reading room work environments.

STABILISING RELATIVE HUMIDITY AND TEMPERATURE

For library collections, stabilising relative humidity arguably is more important than stabilising temperature for two reasons:

1. Changes in relative humidity can cause mechanical damage from materials' internal pressures to shrink and expand; they literally tear themselves apart.
2. Reasonable fluctuations in temperature around a design specification

do change the rate of deterioration of collection materials, but cumulatively have an impact little different from maintaining a single constant temperature.

Most HVAC systems are designed to favour stabilising the system at the design temperature with the expectation that a stable relative humidity will follow. This system design works because relative humidity is dependent upon temperature and is destabilised by relative small changes in temperature. The reason for this dependency is that the percentage of relative humidity is "relative" to the amount of moisture air can hold at a given temperature. As the temperature goes up, the amount of moisture the air can hold rises with it; as the temperature goes down, the amount of moisture the air can hold is reduced.

Consequently, in a closed environment with a given amount of moisture in the air (a book stack, for example), if the temperature goes up, the relative humidity goes down because the capacity of the air to hold moisture has increased. Conversely, if the temperature in the book stack goes down, the relative humidity rises. The relationship between temperature and relative humidity can be exploited to the benefit of the collection by using it to correct fluctuations of relative humidity beyond acceptable limits.

HVAC system controls should be designed to adjust the temperature, if necessary, to maintain relative humidity fluctuation within the acceptable range, limiting the amount of expansion or shrinkage of materials, and thereby avoiding collection damage and extending service life. (Warning: the relationship between temperature and relative humidity cannot be exploited effectively by raising the temperature of the building's HVAC system to "dry out" the collection following a water disaster, *e.g.*, a sprinkler discharge or major roof leaks, because there is a great excess of water in the wet collection, furnishings, and carpets.

Raising the temperature only releases yet more moisture into the air, creating a high temperature, high humidity environment—ideal for rapid mold growth. The recommended alternative is to set the HVAC system to its lowest possible temperature and relative humidity settings, and increase the airflow to maximum volume, or to use as much outside air as possible if the outside air is cooler and drier than can be produced by the HVAC system.)

AIR POLLUTANTS

Gaseous pollutants (compounds of hydrogen, nitrogen, and sulfur in particular), and all kinds of particulates degrade organic materials. Too little is known about the costs relative to benefits of filtration systems for gaseous pollutants to make recommendations other than to generalise that fewer gaseous pollutants are desirable because they are known to be absorbed by collection materials, and then to combine with moisture to form acidic compounds known to attack paper and film-based library materials. (Some research on damage to museum and library materials from gaseous pollutants is documented in the *2003 ASHRAE Applications Handbook.*) One sensible precaution, however, is to locate fresh air intakes to the HVAC system well away from loading docks or other areas where exhausts of vehicles and other petroleum-powered equipment can introduce unwanted pollutants.

Particulate filtration can be recommended because it provides tangible and visible benefits in reduced soiling of collections as well as reduced maintenance costs for building interiors, furniture, and equipment. Most damaging among particulates is soot, which is a product of combustion of organic compounds and very small in size, less than a micron in diameter. Unlike dust, it is not easily removed from collection materials by vacuuming, making efforts to prevent its entry into the collection environment doubly advantageous.

LIGHT SPECIFICATIONS

Light degrades paper, bookbinding materials, and other library media, reducing their service lives. Ultraviolet (UV), infrared, and visible light all cause degradation of outer surfaces, so each source of light damage needs to be addressed and controlled. Damage is directly proportional to exposure (*i.e.*, intensity x time); more exposure results in more damage. To the extent possible, people should be located in areas with natural light, and library materials in areas with artificial light, in order to better control collection exposure. Visible light levels recommended for preservation storage and display usually are much below the 30-60 footcandles recommended for task lighting for reading, and natural lighting usually greatly exceeds light levels recommended for task lighting. Since, less light is better, light levels for the stacks should be set to the minimum acceptable to enable book titles and call numbers to be read.

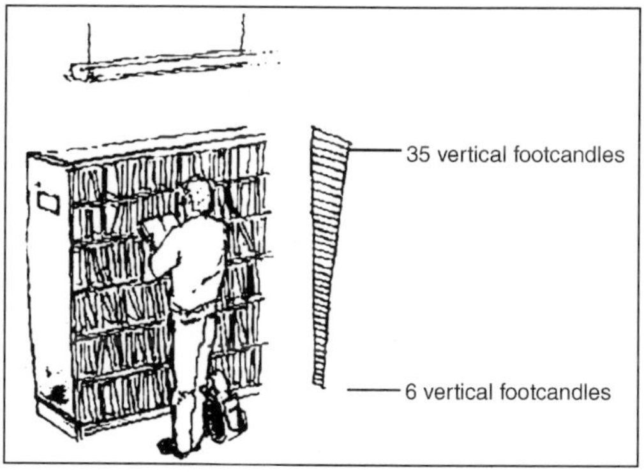

Fig. Ideal Vertical Footcandle Distribution at Book Stacks (from Dean).

Natural and fluorescent light contain ultraviolet (UV) rays, which are damaging to library materials. General collections in areas with natural light should have ranges of shelving set perpendicular to and away from windows whenever possible to avoid direct sunlight on spines of books. Special collections storage areas should have no natural lighting; artificial lighting should be equipped with staff-operated local switches so lights can be employed as needed rather than left on continuously or for extended periods when not needed for staff work. Fluorescent lighting should be equipped with UV shields to eliminate much of the UV light. Windows can be tinted with a UV filtering layer, or retrofitted with UV filters.

Both actions will substantially reduce expenses for rebinding and repair of otherwise exposed collection materials. Limiting the intensity of UV light as a portion of total light exposure to a maximum of 75 microwatts/lumen is recommended. Infrared radiation damage is most noticeable when light sources are close enough to collection materials to heat them, causing local damage. This situation can be witnessed in older, over-crowded stacks with collection materials stored high on the shelves near incandescent stack lighting. A more common situation in modern libraries occurs in display areas that use hot, high intensity lighting. The lighting can heat up objects even at a distance from them; when lighting is mounted in cases, it raises the temperature of the case environment.

Most collection materials receive more exposure to light when on display than at any other time during their service lives. Display lighting that is left on during all open hours (if not around the clock) cumulates very high levels of exposure and light damage. In an effort to limit damage, visible light levels most often recommended for display of paper-based materials are 5-15 footcandles, a level often lower than surrounding ambient lighting, and often too low to attract visitors to the exhibit. Unless exhibits can be housed in a separate space with low levels of ambient lighting, an alternative strategy is to raise exhibit lighting at least to ambient lighting levels, make sure the lights are turned off when not needed, and to limit the length of time materials are allowed to remain on display.

MONITORING THE STORAGE ENVIRONMENT

The storage environment may need to be monitored independently from managing the HVAC system for technical and administrative reasons. The technical reason is the system may be relying on sensors built into the supply or return air ducts, which are not monitoring the conditions in which the collection lives some feet away from the air ducts. The collection can absorb and release moisture to the surrounding air to achieve a relative humidity equilibrium, leaving supply air ducts reporting to the monitors only what the system delivered, not the conditions in which the collection lives.

Sensors in return air ducts will measure only the condition of the returned air, which also could differ markedly from the conditions in the stack.

System thermostats and humidistats should be located in collection spaces away from air ducts when possible. Even when system sensors are well placed to monitor conditions, independent sensors need to be placed in several locations among the items in the collection and away from all air ducts to aid discovery of microclimates, that is, locales within the stack where conditions differ from the typical conditions in the stack as a whole, and to double-check the accuracy of the system sensors, which can malfunction.

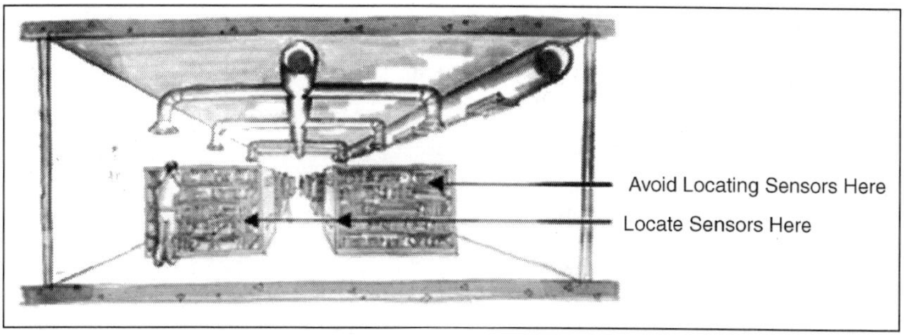

Fig. Place System Sensors away from Air Supply Outlets.

The administrative reason for independently monitoring the environment is that building maintenance engineers often are invested in the performance of the system, not in maximizing the service life of the collection. When there is a potential conflict of interest between system performance and collection preservation, the stack conditions need to be monitored by staff independent from staff assigned to manage the HVAC system.

In new buildings, temperature and relative humidity need to be monitored on a continual basis for the first year of operation of the HVAC system because conditions can fluctuate during the 24-hour day and from season to season in response to changes in climate. Two types of equipment capture and record multiple readings over time, and both are self-contained so they can be placed where needed in the collection storage area: recording hygrothermographs that are constantly reading and recording temperature and relative humidity to a chart, and electronic devices (generically referred to as "dataloggers") that periodically (from seconds to hours) measure the conditions and store the data to electronic memory.

Visible and ultraviolet light measurement usually can be spot-checked with a meter to determine if corrective action is necessary; unlike temperature and relative humidity, continuous measurement usually is not required because conditions don't change unless the lighting equipment is changed. Equipment for monitoring environmental conditions is widely available. Equipment for monitoring the performance of an HVAC system can be purchased for a few hundred to a few thousand dollars, depending upon the features of the equipment, a very modest price relative to the cost of the HVAC system, not to mention the value of the collection. Light meters for visible light are available for a few hundred dollars, but UV monitors are less widely produced and cost more.

STACK SHELVING

SHELVING DESIGN

From the perspectives of utility and protection, dry process ("powder coat") finish, steel shelving is the best choice to avoid possible damage to the collection materials from direct contact with the finish. Care should be taken that the shelving system design does not have shelf or brace fasteners that protrude into shelf space with the possibility of causing damage to volumes. Wooden bookcases are less functional, *i.e.*, wood has problems with acidity, outgassing chemicals that deteriorate paper, surface finishes that stick to collection materials, and too little resistance to insect infestation. However, aesthetic considerations may lead to their use in public or "donor" areas. One compromise is to use metal shelving with decorative wooden end panels.

Fig. "Shelving Through" Oversized Materials.

Shelves should be deep enough to fully support the bottom edges of books. Oversised materials should have deeper shelves; some shelving designs permit "shelving through" in order to take advantage of shelves on either side of the section. The height of stack ranges and width of aisles need to take into account the challenge of retrieving materials from the high shelves. If a shelf height requires a stool or ladder, aisles must be wide enough to accommodate the ladder and a space to place materials being transported to and from the shelves. Bottom shelves should be positioned well above the floor to minimize dirt buildup and book damage from booktrucks bumping into the shelving. The shelving system should have an easily removable base cover so the area under the bottom shelves of the range can be dried easily if it gets wet.

BOOKENDS

The surface of book supports in contact with the books should be solid to avoid imprinting the book covers with the outline of the supports, and should have a wide end profile to avoid books being "knifed" over the supports and damaging the text leaves. Wire bookends that clip to the shelves overhead are a classic example of a book support system that leads to damage to the collection.

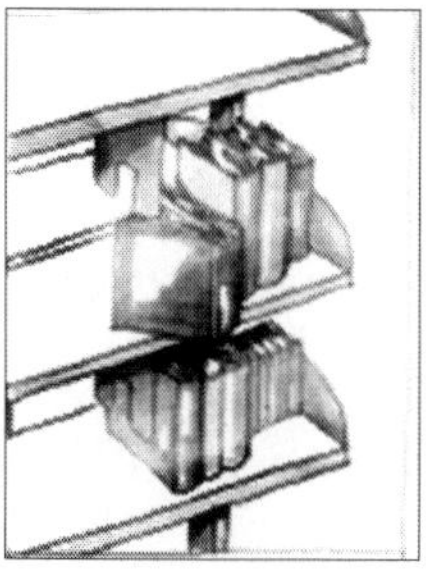

Fig. Avoid Narrow End Profiles for Book Supports.

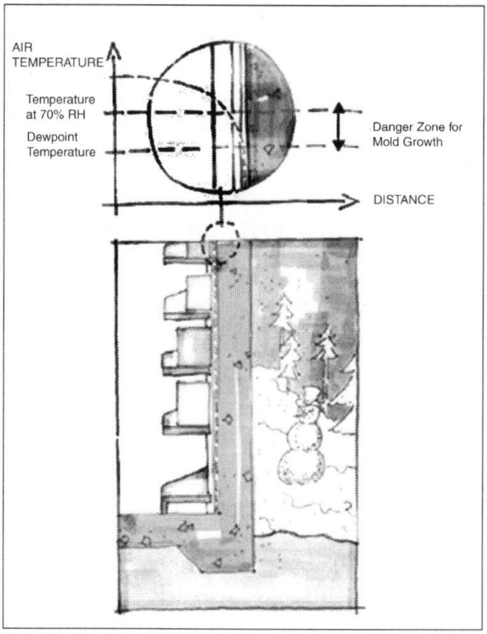

Fig. Microclimate of High Relative Humidity against Exterior Walls.

EXTERIOR WALLS AND PLACEMENT OF SHELVING

Stack ranges should not be placed flat against exterior walls. Differences in the interior and exterior environmental conditions can result in exterior walls that are warmer or cooler than the interior. High humidity thin layer microclimates can develop against the interior side of exterior walls, leading to mold growth, a problem most likely to occur on "weather walls," that is, the wall facing the direction from which storms predominantly come.

STACK CARPETING

Salvage of collections and facilities is greatly facilitated by eliminating wall-to-wall carpeting from stack areas wherever possible. Carpeting traps water, making it difficult to dry out the stacks after a water discharge.

COMMON PRESERVATION CHALLENGES IN LIBRARY BUILDING PROJECTS

AESTHETICS TRUMP PRESERVATION

Architects often are tasked with creating aesthetically pleasing and functional spaces, leading to potential conflicts between the requirements for each goal. A successful solution for both goals is to separate spaces for collection storage and spaces for reader and staff use. Short of complete separation, a workable compromise is to house the general collection in spaces designed to please readers and staff, and to house special and local history collections in a separate space designed to promote collection preservation.

PRESERVATION PRIORITIES GET SCRAMBLED

Too often the budget proves not to be adequate to support the ideal building programme; compromises need to be made, including compromises to preservation goals for the collection. Setting priorities among preservation goals is a solution; a good rule of thumb is to prioritise collection protection actions above environmental control actions. Within environmental control, favour a separate controlled environment for special and local history collections above environmental control for all collections. When funds are not sufficient to meet all environmental control goals, even for special and local history collections, favour meeting relative humidity and temperature goals at the expense of first gaseous, and second particulate, filtration.

PRESERVATION COSTS ENERGY

Library buildings are designed to save collections. Minimizing energy use is an important, but subordinate, priority to maximizing the service life of permanent and special collections. Consequently, continual advocacy for preservation is needed during the building programme process, and continuing vigilance is necessary during the design process to ensure that the design specifications for the HVAC system are responsive to collection preservation needs.

SOME HVAC ENGINEERS DON'T UNDERSTAND COLLECTION NEEDS

An important difference between HVAC system designs for libraries and for other buildings is the major emphasis on creating and maintaining an environment appropriate for maximizing the service life of the collection.

If the engineering team does not understand or appreciate this special need, engineers will argue for changing the design specification based on their experience working with standards and specifications for office, commercial, and residential buildings. Work with the architect to select an engineering firm with experience in HVAC design for stringent environmental control applications and, if possible, interest in care of cultural property.

HIGH-TECH SYSTEMS ARE TOO SMART FOR THEIR OWN GOOD

When systems (*e.g.*, fire protection, air-conditioning) fail due to lack of required maintenance, the problem often is in part too little staffing and in part lack of adequate skills among onsite maintenance staff. A highly sophisticated system that requires special training and unusually attentive operating engineers is a system likely to fail in many library building maintenance situations.

The realities of limitations of library building maintenance staff need to be included with other fundamental criteria in the design and operation of all building systems.

DISASTERS HAPPEN DURING CONSTRUCTION

The potential for damage from fire and water is significant during any project that involves a major renovation or addition to an existing library building. Workers whose primary focus is on completing construction as quickly as possible emphasise convenience to themselves rather than minimizing risks to the collection.

BUILDINGS BELOW THE WATER TABLE GET WET

Buildings designed with underground levels below the water table need special attention to drainage in addition to sealing exterior walls. Relying on sealing the walls alone is very risky because ground shifts, subsequent construction work, and deterioration over time lead to breaks in the water seal and to major problems with water leaking into the building. Special measures can be taken to provide exterior drainage and/or secondary barriers within buildings to compensate for inevitable problems with water when buildings are below the water table.

COLLECTIONS ARE MOVED BEFORE THE BUILDING IS READY

Pressure to take occupancy of a new building before it is ready (often due to unforeseen delays or time overruns in construction) is not uncommon. There are significant risks to the collection when this happens: new construction materials and interior finishes still can be outgassing air pollutants, and remaining construction work continues around and over the collection, risking damage to the materials already on the shelves. Find opportunities to rearrange schedules of events to delay moving the collection until the end of the schedule in order to reduce risk of damage.

5

Electronic Reserve and On-demand Publishing

INTRODUCTION

The term 'electronic reserve collection' may be a misnomer as it implies rationed access whereas 'the digital environment removes the need for this form of rationing as a single digitisation can simultaneously be accessed by any number of readers'.

Nevertheless, the term is used to describe collections of resources, including journal papers and extracts from texts and newspapers, that have been digitised and mounted on campus networks to be accessed by students.

The rationale for this is that hard copy can be accessed by only one person at a time but access to digital copy is limited only by the infrastructure required to use it. Electronic reserve collections (ERCs) have been developed with a view to meeting more effectively the needs of large undergraduate classes which rely increasingly on the library for core reading materials. Development of ERCs is more widespread in the US than it is in the UK.

In the early 1990s, many of those developing ERCs in the US considered it 'fair use' to digitize copyright resources and make them available electronically.

The Conference on Fair Use (CONFU) guidelines were intended to formalise this reading of the law but publishers and librarians were unable to agree on guidelines for electronic reserve use of copyright materials.

Nevertheless, many libraries continue to interpret the law in this way (follow links from the following URL for examples http://www.cc.columbia.edu/~rosedale/#Sites). Use of copyright resources in ERCs in the US must now be licensed just as it is in the UK. In the UK, HE ERC developers have assumed that ER use of copyright materials is not 'fair dealing' and guidelines published recently by the Publishers' Association and the JISC confirm that this is so (http://www.ukoln.ac.uk/services/elib/papers/pa/licence/fairnote.html).

Clearly, the cost of obtaining permissions is important to the economic viability of the whole exercise. This cost includes not only the price for using copyright material but also time spent identifying right sholders, seeking permission to use their copyright material and, often, chasing that request. The total figure can be as high as ten times the actual copyright fee. The cost to rightsholders of administering permissions requests is also significant.

At present the Association for Computing Machinery (ACM) grants blanket permission to copy its copyright materials for educational use because the cost of administering applications exceeds the revenue generated. This suggests that if licensing digital use of copyright materials is to become a viable revenue stream for publishers, copyright fees must be relatively high.

Although publishers have been willing to grant permissions free of charge to limited life ER projects, *i.e.*, during development, they charge fees to use their material in ongoing ER services.

This may not be a viable revenue stream but many publishers consider ER use of their material to be a threat to their core business. Charging deters widespread adoption of ER as an alternative to text provision or recommendation. On the other hand, as long as ER systems do not cannibalise publishers' primary income, a streamlined process may actually generate incremental revenue for them.

Another significant cost associated with ERCs is the cost of digitising text. Odlyzko cites an example of a company that will digitise text for $0.60 per page but recent eLib supporting study established £2.50 as a reasonable estimate. Obviously, cost varies with a number of factors such as the cost of identifying and obtaining the original, the condition of the original, the presence or otherwise of special characters, *i.e.*, the degree of manual intervention required to produce a useful file.

If publishers begin to supply their texts in electronic form and offer the facility to buy subsections of texts, then the need for HEIs to digitise a significant amount of text will vanish. However, unless publishers digitise all back runs of journals and text back lists, there will be a need to digitise older material.

At present, developments in delivering texts in electronic form are embryonic, so material selected for reserve collections from texts must almost always be digitised if it is to be delivered in electronic form. However, duplication of effort may be avoided if institutions collaborate.

Very little has been published on the economics of running an ERC. The ACORN Project at Loughborough University compared the costs of traditional and electronic reserve collections of journal papers.

A more comprehensive study of the costs and benefits of ERCs was published as an eLib supporting study in 1998. This study was informed by all eLib studies in the electronic reserves (ER) and ondemand publishing (ODP) programme areas, including ACORN. Another relevant study comparing charging mechanisms was conducted on behalf of a JISC/PA working party following a seminar on pricing in July of that year.

This study arose from debate among and between librarians and publishers regarding appropriate pricing mechanisms that would not cannibalise publishers' primary income stream. It considered only licensing of digitised copy from printed books and journals; not licensing of electronic products.

The report from the study called for a pricing mechanism that is 'simple and therefore inexpensive to administer ... susceptible to centralised administration [and produces] predictable costs for users and revenues for rights holders'.

Furthermore, the report recommended that two models be adopted to reflect different types of use of digitised material; a 'textbook substitution' model and a 'library substitution' model. The former would be applied to materials that, in print, publishers would expect students to buy.

The pricing mechanism would be based on student numbers and a licence would be granted for a fixed period; probably an academic year. The latter model would be applied to material that, in print, publishers would have expected libraries to buy. In this case, a licence would be granted in perpetuity.

The report referred also to the high cost of digitisation and commended the idea of a central repository of digitised text which would avoid duplication of effort among HEIs and would make it easy for HEIs to identify material for which permission is likely to be granted, as it had been in the past. The report from this study is particularly useful because it resulted from an ongoing collaborative attempt by publishers and HE representative to resolve many issues that hindered progress with ERC developments.

Many of the recommendations in the report appear to have informed the Copyright Licensing Agency (CLA) Higher Education Digitisation White Paper which details the terms on which copyright materials are now licensed by the CLA for digitisation and distribution.

The CLA will continue to require institutions to request rights on a transactional basis and prices will be set individually by publishers. Publishers will differentiate between material that is likely to substitute for sales of texts to libraries and material that is likely to substitute for sales of texts to students. The latter will be more expensive to compensate for many more 'lost sales'.

This differentiation will refer to specific titles; it will not vary between institutions depending on their patterns of use of that title. Thus, although institution A may refer students to title X for further reading while at institution B it is required reading for all students in a class, both institutions A and B will be required to pay at the prescribed rate, be it 'text substitution' or 'library substitution'. This system is not ideal but the alternative, *i.e.,* setting prices with reference to both the title and the institution requesting permission to digitise it would be extremely complex and thus expensive.

The CLA White Paper also specifies the format of digitised text; it should be an 'exact page representation' of the print original. As pages designed to be printed tend not to be suitable for on-screen reading students can be expected to print.

At present, students tend to photocopy materials borrowed from a reserve collection so the library could recover print costs from students without increasing student expenditure. However, support for networked printing is likely to be a significant cost associated with the introduction of an ER system.

The CLA does not expect institutions to comply with the 'exact page representation' criterion by creating and delivering bitmapped images from printed originals. The White Paper acknowledges that bitmapped images are large files and thus are bandwidth hungry.

However, licences may specify the degree of qualitative and quantitative accuracy in digitised text. It may be possible to comply with terms by using suitable software and including disclaimers regarding accuracy (and the CLA anticipates that this will be the case) but there is no guarantee that this will be the case. As OCR programmes tend to generate errors, it may be necessary to proof-read digitised text.

This adds considerably to the digitisation cost. It is not immediately apparent that the eCLA (the name of the new CLA service) will be more efficient than the often criticised CLARCS system for clearing rights in materials to be used in course packs (containing photocopies).

A transactional payment mechanism is expensive. The Copyright Clearance Centre in the US has operated a transactional system for electronic reserve materials since 1997.

In addition to any permission fee it charges $5 per request regardless of whether or not permission is obtained and claims that this charge is required to cover costs. The CLA requires from each publisher a mandate to license that publisher's material for use in electronic form in HEIs. The Publishers Licensing Society (PLS) has published a template which publishers can use to mandate the CLA

Some of the terminology in this template differs from that used by the CLA, *i.e.,* the PLS refers to a 'Bookshop Materials' model and a 'Library Materials' model instead of, respectively, a 'text substitution' and a 'library substitution' model. One more substantial difference between the CLA White Paper and the PLS mandate is that the latter restricts a licence for 'library materials' to 5 years rather than granting it in perpetuity.

The PLS mandate also sets the 'Bookshop Materials' model as default and recommends a default price of 5 pence per page. Thus, libraries will be expected to pay for copyright at a rate of 5 pence per page per student in a class. A single 20-page extract for a class of 200 students would cost £200 (£235 inc. VAT) in copyright fees alone. If widely adopted, the terms of this mandate will probably render ER prohibitively expensive.

HERON

HERON is an eLib-funded project developing a national database and resource bank of electronic texts to be selected and accessed by HEIs throughout the UK. HEIs will supply details of materials that they require in digital form. HERON will obtain permission for their use and will digitise these materials.

HERON is collaborating with rights holders and representative bodies to determine appropriate fee levels and conditions of digitised text and to streamline copyright clearance procedures.

The Project will normally clear rights through the CLA and when an institution requires permission to use material that is owned by a publisher or other person who has not mandated the CLA, HERON will seek to secure an agreement directly with the rightsholder.

Thus, when HERON has agreed terms with a publisher and an institution seeks to use material owned by that publisher, HERON can approach the company with confidence not only that permission will be granted but that the terms agreed previously will suffice and no lengthy negotiation will be required. Gradually, HERON will accumulate a collection of such agreements making it more efficient for HERON than for any individual institution to seek to clear rights in material to be included in an ER system. Furthermore, HERON aims to become a repository for digital copy.

HEIs seeking permission to digitise material from the CLA, either through HERON or directly, will be asked by the CLA to place a digital copy in a repository such as HERON so that it may be accessed by other users thereafter, thus avoiding duplication of effort.

Clearly, any future use of the digital copy would also have to be licensed. The model described later in this report is informed by the eLib supporting study of ODP/ER services, by cost and charge developments such as those published by the CLA and the PLS, and by HERON. The economic impact of rationalisation of licence negotiation and of digitisation will be explored using the model as will the ramifications for libraries of the CLA White Paper and the PLS mandate.

For example, the textbook substitution model (referred to by the PLS as the Bookshop Materials model) reflects the fact that libraries increasingly provide access to core reading materials that, previously, students would have bought from booksellers. Libraries cannot afford to pay to provide all students with core texts and further reading.

The crisis that libraries now face has been precipitated to some degree by student demands that they do so. However, librarians are uncomfortable with the prospect of charging for student reading materials. To do so would be to qualitatively change the role of academic libraries which would then be open to competition from other organisations which charge to supply information. Booksellers also would be affected by a move to supply core texts directly through the library.

INFORMATION GATEWAYS

Very little work has been done on the economics of information (or subject) gateways, also known as portals and hubs. Cataloguing the Internet is an activity undertaken by various types of organisation to attract users to their sites with a view to promoting their primary products/services or enhancing their reputations. Examples of this type of activity include:

- BioMedNet which, offering pointers to useful sites among many other discipline-based services, is effectively a discipline-based Internet community owned by Elsevier Science and funded, in part, by advertising (http://www.biomednet.com/gateways/bac);
- The Wiley student resource centre which includes subject-specific sub-sites each of which revolves around specific high-volume Wiley texts (http://www.wiley.co.uk/products/worldwide/canada/src/index.htm#links);
- Oppedahl and Larson LLP Patent Law Web Server, a site created and maintained by a professional law firm, which includes links to sources about all aspects of intellectual property (http://www.patents.com/index.sht);
- Various HE sites which having created pointers for their own users make them universally available (http://www.stir.ac.uk/infoserv/).

The perceived quality of these types of pointers is related to the site on which they are located. For example, links from an HEI may be considered more credible or impartial than those from a commercial organisation. Information gateways whose primary purpose is to provide pointers to other networked resources without promoting a different primary product would appear to be unique to the UK.

The eLib subject-based gateways (SBGs) have co-ordinated identification and evaluation of Internet resources and provide links to Internet resources within specific subject areas. Every resource which is linked from an SBG has been assessed by an expert in the relevant subject area and deemed to be of high-quality.

None of the SBG projects developed an economic model for maintenance and development of a service beyond the grant-funded period. However, an eLib supporting study conducted by Haynes *et al.* evaluated three different models for the transition of the SBGs from project to service status.

These models varied depending on the proposed funding sources. The first was a JISC-funded service, *i.e.,* one which would continue to rely on 100% grant funding. The structure of SBG organisation would remain unchanged.

The second model would increase JISC funding in the first two years with a view to migrating to a service funded 50:50 between JISC and other sponsors. This model includes a considerable degree of rationalisation in the organisation of SBG activities. The third model would end JISC funding and require services to find alternative sources to fund their activities.

The Haynes report recommended that the JISC pursue the second of these models. This required additional JISC funding for two years to employ a managing director who would seek complementary funding for an ongoing service.

Many of the functions undertaken individually by eLib SBG projects would be rationalised and centralised to reduce duplication of effort and to allow for greater

PRESERVATION AND ARCHIVING

Acceptable archiving and preservation strategies are essential preconditions to the widespread acceptance of electronic journals by authors and librarians. Many questions relating to archiving and preservation require answers before economic factors can be explored. For example, there is the question of who should archive. Publishers are reluctant to accept what, traditionally, has been a library responsibility.

They are waiting to find out what the role of national libraries will be in a digital environment before they commit themselves in this regard. Furthermore, the long-term commitment of publishers and other stakeholder groups is questionable. It has been suggested that the only way to ensure 'systematic archiving of electronic publishing would be to assign that role to national institutions funded to do so and backed up by legislation'.

The UK research community generally agrees that preservation should be the responsibility of a publicly funded national agency. Preservation issues are of great concern to the UK HE community.

They have been the subject of several eLib supporting studies, of a British Library Research Study and issues continue to be explored by the CEDARS project. Economic modelling however, has not yet been undertaken.

JSTOR

Successful attempt to develop a model for archiving and preservation in electronic form of scholarly journals is JSTOR. One of the aims of JSTOR is to help libraries with space problems. JSTOR is also designed to be a trusted archive. Development of the archive has depended on the cooperation of publishers holding copyright in the journals included therein. It is important to those publishers that JSTOR should not cannibalise subscription income.

Thus, current issues of journals are not included in the JSTOR archive. JSTOR operates a 'moving wall' whereby entire backruns of journal issues are included in the archive except those published during the previous X years. Every year the contents from X-1 years ago are added to the archive.

The duration of X varies from publisher to publisher but generally is between 3 and 5 years. The JSTOR archive is funded by fees from institutions accessing the contents. The JSTOR team has calculated and compared the costs associated with:

- A centrally managed electronic text archive (including the cost of migrating content to keep pace with technological development);
- Storage, processing, reshelving and maintenance of a hard-copy collection.

A key factor in making JSTOR financially viable is that it is available widely and thus, costs are spread across a large number of institutions both in the US, and now also in the UK. JSTOR aims to be as equitable as possible in pricing access to the archive. Price discrimination is applied with a view to setting prices according to the value derived by each institution.

Thus, institutions are banded according to size and annual access fees are varied on that basis. Pay-per-use was dismissed as a possible pricing mechanism because it 'usually yields prices higher than the marginal cost of providing the product' and JSTOR 'did not want to force students and scholars to have to decide whether it would really be 'worth it' to download and print an article'.

This contrasts with the view that it is prudent to charge a print fee as this discourages indiscriminate use of printing resources, *i.e.,* a fee would encourage users to filter information before rather than after they have printed. JSTOR received start-up funding from the Andrew Mellon Foundation but is expected to be self-sustaining over the longer term.

JSTOR appears to be a pragmatic and useful model for archiving and providing electronic access to backruns of journals. The capacity of JSTOR, however, is limited; currently the project aims to include backruns of a minimum of 100 journals before the year 2000.

To preserve in electronic form and make available worldwide all developments in scholarly communication is a monumental task requiring co-operation on an international scale.

It is notoriously difficult to secure international agreement for any type of activity and it is beyond the scope of this project to explore the ramifications of such an initiative.

PRE-PRINT ARCHIVES

The most famous example of an electronic pre-print archive is the Physics archive developed by Paul Ginsparg at the Los Alamos National Laboratory (LANL) (http://xxx.lanl.gov). The archive is very successful and is used by authors and readers throughout the world.

Development of the archive was funded by a grant from the US National Science Foundation. The full cost of developing and running the archive is not clear. Odlyzko estimated the cost per paper at $5. Then, to pre-empt disagreement on this figure he recalculated using wildly extravagant estimates of the costs of personnel and storage space.

He estimated that the upper limit would be $75, *i.e.,* that it could not possibly cost more than $75 per paper to run such an archive. In the absence of grant funding, a cost-recovery model would be required.

Given Odlyzko's figures, if the international physics community were to subscribe to this service either on an individual or institutional basis, the subscription charge would be small. Nevertheless, the administration of subscriptions would increase the total cost. An alternative model might charge authors to place pre-prints in the archive.

This would be unlikely to succeed however as authors are reluctant to pay page charges even to submit papers tojournals where the benefits of publication are clear. Harnad is trying to establish a similar pre-print archive in the cognitive sciences. This project (CogPrints) is funded by eLib.

Other than grant funding, no economic model for a pre-print archive has been published and so no model will be explored here.

It should be noted however, that increasing use of preprints effectively transfers the information filtering function either to libraries or to end users.

Publication in a specific journal confers on a paper a mark of quality that is recognised by the readers. When all papers are freely available and unrefereed, the user must seek to identify high quality papers for herself.

The time taken to do so is a cost; thus, in economic terms, preprints are not free. Physicists reading material from the Ginsparg archive tend to read only articles written by colleagues with whose work they are familiar This suggests that they are unwilling to filter the material for themselves. It also makes it difficult for newcomers to establish themselves in the field.

Issues Related to Digital Library Service and Resource delivery

Licensing

The application of national copyright law to the electronic environment is not straightforward; legislation tends to predate the digital era. Furthermore, the business of providing access to copyright materials in electronic form tends to be international.

Combined with the Internet 'gift culture' whereby users expect electronic content to be available free of charge, copyright on its own is inadequate for regulating use of copyright materials. Rather than relying on copyright law, content suppliers tend to use licences to detail precisely the terms on which their copyright material is made available to end users.

In the words of Karen Hunter of Elsevier Science, 'publishers view licences 48 and contracts as a more robust, clearer method of resolving what might otherwise be ambiguities as to permitted use and limitations'. Licence terms have important implications for libraries.

As the availability of an increasing proportion of library material depends on relationships beyond the organisational boundary, library managers must consider the impact that this has, among other things, on their ability to control budgets and guarantee access beyond the current licence term.

Clearly, the pricing model detailed in a licence and the level of prices are important in determining the costs and benefits to licensor and licensee. At present, prices tend to be very high for a variety of reasons including:

- That publishers often tie the price of electronic copy to the print price and offer both formats as a bundle;
- That by becoming the source site, the publisher takes on some of the library roles and costs.

Although pricing is an important element of a licence agreement it is only one of many issues that determine the costs and benefits conferred on the licensor and licensee. At present, pricing models offered by individual publishers vary considerably and are complex. Negotiation on a licence terms requires expertise, and takes a great deal of time. As licensing becomes increasingly important and common so do legal advice and staff with the knowledge and experience required to negotiate favourable and consistent licence terms.

Guidelines published by the US Association of Research Libraries (ARL) in 1997 recommend that institutions 'create a contract team' consisting of 'appropriate staff from the library, legal office, purchasing department and information technology division to provide information and develop contract expertise'. This type of recommendation suggests that licensing electronic resources is very much more expensive in terms of personnel than acquisition of print resources by library staff.

Furthermore, it illustrates the importance to all stakeholders that licences be kept simple and terms be standardised wherever possible. This is the rationale behind CHEST and behind initiatives like the UK National Electronic Site Licence Initiative (NESLI).

NESLI has based its model licence on one developed by a collaborative working party of representatives from the JISC and from the Publishers Association (PA) (http://www.nesli.ac.uk/nesli-licence.html). This model has been revised by NESLI in an iterative process involving all stakeholder groups.

When electronic resources were first offered to libraries by publishers, licences tended to be extremely restrictive with regard, for example, to use and users. This can be understood with reference to the size and importance of the market to academic publishers and the apparent naivety about copyright among users accustomed to the internet 'gift culture'. A great deal of progress has been made towards increased trust, goodwill and understanding between different stakeholder groups.

Librarians have identified licensing issues of importance to them and initiated dialogue with publishers. In the US an informal organisation calling itself the International Coalition of Library Consortia (ICOLC) and representing initially US library consortia, but later also consortia from Australia, the UK and the Netherlands, published a Statement on Current Perspectives and Preferred Practices for the Selection and Purchase of Electronic Infrastructure (http://www.library.yale.edu/consortia/statement.html).

This is essentially a wish list which elicited responses from several publishers thus initiating dialogue which continues at annual meetings of the ICOLC. The most recent (7th) draft of the NESLI model contract, published in September 1998 (http://www.nelsi.ac.uk/nesli7.html) addresses many of the issues raised by the ICOLC 50 and by writers on licensing such as Okerson.

For example, terms dictate that access to licensed material will not be withdrawn when subscriptions are cancelled and that licensees will be given the opportunity to subscribe to electronic copy only. NESLI is also considering the type of usage data that it can feasibly provide and is working towards seamless access from OPAC entry to abstracts, Tables of Contents, and full text.

By offering standardised terms, NESLI aims to minimise negotiation costs for both parties but acknowledges that the terms in this contract will not be acceptable to all publishers.

There are often stark differences between the commercial interests of publishers and the library mission and negotiation is not often straightforward. The US experience to date is that negotiation of terms of use of electronic journals is often adversarial and protracted, and the resulting licences are lengthy and complex but clearly there is a willingness to simplify the licensing process and thus reduce costs for all parties.

User Behaviour in the Online Environment

User acceptance is key to the success of digital library resources and services. A resource can be technically impressive but unless it is acceptable to the target audience it will not be used. Research on user needs should be practical rather than hypothetical as potential users' reported needs differ from those of experienced users.

Thus, studies which provide access over a sufficient period to allow users to learn and repeatedly use a system are likely to be most useful. Research on user behaviour tends to focus on electronic journals but user needs and behaviour with reference to electronic texts and monographs have also been explored.

There is a remarkable degree of consensus among researchers of user behaviour in the online 51 environment. It would appear that researchers consistently identify the same essential pre-requisites for a successful online resource and the same deterrents to use.

Core Functionality

Identification of core functionality is important as journal readers use only those functions that meet their needs. As additional functionality increases production costs and may impact on price, superfluous functions should be avoided.

Users consider the core functions to be the facility to browse, search and print from an electronic journals service. Research repeatedly emphasises the fact that users do not read on screen but prefer to use print copy.

There are various reasons for this, including portability, the facility to annotate and guaranteed future access. Some users claim that a virtual filebox may reduce the need to print.

This would reduce anxiety about accessing materials in the future but does nothing to address the requirement for annotation and portability.

Although Butterworth reports that scientists' interest in electronic journals relates primarily to improved functionality and lists linking to references as one of the required functions, the SuperJournal project found that users consider linking to be 'nice to have' rather than essential.

Creating links to references can be expensive especially for journals that are published in PDF format so it is essential that the importance of this feature to users be established.

Critical Mass and Currency

Users consider it essential that any service should offer a critical mass of resources both in terms of breadth and depth. Access to a limited selection of journal titles, whether they be published by a single publisher or by a range of publishers, is not considered sufficient incentive to learn to use a new system. Users also expect an electronic journal service to offer a backfile of a minimum duration.

The SuperJournal Project found that users consider the minimum requirement for a journal service to be a backfile of 5–10 years. Others consider the minimum useful backfile to be 25 years.

Furthermore, many users expect an electronic journals service to offer a wider range of titles than is currently available in print from the library.

System Performance

System performance is a necessary prerequisite if users are expected to use digital resources and services. Both academics and students are subject to time constraints and users are reluctant to learn to use new systems unless there are clear benefits.

Lowlevel problems demoralise users and it is difficult to entice them back if they have been disappointed. Time taken to download and print materials from a system is also important.

At present many users consider the delay to be excessive and consequently, would not print. Staff from the library at the University of Columbia have found that the online books system is used as a sophisticated catalogue. Users search for items of interest in the digital environment but when they have identified an item and wish to read more than a few lines, they seek a print copy from the library shelf.

This finding echoes that, noted earlier, of the ELINOR project at De Montfort University. It is no surprise that users consider the online books system to be an adjunct rather than a replacement for print.

Convenient, Fast Desktop Access to a one-stop Shop

Desktop access is considered to be important as is speed and ease of use. Users prefer not to have to login at all and complicated login procedures invariably deter use. The SuperJournal project found that when users experienced difficulty with the login procedures they did not attempt to use the system again. Furthermore, 90% of requests for user support from the SuperJournal helpdesk were from users who had forgotten their personal ID for logging in.

Having accessed the system, the time taken to identify and retrieve material is important; users are not prepared to follow long chains of links to access relevant content. A single common interface is also an important feature and the interface should be familiar so frequent upgrading and redesign is unacceptable. Furthermore, users expect an electronic journals service to offer seamless discovery and access. The user should have the facility first to identify material that she wishes to read by searching or browsing tables of contents, second to link to the abstract of any items that interests her, and third to link to the full-text of any article that she wishes to read in full.

Format

A significant proportion of electronic journals are delivered as portable document format (PDF) documents especially when the electronic format is produced as a parallel of the print format. It is claimed that PDF is cheap to produce in these circumstances but is inappropriate for electronic delivery especially when pages have two or more columns.

Nevertheless, PDF currently has advantages over HTML. Users of Super Journal service claimed to prefer reading HTML on screen but when offered a document in either HTML or PDF format, the majority selected the latter.

This may be related to the fact that users prefer not to read on screen and print material if they intend to read more than a few lines. Super Journal users claim to prefer prints from PDF because they look like printed journal pages and, unlike HTML documents, they have page numbers.

Benefits of an Electronic Service

Access to digital library resources tends not to be restricted to library opening hours and generally, two or more users may access an item simultaneously. Improved access is considered to be a benefit of digital library services. However, although Super Journal users claimed that access outside library opening hours is important, most use occurred during office hours.

Users also believe that the digital medium should facilitate faster publication; where items are published in both print and digital formats, users expect the latter to be published before or at the same time as the former.

Benefits of Print and Photocopies

Generally, studies of user needs and behaviour in the digital library have revealed a range of different functions associated with print and photocopies that users consider to be 55 important. Until equivalent or improved features are available in an electronic environment many users will remain attached to print. These features include ease of browsing and reading; most current users have been familiar with print since childhood and are skilled in its use. A ubiquitous equivalent level of familiarity and skill is likely to be available to future users who are currently in the primary education system. Studies also report an emotional attachment to print.

Whether or not this attachment will remain among future lifelong users of electronic media remains to be seen. Another feature of print that currently give it an edge is its portability. Users tend not to read at their computers and often read journal papers at home or when travelling.

The facility to annotate a print copy is also important as is the fact that they can legally cache materials for future use. Finally, some users consider presentation in print resources to be superior to that in digital resources. For example, high-quality graphics cannot be satisfactorily reproduced on prints from electronic resources. This is particularly important with regard to colour images.

Disciplines

Although many research findings apply to all users, differences between disciplines should be recognised. The Los-Alamos pre-print archive is commonly cited as an example of discipline-specific behaviour which has contributed to the success of a digital library resource.

There has long been a culture among physicists of distributing preprints. Physicists differ from other sciences in this respect and it is argued that the success of the Los Alamos archive derives in part from 56 this culture.

It is reported also that electronic journals are embraced more readily by those in disciplines that have not been adequately catered for in a print environment, for example musicology and other disciples to which non-printable elements are important.

Future research on user behaviour in the online environment should differentiate between users from different disciplines. Unfortunately, initiatives such as ATHENS which are designed to streamline delivery of digital resources can subvert attempts to gather data on different types of user.

MEASUREMENT OF USE AND PERFORMANCE INDICATORS IN THE DIGITAL LIBRARY

International Standards for Performance Measurement

The ability to monitor use and interpret the results is essential if any information resource or service is to be deemed a success or otherwise. Internationally standardised performance indicators have been developed for traditional library services.

However, recent studies of usage measurement and performance indicators for digital libraries have found no evidence of standardisation and continue to recommend that international standards be developed and applied.

An initiative in this direction has been taken by the ICOLC who have published guidelines for statistical measures of usage of electronic resources.

An eLib supporting study published in 1997 investigated Management Information Systems and Performance Measurement for the Electronic Library. The authors described a three-fold approach to library management with regard to performance measurement:

- The day-to-day needs of library managers;
- The need for information that can be used by planners for forecasting;
- The need for indicators of value for strategic review.

Although they found that some indicators used in traditional libraries can be adapted, it was necessary to devise other 57 new indicators. For example, the number of documents accessed was considered not to be important in an electronic environment; the range and depth of resources available was deemed far more important.

Furthermore, Brophy and Wynne identified a number of issues which must be addressed if progress is to be made in this area. While acknowledging the significant contribution of the eLib programme in this regard, they called for a clearer definition and understanding of what is meant by the term 'electronic library'.

Non-standard Usage Measurement

A requirement for international standards is clear but development of such standards is a lengthy process. While this process is ongoing, each individual digital library initiative requires feedback to inform development and, thus, must unilaterally adopt an approach to performance measurement.

Electronic library projects in the UK, Europe and the USA have used a variety of different definitions and methods of usage measurement and analysis. Thus, neither analyses nor data from different projects can be compared.

Most Internet usage analysis tools are applicable to digital library activities and WWW server log file analysis programmes still predominate. In 1997 the eLib supporting study referred to above found that most work in the electronic library field relied on transaction logging for management information.

If users are authenticated (*i.e.,* have usernames and passwords), it is possible using these tools, to monitor individual use by logging the username alongside the URL. Hits can also be time stamped. In this way, an individual's progress can be tracked from page to page. It is possible also, using cookies, for a service supplier to track an individual's movements on the Internet beyond that supplier's site. However, this is likely to be considered a breach of privacy and librarians 58 make it an issue in negotiation with content suppliers.

To comply with the library ethos, performance indicators should not rely on information about individuals' reading habits. Many academic subscription services authenticate whole sites by registering and restricting access a list of IP addresses.

Not only does this overcome privacy issues related to individual users as names and time stamps cannot be recorded on accesses, but it also removes the need for costly password management. An alternative means of reducing the cost of authentication in the UK is use of the ATHENS service which provides an individual with a username and password which may be used to access a variety of services.

Unfortunately, use of ATHENS greatly reduces the management information that can be gathered by individual service suppliers. This is deliberate to protect the privacy of individual users. For example, it is not possible for a supplier to monitor use of her service within a specific discipline if neither individuals nor even whole classes are identifiable by user ID.

Limitations of Current usage Measurement Tools

It is important when designing performance measurement activities that they be justified in terms of the benefits derived. Because it is automatic, transaction logging is a cheap way of gathering data in an electronic environment.

Unfortunately, the type of data that can be collected is often restricted by the delivery format. In 1996, when Michigan University intended to test economic models during the TULIP Project, it was unable to do so because 'the Web does not support the kind of data collection required to test economic models'.

Project MUSE is still unable to distinguish between downloading/ printing and browsing as the Web is a stateless environment. SuperJournal know that although users claim to prefer HTML documents for onscreen viewing, given a choice of formats, a large majority 59 chooses PDF over HTML. As most users print documents if they intend to read more than a few lines, it can be assumed that they select PDF as a superior format for printing.

Unfortunately, SuperJournal cannot verify this assumption by monitoring use as it is not possible to differentiate downloading from printing. Thus, although data gathering is cheap, as yet, it is also limited. Furthermore, analysis of such data tends to be time consuming and thus expensive and interpretation is not always straightforward.

For example, it may be assumed that more hits indicate a better service, as a high number suggests that users return and that they recommend a site to others but, of course, this may not always be the case. A subject-based gateway which generates search results that closely match a users needs will record very few hits before that user leaves the site satisfied with the result.

If the search results supplied are poor and include a number of extraneous links or if the user is required to conduct several searches before she retrieves useful links, the gateway will record many more hits before the user leaves.

However, if a subject-based gateway offers not only access to a database of catalogue records but also holds a local archive, it should record a larger number of hits as users are likely both to search the database and to retrieve local resources. Furthermore, attempts to make more efficient use of internet bandwidth by caching and mirroring can subvert attempts to monitor use. Access to resources from site A from a cache or mirror held at site B will not be included in usage measurement unless site B informs site A about the cache and agrees to supply site A with use data. This type of shortfall makes WWW statistics unreliable or, worse, misleading.

Inferring user Behaviour from Transaction Logs

Use of transaction logs for performance measurement requires digital library practitioners to infer meaning from specific types of user act in a digital environment. For example, A. Dawson of the BUBL service (http://www.bubl.ac.uk) suggests that to view a list of journal issues with dates and contents is the equivalent of browsing a library shelf. He also asserts that searching is a deliberate activity which is not easily mistaken and that to access full-text is a likely indication that the user is reading the article.

The latter assertion is qualified by the acknowledgement that the reader may access text to scan for relevance rather than, necessarily, to read the article. However, Dawson argues that this ambiguity need not influence the accuracy of any performance measure as it applies to all journals.

This type of inference helps digital library practitioners to make sense of quantitative data. However, knowledge of user behaviour in the digital environment is limited and it can be dangerous to base inference entirely on assumptions and prior experience.

For example, Dawson's assumption that the frequency with which a reader accessing full text is in fact scanning for relevance will apply equally to all journals is contradicted by the findings of the SuperJournal project.

SuperJournal found evidence that the way in which scientists and social scientists use journal elements differs. For example, scientists are more likely than social scientists to identify a relevant article from its title and to print it on that basis. Social scientists more often read the abstract to establish relevance because article titles in the social sciences can be more ambiguous. There may be similar differences in the way that scientists and social scientists approach full text.

It is clearly difficult to derive qualitative research findings from quantitative information. Qualitative methods such as interviews and 61 observation should be used to inform assumptions about the meaning of quantitative information and for triangulation.

Training and Awareness

Some of the eLib projects in the Training and Awareness programme area have now migrated to a service model and offer training courses in the use of new technologies for teaching and learning. HEIs are likely to continue to pay for this type of training from staff development budgets.

Training of users in the use of IT is unlikely to fall within the remit of libraries although libraries will probably continue to offer training in information skills and the use of specific resources.

It is beyond the scope of this project to explore the economics of this activity and compare the costs and benefits of training academics and students in the use of electronic and print resources. Clearly, the transition from a traditional to a digital or hybrid library involves dramatic changes in the infrastructure that supports the production and use of information resources. At present people prefer not to read on screen so they print articles from electronic journals.

As resources for teaching, learning and research are increasingly delivered in electronic form there is likely to be a mass shift from photocopying to printing; the latter is more expensive than the former but the total opportunity cost of an individual operating a photocopier is not incurred so costs are probably very similar.

As people become more familiar with technology, users may no longer need print copies.

This could lead to a net reduction in the cost of using information. The report of a recent study on the impact of electronic journals on networked printing suggested that one of the reasons for printing material from the Internet is to ensure future access; networked access is not always reliable.

In effect users create a personal print cache of networked resources. The report predicted that improved access to networked resources would 62 reduce the need to print but suggested that it may also increase use of the network, which in turn would increase the print load. The net effect of a combination of such changes is virtually impossible to predict.

Another factor impacting on the economics of digital information is the pace of technological change; new technologies become obsolete at an alarming rate, making it expensive for organisations to meet the changing needs of users. However, technological advances are reducing some costs, for example the cost of storing digital resources.

It is not possible within the scope of this project to estimate the infrastructure costs associated with delivering electronic resources in such an unstable and unpredictable climate. Investment in infrastructure that effectively enables all stakeholders to conduct much of their business electronically will be required. The models described here will be based on the assumption that the HE sector will invest in sufficient infrastructure to support digital/hybrid library activities.

At present there is no coherent model of the digital library, nor is there yet any developed model of the hybrid library. Furthermore, economic issues tend to be tested after solutions have been found to the more pressing technical, cultural and legal issues. Many specific digital library activities are insufficiently mature to have generated economic models. Where a model exists it has been evaluated and where alternatives exist these have been compared.

It is clear that a great deal of progress has been made over the last decade towards a greater understanding of how digital library activities may be integrated in HE. Nevertheless, a considerable amount of work remains, specifically in the areas of preservation and archiving and in standardisation of usage measurement and performance indicators. Conclusions regarding specific issues relating to digital library activities are outlined in the remainder of this report.

6

E-journals: Their Use, Value and Impact

For this research, the authors used Ithink modelling software. Ithink uses a mapping language designed to facilitate visualisation of the 'interrelationships which constitute a process, a strategy or an issue'. The key elements in an Ithink model are described below.

It is thaught to represent graphically the interrelationships that characterise each system modelled. The elements in the models then had numbers or ranges of numbers added and simulations were run. The models were deliberately made simple and aim to capture the essential features of the systems modelled.

They are intended as generic rather than specific examples. Many of the model elements are defined by equations which describe the relationship of that element with one or other elements in the same model. The relationships represented by the equations are generally informed by the literature. However, some assumptions are inherent in these relationships. The bases of the equations and the assumptions in each model are described in 'documents'. These documents may be viewed by double-clicking the element and selecting from the dialogue box a button labelled 'document*'.

The asterisk indicates that a document exists. Some elements are self-explanatory and so are not documented within the model. As these assumptions inform the results of the 'what if' scenarios and sensitivity analyses, they are most appropriately presented alongside those results.

Thus, the assumptions are documented in the Results and Discussion section of this report. Copies of the models described here are available from the authors and can be examined by using the free runtime version of the Ithink software package. This is available at the following URL: http://www.cognitus.co.uk/IS/IS.htm.

The runtime version of the software can be used to view and manipulate our models, but any changes that the user 64 makes cannot be saved. A brief guide for users of this modelling software is appended to this report.

The models were designed to facilitate greater understanding of the economic factors and the economic relationships between different stakeholders in each of the processes modelled. Model variables can be manipulated using so-called 'sliders', and the effects can then be monitored. For example, in a model of electronic journal production and delivery any of the following elements could be varied using sliders: the number of subscriptions; the number of manuscripts submitted; the overhead rate applied to staff costs; the journal acceptance/rejection rate; or the profit margin applied by the publisher.

Holding all other variables equal, a user might, for example, vary the number of subscriptions and observe the effect on subscription price or individual article price. Similarly, in the model of an ER system, the user could vary the number and size of classes to establish how this would affect, for example, total cost, the institution fee, and the fee per student.

MODEL ELEMENTS

Stock

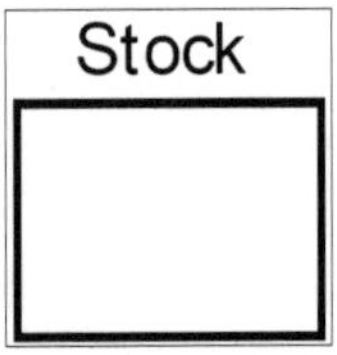

A stock represents an accumulation. For example, in the model of an electronic reserve system the repository of digitised materials is represented by a stock. The items accumulate by flowing into and/or out of the stock. The total content amounts to the inflow minus the outflow at each time period in a model simulation. In many of the stocks represented in the models described here the inflow and outflow are equal.

For example, a journal editor receives a number of manuscripts Stock 65 every year. Of those, she rejects a very small percentage and the remainder are sent for peer review. However, the repository in the ER system has no outflow as items must be stored for possible future use. Thus, its content increases annually.

Flow

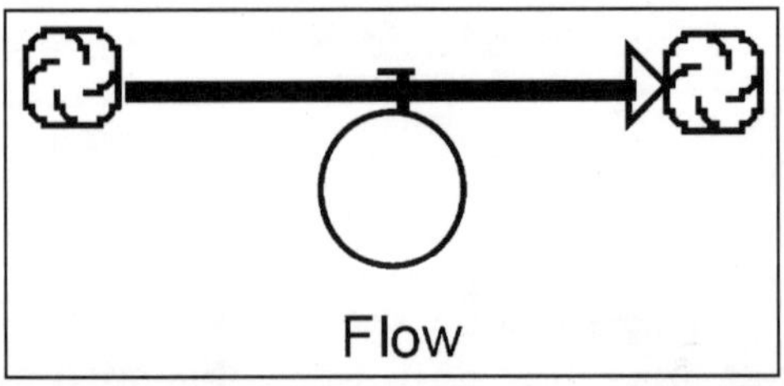

A flow is like a pipe. It either fills or drains a stock in the direction of the flow arrow. A cloud at either end of a flow indicates an infinite source or destination of the 'stuff' flowing to or from a stock.

If the flow source were a stock and that stock were empty, the value of the flow equation would not flow into the destination stock. Thus, a cloud is a device which indicates that the source of 'stuff' passing through the flow is beyond the scope of the model.

For example, where the flow 'journal acquisitions receipts' flowing into the stock 'journal acquisitions budget' originates with a cloud, this means that the entire library or institutional budget is not represented. It is assumed that the library or institution provides funding to acquire journals.

Converter

A converter informs other elements in the model. It may contain a constant value, for example, VAT which is 17.5%, or a variable value which may be manipulated by the model user by means of a slider.

Alternatively, it may represent an algebraic relationship between other elements in the model or it may represent an external input such as the rate at which items selected for digitisation in the ER model are duplicates of items already held in the repository.

The latter may be a ramp, *i.e.*, the initial value is X% and it rises annually by Y%.

A converter may also be the repository for a graphical function which sketches the relationship between an input and an output. For example, the output may be the price of a subscription and the input the number of items in a database. A graphical functions can also be used to sketch non-linear relationships.

Table shows the graphical representations of converters in these roles and an example of a slider which may be manipulated by a user.

Table: Different Roles of a Converter.

Graphical Representation	
 Converter	This is a simple converter which may represent a constant value of the value of an algebraic relationship
 Slider	This is the graphical representation of a slider as it appears in a model.
Profit Margin 	This is the slider which is represented in the model as above. The user slides the button to determine the value of the profit margin before running the model to monitor the effect of this change
 Graphical Function	This converter represents a graphical function, i.e. a sketch of the relationship between and input and an output.

Connector

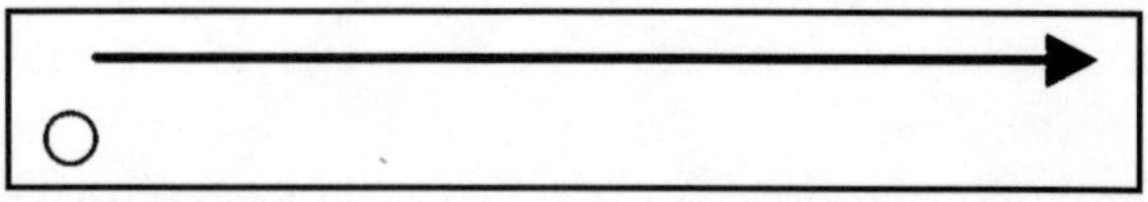

A connector is like a wire which transmits information between elements in a model, *e.g.*, in Figure, the value of the flow labelled 'RDN staff' is determined by the product of the values of the two converters.

The value of the converters is conveyed to the flow by connectors. A connector can connect out of a stock and it can flow into or out of a flow or converter. It cannot connect into a stock as the value of the latter can be altered only by a flow.

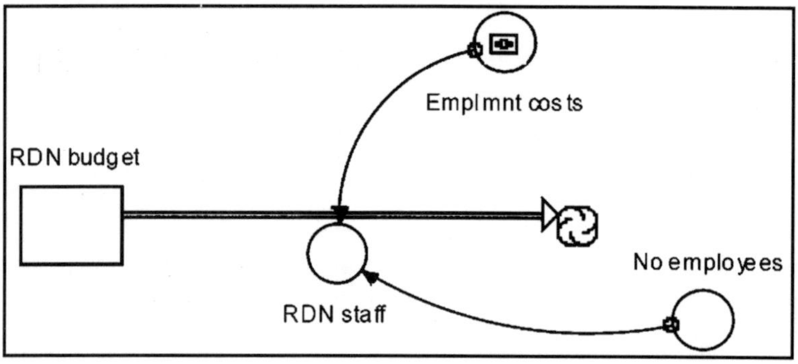

Fig. The Relationship between the flow value RDN staff (costs), the Converter whose value is the number of Employees and the cost of Employing an Individual.

EVALUATION OF ITHINK MODELLING SOFTWARE

Ithink was an effective tool for the research described here. It allowed the authors to map the interrelationships in a system before numbers were introduced.

The documentation supplied with the software is clear and comprehensive. Two versions of the software are available: Ithink Strategy and Ithink Analyst. The latter includes additional modelling features. These features were not required to build the models described in this report. Ithink software is available for educational use at half of the full price.

The educational RDN budget Emplmnt cos ts No employees RDN staff rate for Ithink Strategy is available for $299 and Ithink Analyst for £479. The price includes documentation. There were a few drawbacks. Among them were the fact that the software prohibits circular relationships. For example, in the model of a non-commercial journal, we wished to define the overhead applied when calculating total publication costs as a percentage of sales income.

However, as total publication cost is one factor determining price and price is one factor determining sales income, this relationship would have been circular and was prohibited. Another drawback for this project is the difficulty of printing the models. The software is designed as a learning tool. To be most effective models should be manipulated by users. Thus, prints of the models are considered to be of limited value. Nevertheless, the output of this research project had to be documented and published. Although the authors expect interested parties to request copies of the models, they also believe that illustrations would contribute to understanding of written reports and papers.

Unfortunately, several of the models would be illegible on anything smaller than an A2 sheet of paper. It is for this reason that we recommend that interested readers should download the runtime version of Ithink software and request copies of our models. Requests for discs with the models should be addressed to either of the authors of this report (l.l.halliday@lboro.ac.uk or c.oppenheim@lboro.ac.uk).

The authors built six Ithink models based on economic models of different aspects of the digital library. These include four economic models of electronic journal production and delivery. Development of electronic journals is more advanced than most other areas of the digital library. The selection of models evaluated here reflects this.

The other two models evaluated are a resource discovery network and a National Electronic Reserve Service (NERS). The former is based on a recent eLib supporting study of subject-based gateways and is informed by the JISC call for proposals to develop a Resource Discovery Network Centre (JISC circular 10/98). The latter model is based on the eLib-funded national electronic resource service, HERON and is informed by relevant eLib publications and by publications of other stakeholders such as the CLA and the PLS.

ELECTRONIC JOURNALS MODELS

There are four Ithink models of electronic journal production and delivery. The first is a model of a non-commercial electronic journal with traditional economic characteristics. In this model, costs are recovered from sales of subscriptions and individual articles.

A "Traditional model" is presented first to facilitate easy comparison with journal production and delivery in a print environment. The second model is based on the economic model proposed by Harnad and Hemus and is hereinafter described as the "Harnad model". The third is a 'market' model based on Fishwick *et al.*'s eLib supporting study on the economic implications of different models of publishing scholarly electronic journals and is hereinafter referred to as the "Fishwick model".

The fourth model is an alternative model, proposed by the authors, which is informed by the other three models. The Traditional model is presented first and assumptions informing different elements in the model are explained.

The Harnad model, the Fishwick model, and the authors' alternative model are then described. Where elements and assumptions in these models differ from those in the Traditional model these are documented.

The values of several elements in each of these models were varied and the models run to monitor the effects. The costs and benefits for different stakeholders of manipulating model elements was established and model sensitivities were identified. The results are described.

Non-commercial Electronic Journal with Traditional Economic Characteristics

The characteristics of this model are very similar to those of the scholarly print information delivery chain. Editors and referees are unpaid other than a contribution from the publisher towards editorial office costs.

A traditional pricing mechanism is applied, *i.e.,* costs are recovered through sales of subscriptions and of individual articles. The model differs from the print system in that the entire editorial process is conducted electronically and the product is delivered in electronic form to libraries.

Libraries are free to obtain subscriptions/individual articles directly from publishers or to obtain them from an information broker. It is assumed, if a library chooses the former, that terms will be negotiated between the library and the publisher. The model consists of four interconnected sectors: content origination, publication, information brokerage, and the library function.

Content Origination

In this sector, manuscripts are first submitted to the editorial office for review. The number of incoming manuscripts is specified so that the number of papers published was limited to a realistic level. The model simulates production of a single journal. We assumed that the journal publishes approximately 120 papers per annum.

Theoretically, an electronic journal need not be constrained by a pre-determined limit on the number of papers that it can publish annually because distribution and storage costs are low. However, other resources required for production are related to journal size and these are likely to restricts growth in the short to medium term.

For the purpose of the modelling exercise, the authors assumed that the number of papers published per annum in an electronic journal is similar to the number published in a print journal. The rate at which manuscripts are submitted to any journal fluctuates. However, if an excess of manuscripts is accepted and, in turn, the publication delay is unacceptable, it is reasonable to assume that potential authors will be discouraged from submitting to that journal.

The editors also would regulate the number of papers accepted by increasing the rejection rate to maintain an acceptable publication delay. In the model, the number of papers submitted was specified with reference to the rejection rate to ensure that 120 papers were produced per annum. Most manuscripts submitted for publication are refereed but a small percentage is rejected immediately usually because the subject matter is unsuitable for publication in that journal.

The immediate rejection rate wan this model is 2% and is based on an established print peer reviewed journal. The total rejection rate in the model is varied to monitor the effect. Rejection rates vary between journals, and vary significantly between disciplines (*i.e.,* in the humanities 90% is not uncommon whilst in the pure sciences 10% is common). It is assumed that the editor spends a total of 30 minutes per paper.

This represents time spent scanning the manuscript content, deciding whether or not to have the paper refereed, selecting referees, and considering revisions and whether or not to return the paper to the referees. We assumed that all but 2% of manuscripts are refereed, each of them by two peers. The average paper is revised once.

It was assumed that each referee spends two hours reviewing the manuscript in the first instance and that revision takes one hour. Thus, each referee spends three hours per paper and therefore, each paper takes six referee hours to process. It was assumed that one hour of an average editor or referee costs £50 including full employment costs and overhead.

This is a conservative estimate which does not vary with overhead rate. The total cost to HE is calculated as the cost of editorial and refereeing work minus the contribution from the publisher towards the costs of the editorial office. This cost to HE is an opportunity cost as it is not accounted for in the financial transactions between different stakeholders.

It was assumed that the publisher contributes £160 per accepted manuscript towards the costs of the editorial office. This assumption is based on figures given.

The model includes no clerical administration cost, as most of the clerical administrative tasks are automated and journal production staff undertake what remains. Thus, the editorial and production functions are interlinked. This organisational model is based on that of the *Conservation Ecology* Project.

Publication

Production costs in the model vary with the overhead rate applied. It was assumed that overheads cost 120% of production costs, but a rate of 60% was also tested. The authors would have preferred to calculate overhead as a percentage of sales income because distribution incurs additional administration costs and thus costs vary with the size of the subscription base.

However, calculation of the overhead in this way would have required a circular connection between elements in the model which is prohibited by the software package.

As the model is non-commercial, it was assumed that the publisher does not seek to make substantial profits. However, some profit margin is required to develop the journal. We applied margins in the model at a rate varying from 0% to 20%. The journal is produced by a half-time production editor and a half-time systems administrator.

The cost per paper was estimated at £275. This is based on a part-time journal production editor and a part-time systems administrator each earning, pro rata, £25 000 who also cost an additional 20% of that figure in national insurance contributions (NIC) and pension contributions.

This gives a total employment cost of £30 000. An overhead was not applied to staff costs in this instance. Assuming that these staff members can produce a journal consisting of 120 papers per volume (per year), the cost per paper is £250. An additional £25 was added to this figure to cover any other expenses. Subscription fees in the model vary with the level of use.

The price increases as the user base decreases because there are fewer subscribers or purchasers of individual documents to share the costs.

The price of an individual paper is double that of a paper sold as part of a subscription to reflect the increased risk to the publisher when she sells papers individually rather than in volume sized bundles. This price may be calculated by dividing the subscription price by 120 to generate a per-paper price and multiplying the resulting figure by two. All subscription and article prices include VAT at 17.5%.

HEIs in the UK are currently required to pay VAT on purchases of electronic information, but not on print information. The authors acknowledge that it can take several years for journal start-up costs to be amortized and the duration varies considerably. In the interests of simplicity, the journal modeled here is assumed to be an on-going concern, *i.e.*, start-up costs are not included.

The flow element 'other publisher income' represents sources of income derived from the journal publication other than sales of subscriptions and individual articles. Other source of income may include, for example, advertising or sponsored supplements.

This figure is calculated at 4% of subscription and individual article income. This figure was derived from the journal costing form referred to above.

COST OF STORING DIGITAL JOURNALS

The cost of storing digital journals is currently very low and is falling. It is assumed that this cost is incurred by the publisher and that the work related to storage would be undertaken by the Systems administrator in the normal course of her duties.

The cost of storage space itself is based on a rough estimate that it costs £100 per gigabyte per annum to store digital content. It is estimated that an HTML journal volume occupies approximately 30 Mb. This is a liberal estimate based on figures supplied by Stuart Peters with reference to the electronic journal *Sociology Online*.

Thus, a volume costs £2.93 per annum to store. After 13 years the cost of storing that journal is £26 per annum. Storage costs are likely to decrease significantly over the period but no attempt is made to predict the degree of this decrease.

Information Broker Function

The information broker (subscription agent) undertakes administrative work that saves time and money for both the library and the publisher.

The various tasks involved are not represented. The information broker also generates management information which she supplies to both the publisher and the library as appropriate. As the type of information and thus its value and the cost of processing it are unknown as yet, this function is not represented. It is assumed that the information broker negotiates favorable licence terms for libraries. Libraries pay an annual fee to the information broker. In the model, this is based on the fee charged by NESLI. NESLI charges institutions a fee to use SwetsNet which amounts to £1 per title subscription up to a maximum of £560 (A. Prior, personal communication, 17 March 1999).

In the model, the fee paid by an institution is determined by the amount of service delivered to the institution as determined by number of subscriptions and number of individual articles delivered; the latter is divided by 120 as a proxy for a single journal title.

It is assumed in the model that when an individual at an HEI has received a document electronically, the document will then be available to other researchers at the institution free of charge. This assumption is based on the practice of Elsevier Science with regard to institutions participating in the PEAK project. Publishers pay for the services of information broker by supplying publications at a discounted rate. Generally, discounts from publishers to subscription agents are in the region of 7%. This figure is used in the model.

It was beyond the scope of this study to explore the costs to information brokers of the variety of services that they provide. It was assumed that the discount from the publisher and the fee from the library is sufficient remuneration.

HE Library Function

The cost to the library of negotiating the licence terms on which journals and/or individual electronic articles are supplied is represented by a negotiation fraction for each of these resources. This fraction is based on the cost of an individual, professional negotiator working at full capacity plus the cost of 1 hour per week to five other senior staff members in HE.

This is a modest estimate of the cost based on current practice in the US where licence negotiation often involves a team of senior staff who sometimes meet as frequently as every week.

The hourly rate for employing a senior staff member (including employment costs and overhead) is £50. Electronic Individual Article Supply (EIAS) directly from the publisher is likely to be negotiated based on access to a bundle of titles, perhaps within a single subject area or perhaps the publisher's entire list. The negotiation process itself is likely to take longer than negotiation for a single title as both parties have more at stake. However, the cost of the negotiation may be spread across all EIAS acquisitions for, at least, a single year.

In the model, the cost of negotiation for EIAS directly from the publisher is based on 33 senior staff hours at £50 an hour (representing three 1-hour meetings attended by the negotiator and five other participants and 15 hours of negotiation and related tasks by the negotiator).

It is assumed that negotiation reduces the subscription cost and the EIAS cost to the library to 10% less than the standard price. It was assumed also that the library acquisitions budget is £505 per active researcher.

This figure is based on SCONUL figures for an average academic library acquisitions budget and on the number of active researchers. It was assumed that an average institution has 1174 active researchers. This is a rough estimate based on SCONUL figures.

It includes the total mean number of teaching and research staff which is (arbitrarily) divided in half, the mean number of research only staff, and the mean number of postgraduate research students. In the model, the cost of licence negotiation is deducted from the library acquisitions budget.

This does not reflect reality. However, the cost of licence negotiation is directly related to the acquisition of journals and it is deducted from the acquisitions budget in the model so that the total cost of acquiring journals directly from the publisher may be compared with the cost of acquiring them from via an information broker.

It was assumed that the publisher commits as much time and effort to negotiating licences as the library. Thus, the negotiation fraction deducted from the library journals acquisitions budget is also deducted from the publisher gross income to indicate publisher spend.

COSTS OF PROCESSING, STORING AND ISSUING PRINT JOURNALS

The cost of processing, storing, issuing and other tasks related to print journals is included in the model for comparison. Odlyzko claims that these costs are the cause of the serials crisis and suggests that for every $1 that a library spends on journal acquisitions, it spends another $2 on these related activities.

He based this assertion on the fact that Association of Research Libraries (ARL) statistics consistently show that acquisitions represent approximately 30% of the budgets of research libraries in the US and Canada.

The assumption is that if this material is acquired in digital form, these additional library costs can be eliminated. This assumption is, it must said, contentious. The cost of storing digital journals is likely to be much lower than the cost of storing print but the cost of maintaining that store and of technical migration to ensure that the content is available in the future will be significant. Furthermore, it is likely that in a digital library, the tasks currently undertaken by librarians will be as important as they are now.

These tasks may be undertaken by other stakeholders and the nature of the tasks will change to some degree. Nevertheless, the costs of undertaking them will be incurred and will be included in the price of scholarly literature. Figures used for calculating these costs are based on those calculated for use in planning the JSTOR project.

The cost of storing a single volume of the journal *Ecology* for 1 year is $3.07. This figure is used here as a basis for calculating storage costs for journals.

It has been inflated and converted at the current rate to give £2 per volume. Bowen estimated that circulation costs for current issues of journals amount to a total of $45 (currently £29) and that circulation costs for past issues also cost $45. In the model, the term 'current issue' refers to the current year and two previous years.

After that period has elapsed, the cost of circulating back issues will be added to library costs at the same rate as circulation of current issues. Bowen estimated that binding of current issues costs $20 (currently £13) and processing and check in a further $20 (currently £13). Finally, he estimated that the cost of conserving and preserving backruns is $5 (£3).

The total cost per title per annum ranges from £60 in year 1 to £113 in year 13. As a percentage of the current mean journal subscription fee in the UK this represents 58–109%. These figures are lower than Odlyzko suggested, but are still significant when scaled up for a whole journal collection. For example, the cost of processing, storing and issuing a collection of only 1000 titles ranges from £60 000 in Year 1 to £11 3000 in Year 13. The mean number of titles held by a library is 4880.

The cost to the library of processing, storing and issuing a print collection of this size ranges from £292 800 in Year 1 to £551 440 in Year 13. As a percentage of total gross library expenditure, this represents 9–18

COST TO THE LIBRARY OF USERS PRINTING FROM JOURNALS

At present, researchers use the library to browse but photocopy papers that they intend to read. In an electronic environment, they will print from a laser printer. A photocopy costs about 2.5p/page. A laser print costs approximately double.

However, printing from a laser printer does not require the researcher to stand at the machine and photocopy each page of the journal in turn. When this opportunity cost is taken into account the difference in price between photocopying and laser printing is likely to be negligible.

However, were researchers to begin to read on screen rather from than from printed copy, this cost would be saved. For this reason, the model calculates a very approximate print cost as follows. It is estimated that each active researcher prints 2160 pages per annum. This figure is based on a rough calculation of the number of pages per paper multiplied by the number of papers read by an active researcher per annum.

A selection of 36 papers printed from a variety of electronic journals was sampled and the average number of pages was found to be 10. The number of papers read by each active researcher is based on figures derived from a citation analysis conducted for the FIDDO project. On average, each of 1500 authors cited 18 papers. It has been estimated that one third of all influences is cited so it is assumed that each author reads 54 papers when preparing a paper for publication.

As many academic departments in the UK currently require research-active staff to publish four papers per year, this is taken as a standard and it is assumed that researchers read a total of 216 papers per year. If each paper consists of 10 printed pages, in an electronic environment, each researcher will print 2160 pages. Thus, an institution with only 200 research-active staff will incur print costs of £21 600.

It is assumed that an average institution has 1174 active researchers as calculated above. Based on this figure, the cost to an institution for printing is £126 792. The size of the fund supplied to the library for acquisitions is based on the number of active researchers multiplied by a financial sum per active researcher.

The sum per active researcher is based on SCONUL 1996/97 figures and reflects mean subscription costs plus mean binding costs plus mean ILL transaction costs divided by mean number of active researchers.

Model Simulations

The overhead rate, the profit margin applied by the publisher, and the number of subscriptions were varied and the effect on subscription fees monitored. The results are recorded below.

At an overhead rate of 120% and a profit margin of 20%, subscription fees for 200, 500, 1000, 2000, and 20 000 subscriptions are £809.62, £323.84 £161.92, £80.96, and £8.10 respectively. If the overhead is maintained at 120% and the profit margin is reduced to 10%, the subscription fees for 200, 500, 1000, 2000, and 20 000 subscriptions are £742.15, £296.86, £148.43, £74.22, and £7.42 respectively.

If the overhead is maintained at 120% and the profit margin is reduced to zero, the subscription fees for 200,500, 1000, 2000, and 20 000 subscriptions are £674.69, £269.88, £134.94, £67.47, and £6.75 respectively. If the overhead is reduced to 60%, at a profit margin of 20%, the subscription fees for 200, 500, 1000, 2000, and 20 000 subscriptions are £588.82, £235.52, £117.76, £58.88, and £5.89 respectively.

If the overhead is maintained at 60% and the profit margin reduced to 10%, the subscription fees for 200, 500, 1000, 2000, and 20 000 subscriptions are £539.75, £215.90, £107.95, £53.97, and £5.40 respectively. If the overhead is maintained at 60% and the profit margin reduced to zero, the subscription fees for 200, 500, 1000, 2000, and 20 000 subscriptions are £490.68, £196.28, £98.14, £49.07, and £4.91 respectively.

It is clear from these figures that a non-commercial journal making a modest profit and recovering full costs (120% overhead) can be supplied to users for a modest fee as long as the subscription base consists of at least 500 subscribers.

HARNAD MODEL

The Harnad model differs from the traditional model in that all costs are recovered through author submission fees. Again the entire editorial process is conducted electronically. Journals are available on the Internet free of charge to any user.

However, as delivery through a common, familiar interface is important to users and one function of the information broker is to deliver material through a common interface it is assumed that the library pays to use an information broker to deliver Harnad-modelled journals.

Even if all journals were produced on a Harnad-type model, the library would seek to obtain such a service. It is beyond the scope of this project to determine the feasibility of the latter scenario for the information broker.

Content Origination and Publication

Manuscripts are submitted to the editorial office for review. The model simulates production of a single journal consisting of 120 papers per annum. Only authors of papers which are refereed are charged a submission fee. Thus, the 2% of authors whose papers are rejected immediately do not contribute to publication costs.

The contribution of editors and referees is the same in this model as in the traditional model and again, the cost of this contribution is an opportunity cost as this work is unpaid. The total publication cost is calculated based on journal production staff costs which are the same as those in the traditional model, overhead and storage of the back list as it accumulates.

Overhead is applied at a rate of 120% and of 60%. Clearly, the alternative method of calculating overhead referred to above could not have been used in this model as there is no sales income. The submission fee is calculated as the total production cost divided by the number of papers refereed. No profit margin is applied.

Harnad's is a model in which publication is conducted by, and for the benefit of, HE. It is assumed that future development would be funded by HE grant or other HE sources of income. The cost of storing the journal back list is calculated as above.

Information Brokerage and HE Library Function

In the model, the cost to the library of obtaining information brokerage services is based on the charges levied by NESLI. There is no requirement for the information broker to negotiate with a publisher on behalf of the library.

This would represent a significant proportion of the cost of NESLI services. However, it is assumed that the information broker in this model provides the other services offered by NESLI such as management information and catalogue records as well as the common interface for delivering journals. The fee charged by NESLI for using SwetsNet is £1 per title subscription up to a maximum of £560.

The NESLI pricing mechanism would appear to be based on a traditional model, *i.e.,* one in which publishers charge subscription fees, as NESLI also plans to seek fees in the form of a discount on subscriptions from publishers.

This is likely to be at a rate of approximately 7%. Where subscriptions are free of charge, the library would be expected to pay for that part of the NESLI fee that, otherwise, would be recovered from publishers.

The rate applied in the model is based on the average cost of a journal subscription and the fee per institution is based on the amount of service delivered, *i.e.,* the number of subscriptions.

The average subscription fee used is the mean subscription fee paid by UK libraries for journal subscriptions in 1997 as indicated by the LISU Library and Information Statistics Tables 1998. NESLI would seek 7% of the subscription price from the publisher (£7.26). In this model, the library pays 20% of that figure, £1.45, up to a maximum of £812.

Thus, the total figure paid by the library is £2.45 per title up to a maximum of £1372. In this model, the library incurs no costs from negotiating journal licences with publishers. It is assumed that the library acquisitions budget consists of £505 per active researcher.

The costs of processing, storing and issuing print journals calculated above are unaffected by differences in the journal models as is the cost of printing from electronic journals.

Model Simulations

The overhead rate applied to production costs and the journal rejection rate are varied and the effect on submission fees is monitored. The results are recorded below. If the overhead on production costs is 120%, at a 10% rejection rate the submission fee is £878.90.

This figure falls to £97.66 for a 90% rejection rate. If the overhead on production costs is reduced from 120% to 60% the submission fee is reduced and ranges from £639.21 for a rejection rate of 10% to £71.02 for a rejection rate of 90%. For a 10-page article, a fee of £639.21 represents a page charge of £63.92.

If the submission fee were £639.21 the page charge for a 20-page article would be £31.96 but for each of those 20-page papers the model requires two corresponding 5-page articles, submitted at a cost of £127.84 per page.

If the overhead on production costs is reduced to 30%, the submission fee is further reduced and ranges from £519.36 at a rejection rate of 10% to £57.71 for a rejection rate of 90%. Clearly, submission fees are reduced in line with reductions in the overhead rate applied to production costs. We argue that an overhead rate of 120% is realistic.

Thus, if the overhead rate is reduced, the remaining overhead must be covered by the host institution as a subsidy. Presumably, this could be justified with reference to the kudos gained from producing a reputable peer reviewed journal and only if journal production responsibilities were spread across the HE sector.

However, even at an overhead rate of just 30%, fees are not reduced to within the range that Harnad would expect. He suggests that fees of tens of dollars a page rather than hundreds of dollars a page would be acceptable and estimates that it would cost approximately $400 to produce a 20-page article. This converts as approximately £250 for 20 pages, *i.e.*, a page charge of £12.50.

In the model, a page charge of £12.50 would not cover the production costs of any journal with a rejection rate below 80%. If an overhead of 120% were applied, a page charge of £12.50 would cover publication only if the rejection rate were 88% or more.

If an overhead of 60% were applied, a page charge of £12.50 would cover publication only if the rejection rate were 84% or more. If an overhead rate of 30% were applied, a page charge of £12.50 would cover publication costs only if the rejection rate were 80% or more.

Nevertheless, fees are reduced to a level close to that charged for submission to many US journals. The latter also charge subscription fees which the Harnad model avoids. Thus, although costs are not reduced to the level anticipated by Harnad, cost recovery by author submission fees is a viable model.

Clearly, in this model, rejection rate is a key factor determining viability as submission fees are much higher for papers submitted to journals with high rejection rates. This effect would make submission fees in the natural sciences much more expensive than those in the humanities. In the former, rejection rates tend to be around 10–20% and in the latter, they tend to be around 80–90%.

This may appear to be reasonable as research in the natural sciences is more likely to be funded by substantial grants, so it may be argued that natural scientists can better afford to pay high submission fees. However, the difference between disciplines of the cost of submitting a paper for publication is misleading.

Most academic papers are published even if they are rejected by the first or second choice of journal. In disciplines where the rejection rate is high, presumably authors often have to submit the same paper to several journals before it is eventually accepted for publication and thus, they would be required to pay several submission fees.

Ultimately, the total cost to scientists and humanities scholars would be similar. It may, however, be argued that in these circumstances cost would regulate quality. In other words, authors would not go to the expense of constantly submitting (and paying submission fees) a paper they knew to be inferior.

This argument, whilst valid, is countered by the argument that rejection rates in the humanities do not simply reflect an abundance of poor-quality material. Humanities subjects are characterised by debate rather than the scientific method.

Quality assessment in these subjects is more subjective than in the sciences. Thus, material that is rejected by referees selected by the editor of one journal may be commended by referees selected by the editor of another journal. It is likely, therefore, that the majority of authors will persist with their articles. As expected, in this model the cost to users of journals is very low.

Thus, any HE subsidy for journal production and development could be offset by savings in acquisitions costs. A library providing 4880 Harnad-modelled titles to its users could expect to pay only £11 956 in fees to an information broker. Compared with subscribing to an average journals collection at the average price (£103.71) for a total cost of £506 104 this represents a huge saving for the library.

New Journal of Physics

Working examples of the journals modelled by those who seek to change the economic characteristics of the scholarly information delivery chain are rare. Many journals available in electronic form are published in parallel with print and the price mechanism is traditional. Many other journals that are produced only in electronic form are grant funded and recover costs neither from authors nor from users.

A new electronic journal, *The New Journal of Physics (NJP)* is published by an established publisher of peerreviewed scholarly journals, the Institute of Physics Publishing (IoPP). The *NJP* is published only in electronic form and is no doubt intended to cover its costs; this it does from its authors.

Thus, to a degree, it exemplifies the Harnad model. However, whereas Harnad suggests that costs be recovered through submission fees, the IoPP seeks to recover the cost of publishing the *NJP* through acceptance fees. Presumably, fees paid by authors of papers that are accepted for publication must cover the cost of all papers submitted.

The IoPP charges $500 for production of an accepted paper in the *NJP* and the journal is available to access free of charge over the Internet. This suggests that the *NJP* can be published for $60 000 per volume (based on a volume of 120 accepted papers).

The IoPP encourages authors to submit only papers that are of the highest quality and of wide appeal which suggests that they wish to keep the rejection rate as low as possible. It is common for physics journals to have rejection rates of approximately 10%.

The Ithink model produced to test Harnad's theory was revised to simulate the characteristics of the *NJP.* This revised model was run and the results show that if the overhead rate on production costs is 120%, the total production cost for a volume of the *NJP* consisting of 120 10-page papers ranges from £114 000 at 2% rejection rate to £115 000 at 10% rejection rate.

If overhead is applied at a rate of 60%, the cost is approximately £84 000. If the journal were to recover these costs through a submission fee then, at an overhead rate of 120% the fee would range from £958 to £882 for rejection rates of 2% and 10% respectively. If an overhead of 60% were applied, the fee would range from £697 to £641 for rejection rates of 2% and 10% respectively.

The submission fee decreases as the rejection rate increases. However, if costs are recovered through an acceptance fee, as proposed by the IoPP, then at an overhead of 120%, fees range from £958 to £960 for rejection rates of 2% and 10% respectively.

If an overhead rate of 60% is applied, fees range from £697 to £698 for rejection rates of 2% and 10% respectively. The fee increases with the rejection rate. Hence the desire of the IoPP to keep the rejection rate of the *NJP* low. These figures suggest that production of an electronic journal costs a great deal more than a sum that can be recovered from acceptance fees of about $500 (£311).

Presumably, over the longer term, the IoPP expects to recover costs from some other sources. It will be interesting to monitor the success of this new journal.

Fishwick Model

The Fishwick model is significantly different from either of the other models in that it introduces 'normal' market feedback mechanisms into the academic information delivery chain. Both submission fees and subscription fees are used to recover costs as Fishwick argues that both users' requirement for reading material and authors' requirement for publication create demand.

The financial cost of producing a Fishwick journal is much higher than the cost of the other journals modelled because the editor and referees are paid for their contributions. Again, the entire editorial process is conducted electronically and journals are delivered in electronic form.

Libraries are free to obtain subscriptions/individual articles directly from publishers or to obtain them from an information broker. It is assumed, if the library chooses the former, that terms will be negotiated between the library and the publisher.

Content Origination

In this sector manuscripts are submitted to the editorial office for publication and authors are required to pay a submission fee. Only authors of papers which are refereed are charged a submission fee. Thus, the 2% of authors whose papers are rejected immediately do not contribute to publication costs.

Fishwick *et al.* propose that a submission fee should contribute to refereeing, editorial and production costs. Thus, all authors submitting a paper for publication contribute to production costs regardless of whether or not the paper is accepted.

The alternative would be to charge a submission fee which covers only editorial and refereeing costs and, on acceptance, charge an additional publication cost. However, this would incur an additional administration cost. The contribution of editors and referees is the same in this model as in the traditional model. However, both referees and editors are paid for their work at an hourly rate of £50 including overhead and any other related employment costs.

The submission fee consists of the total cost of editorial, refereeing and editorial office work on the manuscript plus a contribution to publisher costs. Fishwick *et al.* do not suggest an appropriate rate at which authors should contribute to publication costs nor do they suggest a suitable rate at which authors should be paid royalties on sales of their papers. In the model, authors contribute 10% of the production cost and receive royalties at a rate of 5% of usage fees.

Generally, authors, their employers, or their funding sources will pay the fee but a small number of papers will be submitted by authors who cannot pay the fee. In these cases, the editorial office will apply, on behalf of the author, for publication assistance from public/charitable bodies. Any royalties accumulated from publication of these papers will be paid to the body which funded publication.

Publication

Production costs in the model vary with the overhead rate applied. It is assumed that overheads cost 120% but a rate of 60% is also tested. As in the traditional model, a profit margin varying from zero to 20% is applied. Fishwick *et al.* suggests that the basic product be simple unedited text and that a more sophisticated product be available at a higher price.

Research suggests that users and librarians expect electronic journals to have additional functionality and would not consider it worthwhile learning how to use a system simply to access text which they would then print.

It is assumed in this model that users would subscribe only to a more sophisticated product, *i.e.,* that the minimum requirement would be hotlinks to cited papers.

Production costs are based on this assumption and consist of the two part-time staff members described above with reference to the Traditional model. Authors contribute 10% towards production costs and the remaining 90% is recovered through subscription/individual article fees.

This journal would be more expensive than the others to administer because of the additional tasks associated with unfunded papers. As well as manuscript management administration, the cost of the following tasks would be incurred:

- Receiving applications for assisted publication;
- Applying to funding bodies on behalf of those applying for assistance;
- Administering receipt of submission fees;
- Administering royalty payments.

It would cost £19 500 to employ a part-time secretary on a pro-rata salary of £15 000 if the overhead applied were 120%. If the overhead were 60%, it would cost £14 400. A cost per-paper is required for the model.

It is assumed that the cost of applying for assistance with publication costs would be spread across all papers and that the secretary could administer 600 papers per annum. This would be the number received by a journal with an 80% rejection rate. Thus, the cost per paper is £32.50 (£19 500/600) if the overhead rate is 120% and £24 (£14 400/600) if the overhead rate is 60%. Fishwick *et al.* suggest that published papers be sold to users either by subscription to the publisher's whole list, by subscription to specific parts (*e.g.* within a specific subject areas), by a two-part tariff which consists of a reduced subscription price combined with reduced transaction costs relating to individual articles, or simply on a pay-per-use basis. These different pricing mechanisms are different risk-sharing schemes. When the publisher shoulders most of the risk in a pay-per-document model the price is higher but when the library shoulders most of the risk by subscribing to a whole database from which users may select only a small proportion of the content, the price per paper is lower.

These different pricing mechanisms were not modelled. To include them in the model would be to introduce too many variables and thus, simulations would reveal economic factors that apply only in very specific circumstances.

Only subscription and individual article fees are included in the model. Subscription fees vary with level of use as in the Traditional model. It is assumed that the journal is an ongoing concern, *i.e.,* that journal start-up costs need not be amortised

Information Brokerage

Assumptions informing the role of the information broker were the same in this model as in the Traditional model.

HE Library Function

Assumptions informing the HE library function were the same in this model as in the Traditional model.

SUBMISSION FEES

The submission fee covers the cost of the editorial process and contributes to publisher income for use in the production process. However, it is not informed by subscription price or any of the elements affecting price and thus, it is not affected by the profit margin applied by the publisher.

It varies only with rejection rate and the rate at which overhead is applied. The latter alters the submission fee because the fee includes the cost of administering the manuscript which is not insignificant in this model.

If the overhead is applied at a rate of 120%, submission fees will range between £446.56 for a journal with a 10% rejection rate to £368.44 for a journal with a 90% rejection rate. If the overhead is applied at a rate of 60%, submission fees will range between £413.92 for a journal with a 10% rejection rate to £357.10 for a journal with a 90% rejection rate.

These fees fall within the range charged by many US journals and thus, are not entirely unacceptable. Unlike the Harnad model however, they contribute little to a reduction in costs for the user.

SUBSCRIPTION PRICE

The subscription price does not vary with rejection rate because it is determined by the cost of producing the 120 papers published in the journal. It does not include the editorial process which is covered by the submission fee.

If the overhead is applied at a rate of 120% and the profit margin is 20%, the subscription price if 200 subscriptions are sold is £728.66. The subscription price if 500 subscriptions are sold is £291.46.

The subscription price if 1000 subscriptions are sold is £145.73. The subscription price if 2000 subscriptions are sold is £72.87 and the subscription price if 20 000 subscriptions are sold is £7.29.

If the overhead is applied at a rate of 60% and the profit margin is 20%, the subscription price if 200 subscriptions are sold is£529.93. The subscription price if 500 subscriptions are sold is £211.98. The subscription price if 1000 subscriptions are sold is £105.99.

The subscription price if 2000 subscriptions are sold is £52.99 and the subscription price if 20 000 subscriptions are sold is £5.30. If the overhead is applied at a rate of 120% and the profit margin is 10%, the subscription price if 200 subscriptions are sold is £667.94. The subscription price if 500 subscriptions are sold is £267.18. The subscription price if 1000 subscriptions are sold is £133.59.

The subscription price if 2000 subscriptions are sold is £66.79 and the subscription if 20 000 subscriptions are sold is £6.68. If the overhead is applied at a rate of 60% and the profit margin is 10%, the subscription price if 200 subscriptions are sold is £485.77. The subscription price if 500 subscriptions are sold is ££194.30. The subscription price if 1000 subscriptions are sold is £97.15. The subscription price if 2000 subscriptions are sold is £48.58 and the subscription if 20 000 subscriptions are sold is £4.86. If the overhead is applied at a rate of 120% and the profit margin is zero, the subscription price if 200 subscriptions are sold is £607.22.

The subscription price if 500 subscriptions are sold is ££242.88. The subscription price if 1000 subscriptions are sold is £121.44. The subscription price if 2000 subscriptions are sold is ££60.72 and the subscription price if 20 000 subscriptions are sold is £6.07. If the overhead is applied at a rate of 60% and the profit margin is zero, the subscription price if 200 subscriptions are sold is £441.61.

The subscription price if 500 subscriptions are sold is ££176.64. The subscription if 1000 subscriptions are sold is £88.32. The subscription if 2000 subscriptions are sold is £44.16 and the subscription price if 20 000 subscriptions are sold is £4.42.

AUTHOR ROYALTIES

Author royalty is based on income from subscriptions and sales of individual articles, *i.e.*, it is based on the price of subscriptions and individual articles. It is not affected by the rejection rate because editorial and associated administrative costs are covered separately by submission fees. Nor is author royalty affected by the number of subscriptions sold.

Subscription price varies with the number of subscriptions sold so that journals/individual articles may be delivered to users at the cheapest rate possible; this a non-profit initiative.

The royalty is affected, however, by the overhead applied to production costs and by the profit margin applied by the publisher as both of these things vary the price of the product. If overhead is applied at a rate of 120%, a profit margin of 20% is applied, the mean royalty received is £24.03.

If overhead is applied at a rate of 60%, a profit margin of 20% is applied, the mean royalty received is £17.48. If overhead is applied at a rate of 120%, a profit margin of 10% is applied, the mean royalty received is £22.03. If overhead is applied at a rate of 60%, a profit margin of 10% is applied, the mean royalty received is £16.02. If overhead is applied at a rate of 120%, a profit margin of zero is applied, the mean royalty received is £20.03.

If overhead is applied at a rate of 60%, a profit margin of zero is applied, the mean royalty received is £14.56. Individual articles are priced at double the rate of a paper sold as part of a subscription. However, prices of papers and subscriptions vary with the number of subscriptions and individual articles sold, *i.e.*, with income from sales. Thus, although a single paper may sell well on an individual article basis, the mean author royalty will be static.

The royalty is included in Fishwick's model as an incentive to publish only high-quality material. A very successful paper could recover the submission fee through royalties such as these.

For example, the royalty for a journal produced when an overhead of 120% and a profit margin of 10% are applied is £16.02. In this case the submission fee is £413.92. To recover the submission fee, the author would be required to attract 22% of the royalty funds available for that title in a single year.

The Fishwick model is expensive. Submission fees are not insignificant and, primarily, they pay for work that is unpaid in other models.

Furthermore, although authors contribute 10% to production costs, the effect on subscription fees is small. Thus, in financial terms the model does not compare well with the others. Nevertheless, like the other models, subscription fees generated for this model are modest compared with fees of commercial publishers.

Alternative Model Proposed by Authors

Like the Fishwick model, the alternative model proposed here recovers costs through a submission fee and a subscription fee in recognition that both authors and users create demand for publication of scholarly articles.

However, this is not a market model and does not introduce payment for editors and referees. The model differs from the standard non-commercial model only in that a proportion of the production cost is recovered from submission fees.

Content Origination

In this sector manuscripts are submitted for publication and authors pay a submission fee. Only authors of papers which are refereed are charged a submission fee. Thus, the 2% of authors whose papers are rejected immediately do not contribute to publication costs.

The authors attempted to establish an acceptable rate at which page charges may be levied. Figures charged for publication in some leading US journals were compared. These tend to fall within the range $25–$75 per page.

At current UK prices, these charges represent £15.53–£46.58 per page which, for a 10-page article, amounts to £155.30–£465.80. The model is used to explore the effect on subscription costs of varying submission fees from £200–£50. The former falls comfortably within the lower end of the scale of charges common in the US and the latter is a fraction of those charges.

The contribution of editors and referees is the same in this model as in the traditional model. It was assumed that clerical and administrative tasks are undertaken by journal production staff.

- *Publication* Other than that authors contribute to production costs, the assumptions informing the publication sector were the same as in the Traditional model.
- *Information brokerage* Assumptions informing the role of the information broker were the same in this model as in the Traditional model.
- *HE library function* Assumptions informing the HE library function were the same in this model as in the Traditional model.
- *Model simulations* The effect of variations in overhead rate applied, profit margin, rejection rate and submission fee were explored.

The results follow. If the submission fee is set at £200 per paper, the overhead is 120%, the profit margin 20% and the rejection rate 10%, subscription prices range from £6.25 to £625.38 for 20 000 and 200 subscriptions respectively. The subscription price if 500 subscriptions are sold is £250.16, if 100 subscriptions are sold, £125.08 and, if 2000 subscriptions are sold, £62.54.

If the submission fee is £200 per paper, the overhead is 120%, the profit margin 10% and the rejection rate 10%, subscription prices range from £5.73 to £573.27 for 20 000 and 200 subscriptions respectively.

If 500 subscriptions are sold the price is £229.30, if 1000 subscriptions are sold, £114.65, and if 2000 subscriptions are sold the price is £57.33. If the submission fee is £200 per paper, the overhead is 120%, the profit margin is zero and the rejection rate 10%, subscription prices range from £5.21 to £521.15 for 20 000 to 200 subscriptions sold respectively.

If 500 subscriptions are sold the price is £208.46, if 1000 subscriptions are sold, £104.23, and if 2000 subscriptions are sold the price is £52.12. If the submission fee is £200 per paper, the overhead is reduced to 60%, the profit margin is 20% and the rejection rate 10%, subscription prices range from £3.71 to £370.86 for 20 000 to 200 subscriptions sold respectively. If 500 subscriptions are sold the price is £148.34, if 1000 subscriptions are sold, £74.17, and if 2000 subscriptions are sold the price is £37.09.

If the submission fee is £200 per paper, the overhead is 60%, the profit margin is 10% and the rejection rate 10%, subscription prices range from £4.05 to £404.58 for 20 000 to 200 subscriptions sold respectively. If 500 subscriptions are sold the price is £161.84, if 1000 subscriptions are sold, £80.92, and if 2000 subscriptions are sold the price is £40.46.

If the submission fee is £200 per paper, the overhead is 60%, the profit margin is zero and the rejection rate 10%, subscription prices range from £3.37 to £337.15 for 20 000 to 200 subscriptions sold respectively.

If 500 subscriptions are sold the price is £134.86, if 1000 subscriptions are sold, £67.43, and if 2000 subscriptions are sold the price is £33.71. If the submission fee is reduced to £100 per paper, the overhead is 120%, the profit margin is 20% and the rejection rate 10%, subscription prices range from £7.18 to £717.50 for 20 000 to 200 subscriptions sold respectively.

If 500 subscriptions are sold the price is £287, if 1000 subscriptions are sold, £143.50, and if 2000 subscriptions are sold the price is £71.75.

If the submission fee is £100 per paper, the overhead is 120%, the profit margin is 10% and the rejection rate 10%, subscription prices range from £6.58 to £657.71 for 20 000 to 200 subscriptions sold respectively. If 500 subscriptions are sold the price is £263.08, if 1000 subscriptions are sold, £131.54, and if 2000 subscriptions are sold the price is £65.77.

If the submission fee is £100 per paper, the overhead is 120%, the profit margin is zero and the rejection rate 10%, subscription prices range from £5.98to £597.92 for 20 000 to 200 subscriptions sold respectively. If 500 subscriptions are sold the price is £80.12, if 1000 subscriptions are sold, £40.06, and if 1000 subscriptions are sold the price is £59.79.

If the submission fee is £100 per paper, the overhead is reduced to 60%, the profit margin is 20% and the rejection rate 10%, subscription prices range from £4.97 to £496.70 for 20 000 to 200 subscriptions sold respectively. If 500 subscriptions are sold the price is £198.68, if 1000 subscriptions are sold, £99.34, and if 2000 subscriptions are sold the price is £49.67. If the submission fee is £100 per paper, the overhead is reduced to 60%, the profit margin is 10% and the rejection rate 10%, subscription prices range from £4.55 to £455.30 for 20 000 to 200 subscriptions sold respectively.

If 500 subscriptions are sold the price is £182.12, if 1000 subscriptions are sold, £91.06, and if 2000 subscriptions are sold the price is £45.53. If the submission fee is £100 per paper, the overhead is reduced to 60%, the profit margin is 0% and the rejection rate 10%, subscription prices range from £4.14 to £413.91 for 20 000 to 200 subscriptions sold respectively. If 500 subscriptions are sold the price is £165.56, if 1000 subscriptions are sold, £82.78, and if 2000 subscriptions are sold the price is £41.39.

It is clear that if the rejection rate is low, *i.e.,* close to those common in the pure sciences, it would be possible to recover full costs (*i.e.,* 120% overhead) and make a modest profit (*i.e.,* 10%) by charging a submission fee of only £100 whilst reducing subscription fees well below the current level.

If these conditions applied, then with a subscription base of 500–1000 a publisher could afford to set the subscription fee at £131-£263.

A larger subscription base would reduce the price. When the rejection rate is much higher, *i.e.,* close to those common in humanities subjects, both the submission fee and the subscription fee can be lower. If the overhead rate applied is 120%, the profit margin is 20% and the rejection rate is 90% then a submission fee of £200 would more than cover the costs so no subscription fee need be charged.

If the submission fee is £100 per paper, the overhead is 120% the profit margin is 20% and the rejection rate 80%, subscription prices range from £1.74 to £174.28 for 20 000 to 200 subscriptions sold respectively. If 500 subscriptions are sold the price is £69.72, if 1000 subscriptions are sold, £34.86, and if 2000 subscriptions are sold the price is £17.43.

An even lower submission fee may be preferable however, given that an author has an 80% chance of having her paper rejected and may need to pay another fee to submit the paper for publication in another journal.

If the submission fee is £50 per paper, the overhead is 120%, the profit margin is 20% and the rejection rate 80%, subscription prices range from £3.82 to £381.55 for 20 000 to 200 subscriptions sold respectively. If 500 subscriptions are sold the price is £152.62, if 1000 subscriptions are sold, £76.31, and if 2000 subscriptions are sold the price is £38.15.

If the submission fee is £50 per paper, the overhead is 120%, the profit margin is reduced to 10% and the rejection rate 80%, subscription prices range from £3.50 to £349.75 for 20 000 to 200 subscriptions sold respectively.

If 500 subscriptions are sold the price is £139.90, if 1000 subscriptions are sold, £69.95, and if 2000 subscriptions are sold the price is £34.98. At a 90% rejection rate, if the submission fee is £50 per paper, the overhead is 120%, the profit margin is 20%, subscription prices range from £1.74 to £174.28 for 20 000 to 200 subscriptions sold respectively.

If 500 subscriptions are sold the price is £69.72, if 1000 subscriptions are sold, £34.86, and if 2000 subscriptions are sold the price is £17.43. At a 90% rejection rate, if the submission fee is £50 per paper, the overhead is 120%, the profit margin is 10%, subscription prices range from £1.6 to £159.75 for 20

000 to 200 subscriptions sold respectively. If 500 subscriptions are sold the price is £63.90, if 1000 subscriptions are sold, £31.95, and if 2000 subscriptions are sold the price is £15.98.

It is clear that in disciplines with high rejection rates, *i.e.,* close to those common in the humanities, it is possible to recover full costs (*i.e.,* 120% overhead) and make a modest profit (*i.e.,* 10%) by charging a submission fee of only £50 whilst reducing subscription fees well below the current level.

If these conditions applied, then with a subscription base of 500–1000 a publisher could afford to set the subscription fee at £32–64. A larger subscription base would reduce the price. It is possible to reduce the submission fee even further if a higher subscription fee is acceptable.

If the submission fee were £25 and the rejection rate 90% subscription fees could be set at £110.43 and £220.86 for 1000 and 500 subscriptions respectively. If the submission fee were £25 and the rejection rate 80% subscription fees could be set at £64.72 and £129.44 for 1000 and 500 subscriptions respectively.

Journal Submission Fees Subscription Fees

It is clear that the rate of overhead paid on production costs is more important than any modest profit margin. A journal recovering full costs is much more expensive than one that is subsidised by its host institution in the form of a reduced overhead on production costs regardless of whether it seeks to make a small profit or not.

Nevertheless, although a reduction in costs predicted by Harnad and others is unlikely to be realised in an electronic environment, it is clear that prices of non-commercial journals which recover full costs (*i.e.,* 120% overhead) and make a small profit (10%) can be sold at reasonable subscription prices as long as there is a subscription base of at least 500.

A journal recovering costs through subscription only can sell 500 subscriptions at £148.43 and 1000 subscriptions at £74.22. A modest submission fee reduces the subscription fee even further.

Net Benefit to Libraries of Negotiating Licence Terms with Publishers

It is assumed that negotiation will be sufficient to secure a reduction in price of 10%. If a non-commercial journal recovering full costs and making a profit of 20% on a subscription base of 1000 costs £120.38 (exc. VAT), the library can expect to reduce the price to £108.34, a saving of £12.04.

The cost of negotiating this saving would be £550. The net loss for the library is £537.96. Even for a journal costing 10 times as much as the one described above, *i.e.,* £1203.80, the saving would be only £120.38 and the net loss would be £429.62.

It is clear that some rationalisation of negotiation activity is required. Consortia may find that they can efficiently negotiate licences on behalf of their members. It is beyond the scope of this project to investigate this.

It is clear, however, that use of information brokers such as NESLI is very efficient. Furthermore, these organisations understand the business and have established relationships with all other parties, *i.e.,* with libraries and publishers.

It is likely that in an electronic environment information brokers will continue to be useful to both libraries and publishers. It may be difficult for them to survive, however, if all journal prices are significantly reduced. At present, an information broker's income tends to be derived from publisher discounts.

If prices are reduced and publisher operations are necessarily leaner, the current discount rate of 7% will be insufficient and the information broker may find it difficult to negotiate a viable rate.

Resource Discovery Network

This model is based on the eLib supporting study titled *Comparative Evaluation of the Subject Based Gateways Approach to Providing Access to Network Resources* and is informed also by the JISC Circular (JISC 10/98) which called for proposals for a Resource Discovery Network.

The report explores a number of alternative models for the continuation of subject-based gateways and, finally, recommends one of those models. The selected model involves:

- Rationalisation of non-cataloguing tasks such as marketing and training;
- Employment of a Managing Director (MD) with responsibility for finding sponsors to fund SBGs;
- And 50% matched funding from the JISC over a 3-year period.

The report states that 'until a market for these services has been fully developed it will be difficult to predict the long-term viability of fully selfsupporting services'.

The model developed here explores the financial viability of a resource discovery network which is part-funded by the JISC or is self-supporting. The model consists of the RDN centre, the hubs and the RDN income.

Staff Costs

All staff costs in the model include salary plus 20% for national insurance contributions (NIC) and pension payments, plus overhead. The overhead is not broken down into accommodation, consumables, equipment etc. but the authors aim to reflect the true cost to the institution so overhead is calculated at 120% (V. Bruce, Vice Principal (Research), Stirling University, personal communication, August 1997).

The authors are aware that some critics may argue that a lower rate would be applied by University Finance Departments so an alternative rate of 60% is applied and figures generated by the model on that basis are recorded.

The Hubs

It is assumed that the RDN will consist of eight hubs. Development of these hubs will vary. Some of the hubs will be developed from existing subject-based gateways and thus, will have a database of catalogue records from Year 1.

As existing Subject Based Gateways (SBGs) vary in size, the databases of hubs developed from SBGs will also vary in size. It is assumed that some hubs will be developed anew and thus will have no existing catalogue records.

The model developed by the authors would become overly complex if each of eight hubs were included. Thus, although equations within the model will generate figures for eight hubs, only three different-sized hubs are modelled. One is a new hub with no existing records.

The second begins with 2000 records and thus corresponds with a small SBG such as RUDI or ADAM. The third begins with 7000 records, and thus corresponds with a large SBG such as SOSIG.

Hub Income

It is assumed that each hub receives from the RDN a sufficient sum to employ one fulltime individual who catalogues resources and develops and maintains the hub. This individual is paid within the range cited by Haynes et al., *i.e.,* £16 000 - £23 000 (a mean figure of £19 500 each is used). Employment costs consist of a salary of £19 500 plus 20% NIC and pension payments, plus overhead.

Thus, the total cost is either £37 440 or £51 480 if overhead is applied at a rate of 60% and 120% respectively. In addition to funding an individual employee, the centre contributes start-up (SU) costs to any new hub at a rate of £20 000 in the first year. It is assumed that each hub benefits from its own success in that is receives a percentage of the HE subscription income received by the RDN for access to that hub and it attracts more sponsorship.

The latter is difficult to predict and to model because other variables will affect the likelihood that any specific hub receives sponsorship, *e.g.,* it can be assumed that OMNI, like any other medical publishing outlets, is more likely to attract sponsors than an arts and humanities hub.

The total sum required from sponsors for the whole RDN is calculated on an annual basis. It is assumed that the hubs will invest their income in development.

Thus, hubs that receive larger sums as a proportion of subscription income will develop at a faster rate than those that do not. Each hub passes 28% of its work to the RDN centre. The centre pays for hub employee and infrastructure costs and requires the bulk of any income to do so.

It is assumed that although the centre uses a majority share of any income to pay for hub and centre costs, a percentage of subscription income is passed directly back to the hub to invest in development. It is estimated that 12% of current JISC spending on SBGs could be saved through rationalisation such as that represented in this model.

It is assumed, arbitrarily, that 12% of the hub subscription income is returned directly to the hub to invest in development. The rest of the hub income is routed through the RDN centre which pays for hub employee and infrastructure costs.

The number of subscriptions to each type of hub in the model is a variable and is controlled by a slider. Subscription price varies from £100 for a database with 5000 records (those with fewer records are available free of charge) to a maximum of £500 for databases of 25000 records or more.

The effect of doubling these prices is also explored. In reality subscription price may vary with institution size but, for example, the influences determining subscription numbers across different institution sizes are unknown so this additional complexity is not modelled.

Hub Spend

Each hub spends its funds on development of the hub, on creating catalogue records and on maintenance of the database. It is estimated that the cost of a record produced by an individual earning £16 000—£23 000 lies between £13.80 and £19, depending on the overhead rate applied.

These figures were calculated as follows from information supplied by Haynes et al.: during a sixmonth study period, five SBG providers added between 350 and 3057 records to their databases and three of the five producers added between 948 and 1326. It is fair to assume that one provider added 350 records, one added 3057 records and each of the other three added ~ 1137 (*i.e.,* ((948 + 1326)/2) x 3) records.

Thus, the mean number of records added over the six-month period was 1363 ((350 + 3057 + (1137 x 3))/5). Thus, in one year, a provider may be expected to add 2726 records. It is assumed that an individual works for approximately 1628 hours per annum (52 weeks minus 8 weeks holiday at 37 hours per week).

Thus, the individual produces 1.67 records per hour. Her hourly rate is calculated as follows: she is paid within the range cited by Haynes *et al., i.e.,* £16 000–£23 000 (a mean figure of £19 500 each is used).

Her employment cost, including NIC, pension contributions and overhead at a rate of 120% or 60% is £51 480 or £37 440 respectively. Thus, if she works for 1628 hours per annum, her hourly rate is £31.62 or £23 at overhead rates of 120% or 60% respectively. If she produces 1.67 records per hour, the cost per record is £19 or £13.80. Gateway development costs are assumed to amount to 10% of one full-time employee per annum per hub. Haynes *et al.* estimate that as much as 30% of the time of a hub employee will be spent maintaining current records.

Presumably, this is based on the SBGs at the time of the study and thus, it must be based on databases of approximately 2000–7000 records. As 30% is cited as a high figure, it is assumed that 30% time relates to a larger database of *e.g.,* 7000 records. This rate is divided to generate an indication of how many records could be maintained per 1% of an individual's time.

The result is that 233 records (7000/30) can be maintained per 1% of a hub employee's time. This figure is used to relate directly the employee's time spent on maintenance to the number of records in the hub database.

RDN Centre

The RDN centre is modelled as a budget which has four outgoing flows and one incoming flow. The outgoing flows represent RDN staff costs, RDN infrastructure costs, hub income, and Managing Director salary and bonuses.

The incoming flow represents RDN funds and is informed by two converters: non-grant funds and JISC funds. The former consists of HE subscription income and of sponsorship and the latter consists of JISC start-up funds plus and ongoing allowance as described by Haynes *et al.*

However, the JISC will probably not continue grant-funding this enterprise indefinitely, so simulations were run also on the assumption that the JISC provides start-up funding over the first four years as described by Haynes *et al.*, but that there was no further funding beyond that period.

The element in the model determining the number of subscriptions represents the number of subscriptions per hub and is controlled by a slider. The model represents only three hubs but model elements representing the financial figures for the system are based on the existence of eight hubs. Thus, figures calculated for, *e.g.*, sponsorship income required, refer to an RDN with eight hubs. Subscriptions income is determined by the subscription price of each type of hub multiplied by the number of subscriptions. Total subscription funding from the three hubs is multiplied by 8/3 to generate the total figure paid to the centre for subscriptions to eight hubs. It is difficult to predict uptake. There are 174 HEIs in the UK.

However, the subject area covered by some hubs will not be relevant at many of these institutions. Uptake of JISC datasets varies from 23 to 131 subscription according to the dataset and most commonly falls between 30 and 50. Price is not the only factor affecting uptake.

Many institutions do not subscribe to datasets even when they are free of charge. The effect of varying uptake is explored but the authors acknowledge that subscription may not be a viable income stream for the RDN. The financial effect of relying more heavily on sponsorship is explored as is the effect of varying subscription rates from 30 up to 120 per hub.

It was assumed that sponsorship would not be received until Year 2. The MD will spend Year 1 seeking sponsorship. The converter representing funding from 'sponsorship' is a slider which is varied to monitor the effect during model simulations. Sponsorship income attracted by the three hubs is multiplied by 8/3 to reflect the income derived from eight hubs of varying sizes. The JISC contributes £950 000 in Year 1.

This represents current spending on SBGs, plus £50 000 for a Managing Director, plus £50 000 for managing change. In Year 2, this is reduced to £650 000.

This reflects a saving of £100 000 as a result of rationalisation, a reduction in the cost of managing change to £30 000 a reduction in the MD's salary to £25 000 but with an additional marketing bonus of £10 000. It is assumed that the MD will have attracted matched funding, *i.e.,* non-grant of £165 000. In Year 3, the JISC contribution is reduced by £265 000 to £385 000. Matched funding is assumed to have increased by £215 000 to £380 000 while the saving from rationalisation has remained at £100 000.

The MD's bonus has increased by £5000 to £15 000 but she no longer receives a salary from the JISC which saves £25 000 and funds for managing change are no longer contributed by the JISC which saves £30 000. In Year 4, JISC funding is reduced by a further £15 000 to £370 000 as the JISC will no longer contribute a marketing bonus.

This is the sum contributed by the JISC in all future years but the assumption that JISC funding is withdrawn entirely after 3 years is also tested. RDN costs include staff costs, infrastructure and hub income. Haynes *et al* suggested that rationalisation of certain aspects of the work of subject-based gateways could save £100 000 from a budget of £850 000.

This is a 12% saving. Such a saving would be achieved were each hub to pass 28% of its work to the centre and for the work to be undertaken by two full-time employees. RDN salaries are the salaries of these two individuals.

It is assumed that they each earn salaries in the same range as the hub employees who catalogue resources, *i.e.,* £16 000–£23 000 (a mean figure of £19 500 each is used). A further 20% is added to reflect NIC and pension payments (£23 400 each) and overhead is calculated at 120% (total £51 480 each) and 60% (£37 440).

As there is no breakdown of costs in Haynes *et al.*'s report the cost of infrastructure is unclear. In the model, it was assumed that the RDN centre meets infrastructure costs at a rate of 25% of all staff costs. The latter includes hub employee costs, RDN staff costs and MD costs.

Hub income consists of 12% of subscriptions income, plus the cost of employing an individual for each of eight hubs, plus start-up costs for the new hubs. As there are only three hubs in the model, it is assumed that 8/3 of the eight hubs is a start-up hub.

Haynes *et al.*'s report suggests that the MD should be employed for 18 months and that she would cost £50 000 in Year 1 and £25 000 in Year 2. Employment costs of £50 000 would pay a salary of approximately £19 000 or £26 000 assuming that the employment cost also covers NIC and pension contributions (20% of salary) and that overhead is applied at a rate of 120% or 60% respectively.

Haynes *et al.* state that 'we envisage a package with a competitive salary for 18 months and additional incentives in the form of a bonus based on the level of matched funding obtained and payable in the two years after the funding has been secured'.

As the model is based on the Haynes *et al.* report, the effect of paying the MD at that rate is explored. However, the authors of this report would suggest that an MD of the calibre required would expect to be paid at least double that rate and more probably, would expect a salary of around £60 000.

The effect of paying the MD a basic salary of £60 000 is explored. The total cost of such a salary including 20% for NIC and pension contribution would be either £115 200 or £158 400 if overheads are applied at 60% or 120% respectively.

Haynes *et al.* propose that the MD would receive a bonus of £15 000 in Year 2 for attracting matched funding of £380 000. This corresponds to a bonus of 4% of non-grant funding. Thus, it is assumed that the MD receives an annual bonus of 4% of non-grant funding.

Model Simulations

It is assumed in these model simulations that the RDN is expected to be self sustaining within 10 years of starting up. Thus, the RDN budget must always be in the black and, before the end of the 10-year period, the RDN must make a surplus, however small.

The simulations were run with a view to determining the level of sponsorship required if the RDN is to be viable. The sponsorship required is rounded up to the nearest hundred pounds. Table documents the results of the model simulations by listing the level of sponsorship required in each instance.

Simulations include those that assume that the JISC continues to fund the RDN at a rate of £370 000 per annum after the initial 3-year period when higher sums are granted, and those that assume that JISC funding ends after the initial 3- year period.

The subscription price of resources from each hub varies as described above and two rates of prices are tested: those that begin at £100 for a database of 5000 records and increase to £500 for a database of 25 000 records or more and those that begin at £200 for a database of 5000 records and increase to £1000 for a database of 25 000 records or more.

The other variable is the MD's salary. Either she earns £60 000 and overhead is applied at a rate of 120% or 60% or she costs £50 000. If the latter, her salary is £19 000 or £26 000 at overhead rates of 120% and 60% respectively. Simulations are run assuming that the following number of subscriptions is secured per hub: 0, 30, 50, 70, and 120.

These figures are encouraging. Haynes *et al.* suggest that matched funding, *i.e.*, sponsorship, could be secured at a rate of £365 000 within 4 years.

If the JISC continues to fund the RDN beyond the initial 3-year period, all but the most expensive alternative modelled here would be sustained by sponsorship of less than £281 000. The most expensive alternative would be sustainable for £361 000 if it could also secure a modest income from subscriptions.

If JISC funding ends, the RDN will be required to attract much more funding from sponsors. Sale of subscriptions is considered by the authors to be viable as a constituent income source. However, if RDN resources are restricted to the UK HE community, this source will be limited and must be complemented by other sources such as sponsorship. In this model, as in the others, variation in the overhead rate applied to staff costs has a marked effect.

Clearly, staff are a very expensive resources. Nevertheless, if an HEI hosts an initiative such as the RDN and fails to recover full costs, it effectively subsidises the RDN activity. In the present climate, few HEIs can afford to do this.

National Electronic Reserve Service (NERS)

The model of a national electronic reserve service is based on information and assumptions about the HERON project and is informed by an eLib supporting study of ODP/ER services and by cost and charge developments such as those published by the CLA and the PLS. Figures cited here are for a NERS which has migrated from grant-funded status. It is assumed that development during the project phase lasted for 3 years.

Three functions of the NERS are represented: copyright clearance, digitisation, and the repository function. It is assumed that course materials change every 4 years *i.e.,* that there is an annual change of 25%. Thus, in a print environment publishers could expect libraries to have replaced all books for a class by the end of every 4-year period.

This should be a basis for comparison of publisher income in a print environment and in an electronic environment such as the one modelled here. Costs are not inflated over the 13-year period.

7

Application of Data Mining in Library and Information Services

INTRODUCTION

At the beginning of each adjustment in a library, librarians or library managers need to think about which kind of books are going to purchase or what kind of magazines have to be ordered in the coming renewal period of the year. The purpose of project is to provide statistics and analysis software. It will offer librarians or managers sufficient information to make right decisions. The statistical data orchart produced by the programme will easily make librarians sense what changes need to be made. We are going to research the reader's behaviour from these statistical data or charts and then improve or modify our library service.

The library professionals do not know which books a patron wants, which is offered for their studying, or which patron prefers what class of book. The library may offer a book that no patron wants to borrow, or the offered books may not have enough readers. Librarians should make a decision so that this kind of book may never be or seldom ordered in the future. On the other hand, librarians have to use a lot of their budget for much used books to provide the reader more services. Librarians will be helped by this programme. This kind of feedback can be researched and can present some trends. This will be important information for further improvement of the library. Data Mining in a Library System will be a product after we digitalize the library. Librarians may get a lot of worthwhile information immediately such as the students' studying trend, the top 10 of circulation in the library, the hottest field of studying by using this system. Not only librarians want this but also patrons need it. This is also a knowledge management strategy system for the current library. Actually, the system will enhance the librarian's efficiency in controlling library resources. Librarians could imagine the future library from it.

The uncertainties of the Internet challenge the modern workplace but also promise unexpected opportunities. Converting uncertainties to opportunities requires human efforts to enhance the capabilities of technology to benefit professional endeavour. In the library profession, practices of unstructured and unrestricted information dissemination and retrieval from the World Wide Web (WWW) not only create an information explosion but make uncertain the future of the profession as well. Facing the need to adapt to the new climate of the information world, academic librarians are charged to extend their services from the reference desk to the virtual environment on the WWW.

To meet the challenge, new information technologies that can assist in organizing and retrieving information are constantly being investigated by academic libraries. Web mining is one of these new technologies that deserves special attention because of its capability to discover and analyse useful information from the Web.

WHAT ARE DATA MINING AND WEB MINING

Data mining is one of the hottest topics and buzz word in information technology. It automatically and exhaustively explores very large datasets, consequently uncovering otherwise hidden relationships among data.This technology has been successfully applied in science, health, marketing and finance to aid new discoveries and strengthen markets. In addition, data mining techniques are being applied to discover and organize information from the Web.Data mining itself is in the second generation of artificial intelligence; the core concept of data mining is focused on machine learning.This machine-learning ability allows modification of search criteria automatically before the next execution, once particular patterns or trends have been discovered in the data searched.It is important to understand that data mining is a discovery-oriented data analysis technology and not a single product or a system. It is a highly focused data transformation framework.

This transformation process uses a series of analytical techniques, such as clustering, association and classifi-cation.These techniques are taken from the field of mathematics, cybernetics and genetics, and can be used independently or cooperatively. The function is to extract high quality information to identify facts and draw conclusions based on relationships or patterns among the data. Most important, data mining can ask a processing engine to "show answers to questions we do not know how to ask".For example, bank customers' data are kept in different databases, thus, they are isolated from each other.

Data mining technology can search all the different databases together, and provide a better customer view so that the bank can concentrate more on potentially good customers.The rationale is that when asking for specific relationships, more important relationships might be missed. Asking to find relationships that we do not know exist will yield more meaningful data or business knowledge.The combination of these two areas, data mining and the WWW, is known as Web mining.

When data mining is applied to the Web, it can perform several functions including:

- Resource discovery the discovery of locations of unfamiliar files on the network;
- Information extraction the acquisition of useful information from the WWW;
- Generalization the discovery of information patterns from said resources

There are two primary dimensions of Web mining:

- Web content mining and
- Web usage mining.

WEB CONTENT MINING

Web content mining is the "process of information or resource discovery from millions of sources across the World Wide Web ".There are two approaches in Web content mining: the agent-based and database approaches. The agent-based approach involves artificial intelligence systems that can "act autonomously or semi-autonomously on behalf of a particular user, to discover and organize Web-based information ".Some intelligent Web agents can use a user profile to search for relevant information, then organize and interpret the discovered information. Some use various information retrieval techniques and the characteristics of open hypertext documents to organize and filter retrieved information.

Another kind of agent is programmed to learn user preferences and use those preferences to discover information sources for those particular users. The database approach focuses on "integrating and organizing the heterogeneous and semi-structured data on the Web into more structured and high-level collections of resources." These organized resources can then be accessed and analysed. These "metadata, or generalizations, are then organized into structured collections and can be analysed".

WEB USAGE MINING

The other dimension of data mining is Web usage mining. This is the process of discovering user access patterns, as data are automatically collected in daily access logs. Recently, referrer logs, which collect information about referring pages for each reference and user registration, also have been included. Web usage mining is crucial in establishing user profiles for a better structured Web site. "As the manner in which the Web is used continues to expand, there is a continual need to figure out new kinds of knowledge about user behaviour that needs to be mined for".

TEN STEPS OF DATA MINING

The following are ten steps of Data Mining for extracting hidden knowledge from data:

IDENTIFY THE OBJECTIVE

The purpose of Step 1 is creating a list of analyses to perform, questions to investigate, and hypotheses to test. The first of thing is to be clear on what you hope to achieve with your analysis. It includes some advanced planning about what type and level of information you intend to capture from the database. Make sure whether or not the objective is measurable. This advance planning can save you time and money in your data mining efforts.

SELECT THE DATA

The next step is to select the data to meet this objective. In this step, the data is organized for analysis and to produce an effective representation.

The following are some examples for a quick checklist:

- Is the data adequate to describe the phenomena, the data mining analysis is attempting to model?
- Is there a common field in your data that can be used for linking it to other database?
- Are internal and external information available for the analysis?
- Is the data stable—will the data being mined be the same and available after the analysis?
- Is there redundancy in the data sets when they are merged?
- How current and relevant are the data to the business objective?
- Is there lifestyle or demographic data available?

PREPARE THE DATA

Once you've organized the data, you must decide which features to convert into usable formats. The purpose of this step is to produce a "data mining-ready" data set.

- Establish strategies for handling missing data, extraneous noise, and outliers
- Identify redundant variables in the dataset and decide which fields to exclude
- Determine the distribution frequencies of the data

For example, it may be efficient to have an account establish date in the format of YY-MM-DD, but it may be necessary to transform this field to one total account number days like NNNN. You can postpone some of these decisions until you select a data mining tool. For example, if you need a neural network or polynomial network you may have to transform some of your fields.

EVALUATE THE DATA

"*Evaluate the structure of your data in order to choose the appropriate tools*:

- What is the ratio of categorical/binary attributes in the database?
- What is the nature and structure of the database?
- What is the overall condition of the dataset?
- What is the distribution of the data set?

Balance the objective evaluation of the structure of your data against your users' need to understand the findings." For example, neural networks generally work best on data sets with a vast number of numeric attributes.

FORMAT THE SOLUTION

In conjunction with the evaluation of data and business objective determine the format of the solution.

You may think about:

- What is the optimum format of the solution—decision tree, rules, C code, graph, or SQL syntax?
- What are the available format options from the data mining process?
- What is the goal of the solution, classification, and segmentation?
- What does the end-client need—graphs, reports, code?

SELECT THE TOOLS

This step is to select an appropriate data mining tool for the business objectives and data structure.

While selecting a data mining tool, we may consider:

- Is the data set heavily categorical?
- What platforms do your tools support?
- Are the tools ODBC-compliant and incorporated with an end-user interface?
- What data formats can the tools import/export?

A data mining tool should help you understand the results of its analysis and the kind of solutions the tool generates. No single tool is able to provide the answer to your data mining project. Some tools integrate several technologies into a suite of statistical analysis programmes, a neural network, and a symbolic classifier.

CONSTRUCT THE MODEL

At this stage the data mining process begins. "This is the process of searching for patterns in a data set and the generation of classification rules, decision trees, clustering, scores, weight, and evaluation and comparison of error rates. Usually the first step is to use a random number seed to split the data into a training set and a test set and construct and evaluate a model."

Resolve these issues:

- What are the model error rates? Are they at acceptable levels? Can they be improved?
- What extraneous attributes did you find? Can those noisy and redundant be purged?
- Is additional data or a different methodology necessary to improve model performance?
- Will you have to train and test a new data set?

VALIDATE THE FINDINGS

This step involves testing a model. It is important after achieving your data mining analysis that you share and discuss the results of the analysis with the administrator, designer, analysts, managers, and engineers.

Ensure that the findings are correct and appropriate to the objectives:

- Are the findings available and do they make sense?
- Does the process have to return to any previous steps to improve results?
- Can other data mining tools be used to produce the same findings?

DELIVER THE FINDINGS

This step provides a final report to the business unit or client. The report should document the entire data mining process such as data preparation, tools used, test results, source code, and rules. Thus, you will know if the findings meet the objective, if additional data can improve the analysis, what strategic insight you dig out and how it is applicable, and what proposals can result from the data mining analysis.

INTEGRATE THE SOLUTIONS

Finally, you share the findings with all interested end-users in the appropriate business units. This process involves incorporating the results of the analysis into the company's business procedures. Although data mining tools automatically invoke database analysis, they can make some mistaken findings and erroneous conclusions if you're not careful.

ADVANTAGES OF DATA MINING

Data mining uses advanced technology for gleaning valuable insights from database that enable the business user to make the right business decisions. It turns up data that gives business companies just a little edge, but the payoff for this small edge is large. One obtains the competitive advantages required to grow in today's competitive environment. Data mining is simple in theory, but it can get quite involved in practice. That means that users will probably need some help getting set up. Many data mining software solutions are available for small and large businesses in most industries and these tools are constantly improving. The accuracy of mining will make a difference in the bottom line of business. "A recent META Group survey revealed that Fortune 500 firms were using data mining for three general purposes: 64 per cent for strategic planning, 49 per cent for competitive intelligence, and 46 per cent to increase their market share."

So far, the following have been the traditional applications of data mining technology by industry sectors:

- Retailers Database marketing, advertising effective-ness, inventory and category management.
- Banking and Insurance Financial modeling, fraud detection, market and industry profiling, database marketing, customer segmentation.
- Brokerage/Stock Exchange
- Telecommunication call detail record analysis, optimal use of capital equipment, targeted marketing.
- Government Collections, workload selection, logistics, and intelligence gathering.
- Manufacturing Production quality control, supply-chain and inventory control

Data mining provides companies extremely valuable insight that has, to date, been closely guarded as corporate stealth technology to protect competitive advantage. However, there is sometimes a breakthrough when trying something new. Some mistakes will be made. Mistakes can be remedied with statistical expertise, but the technology is becoming more useful for more users.

Data mining is also not designed to fix all business problems or tell you what the real problem is, but it gives a company a sense which can be used to help make intelligent business decisions. "Most of all, data mining is an ongoing process that involves a lot of analysis and refining along the way, so think of it as a worthy investment. And like any investment, even if your data-mining portfolio only uncovers small golden nuggets at first, those nuggets properly managed yield a lot of value."

DATA MINING TECHNIQUES ENHANCE LIBRARY SYSTEM

Suppose a library system has the following goals:

- Increase books borrowing rate.
- Attract more users to borrow books.
- Assist library professionals in making policy on the acquisition of duplicate copies and new publications.

The relationship between Data Mining and Library Management can be shown as in figure

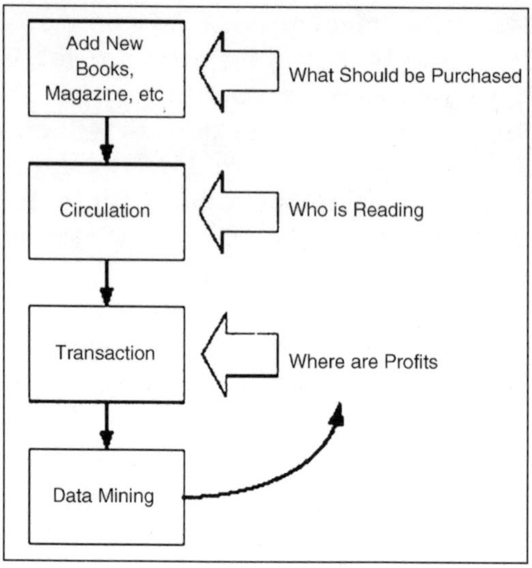

Fig. The Cyclical Relationship between Data Mining and Library Management

EXAMPLE

Consider a library whose books database includes the data of 2000 volumes of books, and the borrowing history of 5000 users who have borrowed books from library. From this database, we have developed a report system to represent the relationship between books and students. And then we use the data mining association rule to analyse the books of the same cluster borrowed by the students. A report chart of books will be produced, so that the library professionals will find references to the books for making a decision. Additionally, the library collection may be used more effectively.

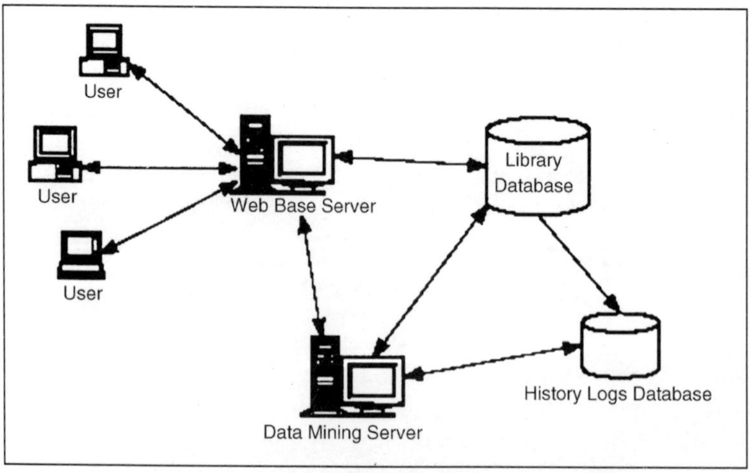

Fig. The Prototype of a Library Architecture

The library database includes seven tables. The first of them is *BOOKS* which contains each of the books' basic information. The table *BOOKS* was improved from *MARCBOOKS* which comes from the previous library system. It kept most of the columns from MARCBOOKS. Machine-readable Cataloguing (MARC) is a kind of metadata to describe a book. *USERS* has part of a student's basic information from the registration system and coordinates with the library system. *COPY* describes the actual volumes in the library. *LOCATION* reports the real location of each book. *CIRCUL* records each circulation of a book. *RESERVATION* has the information that is stored when a user holds a book. Figure shows the schema of these tables. Between each table, there is a key column that sometimes is a primary key in one of them. For instance, the relation key between *BOOKS* and *COPY* is ISBN.

The data mining system is under statistics in a library system. It is an advantageous part of the library system. The process between the main page of data mining and its four functions is shown in figure. On the main page of data mining, the administrator has four functions to execute. The first function is backup the *CIRCUL*. The second one is the list of top ten books. The third one is to execute rule. The final one is rule manager. The following paragraphs are describing them.

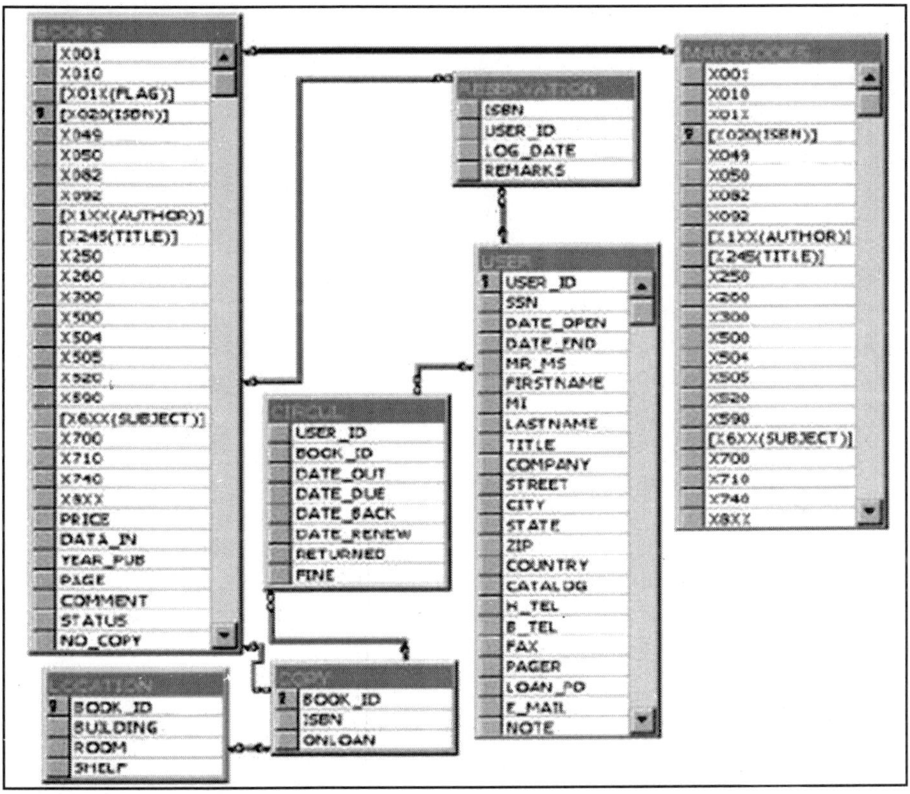

Fig. The Schema of the Library Database

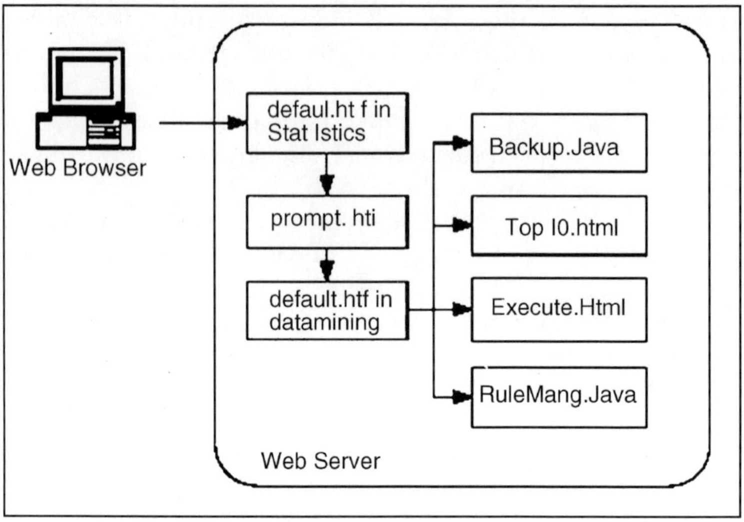

Fig. The Main Process of the Data Mining System

CONCLUSION

It is unlikely that libraries will continue to satisfy users' information needs using the traditional catalogs as the primary access mechanisms. To be certain, online catalogs provide good access to books, films, microfiche, audio tapes, and other materials traditionally kept in libraries. However, few, if any, libraries have succeeded in using their online catalogs to provide adequate access to a significant number of digital materials. In an era where information costs rapidly increase while budgets remain flat, libraries must find alternatives to slow, awkward, and expensive manual cataloguing. The Artificial Intelligence methods such as genetic algorithms and machine learning, or statistics method support data mining tools to accomplish tasks. These methods are fast and thorough and exploit the tremendous power of computers to find nuggets of useful information embedded in mountains of data. In the future, advanced data mining technology will depend on computer architecture and database technology.

exhibited at no more than a gentle angle.

If the book will not remain open naturally, a polyester band closed with 3M double-sided tape no. 415 can be used to hold the book open. Books can be structurally damaged by long-term exhibition in an open position, so exhibit periods must be limited. Turning the pages of a book every few days will prevent overexposure to light on one page.

Index

I

J

L

M

O

P

R

S

T

U

V

W